D0871786

William S. Burroughs

A Bibliography

1953–73

Portrait of William Burroughs by Avedon, July 9, 1975

William S. Burroughs

A Bibliography, 1953–73

Compiled by Joe Maynard and Barry Miles

Unlocking Inspector Lee's Word Hoard

Published for the Bibliographical Society
of the University of Virginia
by the University Press of Virginia
Charlottesville

A Linton R. Massey
Descriptive Bibliography

THE UNIVERSITY PRESS OF VIRGINIA
Copyright © 1978 by the Rector and Visitors
of the University of Virginia

First published 1978

Photographs by Hydon Taylor
and Barry Miles

Library of Congress Cataloging in Publication Data
Maynard, Joe, 1942—
  William S. Burroughs.
  Includes index.
  1. Burroughs, William S., 1914— —Bibliography.
I. Miles, Barry, 1943— joint author. II Virginia.
University. Bibliographical Society.
Z8136.17.M38 [PS3552.U75] 016.813′5′4
77-2663
ISBN 0-8139-0710-1

Printed in the United States of America

To
Ian Sommerville
and to
Donatella Manganotti

Contents

Foreword

Leafing through these titles I glimpse a number of scenes, bits of vivid and vanishing detail. That phrase is from Conrad's *Lord Jim*.

Junkie: I see Carl Solomon who worked for Ace Books, my first publishers. Over lunch he suggested the name of Old Ike for Dave the pusher in Mexico City. Old Dave died there—I heard later from Jack Kerouac, who had the story from Dave's old lady Esperanza. "He just sit down on the curb and die," she said. And the government script for morphine he and I used to split died with him.

One morning Sinclair Beiles came to my room in the Beat Hotel, 9 rue Git-le-Coeur, and said Girodias wanted to publish *Naked Lunch* and quickly. Could I have the manuscript ready in two weeks? Girodias had rejected the first version submitted to him two years before Sinclair's morning visit and the book had made the round of publishers in America and England, some of whom did not content themselves with a form rejection slip but wrote nasty personal letters like Stephen Spender: "Having waded through the yards and yards of entrails, I feel that this book could only interest a student of abnormal psychology."

With the help of Brion Gysin and Sinclair I did get the manuscript ready in two weeks; this meant choosing 200 pages from 600 pages of notes and unfinished sections. However, much of what went into the book had been previously retyped by Alan Ansen and Allen Ginsberg in Tangier. The sections were sent along to the printer as fast as they were typed, and I had planned to decide the final order of chapters when the galley proofs came back. Sinclair took one look at the galleys and said: "I think this order is the best." By some magic the chapters had fallen into place, and the only change was to shift the "Hauser and O'Brien" section from the beginning to the end. One month after Sinclair's visit, *Naked Lunch* was out on the stands, setting a record for prompt publication.

Maurice Girodias had changed his mind about publishing the book after seeing some excerpts that appeared in the *Chicago Review*, which Allen Ginsberg had picked out and sent along to Irving Rosenthal, the editor. The university authorities objected vociferously to the issue of the *Review*. Sex and drugs and four-letter words were by no means acceptable at the time, and certainly not on a university campus. The editorial staff of the *Chicago Review* resigned in protest and started *Big Table*. This move caused quite a local issue, which attracted attention in the press. The conflict, of course, increased Maurice's interest, and he wanted to publish the book as soon as possible, while the issue was still active. So it was publication in a little magazine that led to the publication of *Naked Lunch* at a time when I had almost given up. For many years I sent out pieces to all little magazines that asked me for a contribution, as this bibliography attests.

After the publication of *Naked Lunch* I was visited by a reporter and photographer team from Time-Life, obviously acting the roles of Hauser and O'Brien.

"Have an Old Gold Mr. Burroughs. . . . You know, I have an intuition about you—I can see you on Madison Avenue making $20,000 a year . . . life in all its rich variety. . . . "

One day, returning from lunch with this vaudeville team, I found Brion Gysin with scissors and bits of newspaper and magazine articles which he had arranged into montages, spread out on a table. These were the first cut-ups that later went into *Minutes to Go* . . . "There seems little doubt however that Eisenhower said 'I weigh fifty-six pounds less than a man.' Flushed and nodded curtly. He boasted of a long string of past crimes highlighted by a total eclipse of whoever stood in his way when he redid her apartment. Last seen swimming desperately in sewage. *Ich sterbe*. They were drafted." The cut-ups unloosed an era of total paranoia among the denizens of 9 rue Git-le-Coeur. Gregory said he didn't want people cutting up his poetry. Everyone was into some sort of interplanetary conspiracy involving the CIA, the Venusians, the Scientologists, British Intelligence, the Pondicherry Mother, the Deuxième Bureau, the Russian cosmonauts, the Pope and Chairman Mao, Henry Luce, Hassan i Sabbah, and Paul Getty. And everyone was getting telepathic instructions from his alleged employers or patrons, who were not overly generous when it came to actual cash. I was rich at the time, with $200 per month allowance from my mother and father, who made it in Cobble Stone Gardens, a gift and art store on Worth Avenue in Palm Beach.

There were difficulties about publication of *Minutes to Go*—financial of course—Two Cities couldn't meet a printing bill for

$300, and Mrs. Gaît Frogé of the English Book Shop put up the money. So that publication proceeded, launching the cut-up controversy which flared at the Writers Conference in Edinburgh, 1962, organized by John Calder who came to Paris and persuaded me to attend. I gave a talk on cut-ups which was well received by the audience, who thought it was funny, especially the first virgin cut-ups, and I remember laughing as I hadn't in years. Stephen Spender said it sounded like some medieval superstition to him and I said it was simply a literary technique and if he didn't like it he didn't have to do it. Alliances were emerging. Mary McCarthy praised my work publicly, which lined her up with Alex Trocchi, Colin MacGinnes, and Lawrence Durrell, as opposed to Spender and Kushwant Singh, definitely plugging a conservative antidrug antianarchy line. Coming in from another tack, Hugh Macdiarmid said that Trocchi and me and our ilk belonged in jail and not on the lecture platform. People were easily shocked in those days when Allen Ginsberg would go to an English poetry reading and the academics would tell him, "We want no howling here."

1964 . . . No. 4, Calle Larachi, Tangier. *My Own Mag* . . . smell of kerosene heaters, hostile neighbors, stones thudding against the door. Jeff Nuttall sent me a copy of *My Own Mag* and asked me to contribute. I recall that delivery of the first copies to which I had contributed was heralded by a wooden top crashing through the skylight. In the spring of 1964, when I had moved from Calle Larachi to a flat above the Tangier lottery, I received a book of poems in the mail from Graham Masterton and wrote an introduction to the poems from cuts and juxtapositions. Later I met Graham Masterton in London, where he was an editor of *Mayfair*, and this led to publication of the Academy Series.

The article in the *British Journal of Addiction* in 1956. This brings back the apomorphine cure with Dr. Dent at 99 Cromwell Road. That building has been torn down now and Dr. Dent is dead. My experiences with the apomorphine treatment later served as source material for an article called "The Death of Opium Jones" which appeared, I believe, in the *New Statesman*, and this led to a controversy with Dr. David Cooper. We were later reconciled, and I apologized for the sharpness of my letter.

And here is the *Times Literary Supplement* where I published "The Literary Techniques of Lady Sutton-Smith." This issue, which was called "The Changing Guard," was maneuvered by Father Houdard, the Beatnik priest, who had served with British Intelligence during the war and still had a mysterious and purposeful air when I met him in London, in 1956, at the New Cavendish Hotel where I was waiting to move into my flat at Dalmeny Court. After a long correspondence I visited Carl Weissner in Heidelberg in the spring of 1966, and later published in his magazine *Klactoveedsedsteen*.

Salt Chunk Mary is a character lifted from a book called *You Can't Win*, being the autobiography of a burglar, which I read at the age of fifteen. This was I think my first literary contact with the drug world from a former addict. He mentions extracting opium from lettuce, and this story turned up recently in *High Times* magazine, with detailed instructions. Richard Aaron obtained a copy of this book for me recently, and I found it quite good on rereading after forty-five years.

So many scenes. It is certainly gratifying to see them all collected into this bibliography on which Joe Maynard and Barry Miles have spent so many years of patient work. Leafing through these titles and choosing 200 pages of vivid and vanishing detail—Old Dave, Mexico City alleys, Callejon de la Esperanza. The government script said "This order is the best." Naked lunch in the Beat Hotel, 9 rue Hauser, and quickly to the end publishers did not content themselves with—a man flushed and nodded. Nasty person letters like step of past crimes waded through the yards and yards stood in his way when he redid book desperately in sewage. Ich with the help of Brion, ready in two weeks. Cut-ups some of whom weigh fifty-six pounds less by a total eclipse of entrails. They were drafted into air. . . .

WILLIAM S. BURROUGHS

Introduction

Who has the time to read such big bibliographies? Certainly such readers are very specialized creatures in midwestern libraries appreciatively washing their hands and smoking a little hash before opening up these dreadful tomes. On the other hand, there are young lads and lasses all over the century whose brains have been influenced by Burroughs's implacable egolessness or deathly wit as 'twas said in the presence of Tibetan lamas. These students of manners, culture, letters, poetics, film frame, sound collage, surrealism, futurism and cut-upism, medicalist-hypnosis, cock sucking or out-of-the-bottle genius, needle precision, levitation, and writing-writing will now be enabled to locate precise references and experiments among the multitude of papers that have shifted for decades through Burroughs's dreamy cranium. Burroughs's work has been logical patchwork, a series of psychophysical literate experiments on himself and the Word planet, advances and retreats, overnight flights, tunnelings, stopovers, exiles, and homecomings to different areas of emotion and physical space, bewildering in variety but coherent as our solar system.

I hope this book serves as guide map for myself and others to locate his landmarks and side trips, interzones and galaxies—where we'll find him lurking waiting for us with benevolent indifferent attentiveness, "last of the Faustian men," as Kerouac mythologized him in an earlier decade this century.

August 11, 1976   ALLEN GINSBERG
Jack Kerouac School of Disembodied Poetics
Naropa Institute, Boulder, Colorado

Preface

In early 1964 I obtained Grove Press's eleventh serving of *The Naked Lunch*—a "hot" lunch as few booksellers stocked it at that time—put everything and everybody on "hold," and my whole self went "Out to Lunch" as I went into it. I surfaced I don't know how many hours later, after jumping that uptown A-train with Lee the Agent, vicariously tripping to Texas, Louisiana, Mexico, and farther south to Yage Country, then back to the rebuilding of The City; I had read scenes so real that I felt I was there, right there, living Lee's story as it unfolded; hearing, smelling, seeing, touching, tasting. It takes a master writer to project that sense of reality to a reader, and after reading *The Naked Lunch* I knew William S. Burroughs to be one. *Nova Express* followed shortly thereafter, and it was an express!—by now the cut-ups and fold-ins were being put to full use and the book was a roller-coaster ride at breakneck speed from NYC to the Crab Nebula and back, showing all the control systems and the way to break them, and showing me the genius of William Burroughs.

From 1964 onward, I read and collected everything by WSB I could beg, borrow, steal, or buy, each new book, story, poem, or magazine article revealing some new technique, idea, experience, or facet of an author joyously, totally involved with being a writer and advancing the art of writing, which WSB certainly has in taking the novel form and exploding it out into many levels of meaning, thus making the printed page truly psychedelic; just like looking at a canvas of Bosch, Van Gogh, Picasso, Dali, Klee, or Pollock, it baffles you for the moment, but suddenly you see what the artist saw, and you're out, gone, ZAPPED!

September 1970 found me in Charlottesville managing The Band Box record shop and amassing a large WSB collection for a checklist which I was going to get published just to alert people like myself who admired Mr. Burroughs's writing to his prolific output, when Walker Cowen walked into The Band Box one night and said if I could round-out, beef-up, and blow-up the checklist into a full-scale bibliography, he thought it might be publishable. I bought that outright, and spent the next year reading all the textbooks and all the

really good bibliographies, finding out what kind of an animal a
full-scope analytical bibliography really was—what it was was really
hairy! But by now I had the knowledge without the college, and I had
all the books, and no one else was doing one; so there went me. In
1972 my job went, too; and I completed the bibliography at home in
Delbarton, W.Va.,while sponging off the parents and sister (a big
thanks, Riley, Laura, and Joanne Maynard).

When 1973 arrived, I went back to Charlottesville to clerk at
Boggiano & Son/Books, and got bolder with the bibliography,
sending a first draft to WSB himself for approval. Along with his kind
thanks and interest, Mr. Burroughs told me of Barry Miles' work
and suggested I get in touch with him so that we didn't duplicate
anything. I was able to contact Miles through Am Here Books'
owner, Richard Aaron, and Miles and I met and compared manuscripts in Charlottesville in December 1973. It was beneficial to both
of us that for the past seven years, Miles had done his major work on
the periodical appearances, anthologies, foreign editions, and
ephemera; while I for my three years had concentrated my attention
on the books and pamphlets. Seeing that between us we had a
completed bibliography, Miles graciously proposed a collaboration.
Before he could complete his sentence, I accepted, all eyes and
smiles, and here 'tis.

My first thank-you is a thousandfold one to William Seward Burroughs himself for his invaluable assistance, kind words, and encour-
agements, and for writing all those wonderfully electrical, magical
books and stories which this book is about.

Second thanks go, of course, to Walker Cowen, who has assisted
me very kindly and readily from the formation stage to the completed manuscript, helping me cast the style, advising me on so many
of the finer points, answering questions like, "What is a bibliography,
anyhoo?", and keeping me at it.

Next, a long thank-you to Fred Jordan, Claudia Menza, Carla
Rotollo, Rachelle Bijou, and all the staff at Grove Press without
whom the printing histories would still be a big, fat zero.

Thanks also to Julius P. Barclay, William Runge, Joan St. C. Crane,
Lani Billeaud, Daisy Wright, and all the people in the Rare Book
Department, University of Virginia Library in Charlottesville. I did
most of my work there, and obtained so very much technical assistance and inspiration from Miss Crane.

Thanks go also to Phillip O. Stafford for proofreading the manuscript, and to Cary Bean and Stephen Getlein for reading the proofs.

I would also like to thank Richard Aaron, Norman A. Belanger, Andreas Brown, David Bruce, Jane Butcher, Donald W. Davis, Richard Elovich, Lawrence Ferlinghetti, Maurice Girodias, James Grauerholz, Jan Herman, Claire Humphreys, Ruth P. Ham, Risa Kessler, Larry Kirshbaum, Susan R. Lewis, R. Russell Maylone, Constance Nickel, Jim Pennington, Gaye Poulton, Susan Rada, John Sankey, Richard Seaver, and Hydon Taylor.

And last but not least, a special thank-you to the friends who through their concern about and enthusiasm for the bibliography inspired and encouraged me.

JOE MAYNARD

I began to compile this bibliography in London sometime in 1967, working on it between projects and sometimes taking a day off to visit the British Library. It was not until December 1973 that I met Joe Maynard and, after visiting with him in Charlottesville, that we decided to collaborate. Maynard had already compiled a checklist of WSB's books which the Bibliographical Society of the University of Virginia was interested in publishing. In my work I had concentrated largely on tracing the magazine and anthology publications which form such an important part of WSB's bibliography. I had intended to describe the books last of all as I had them to hand in my own collection. I had, however, taken notes and written for information concerning them shortly after beginning the project. The high standard and the detail of Maynard's work made it obvious that we should combine our efforts rather than each publish separate works.

The bibliography thus falls very much into two parts: The books, which have been described by Maynard, and the anthologies, periodicals, foreign editions and interviews which I have described. We have, of course, been able to help each other considerably within these areas. For instance I had certain information, gathered some time ago, on the printing figures of various titles. This information is no longer available as the records have since been destroyed and I was able to fill some of the gaps in Maynard's description there. Maynard has, of course, been able to draw my attention to many omissions from the Periodicals and Anthologies sections. The creation of the Miscellaneous section is largely Maynard's work though

many of the descriptions are mine and were originally included
among the anthologies. In particular the exhibition catalogue descriptions are mine, and had there been just a few more, we might
have considered a separate section for them.

I was helped considerably by William Burroughs himself in the
preparation of this bibliography, both in the early days of my work on
it and in 1972 when I described and catalogued his archives and those
of Brion Gysin. Burroughs still had them at his London flat at the
time, and so I was able to question him and also Brion Gysin about
bibliographic points which arose from describing their correspondence and papers. I unfortunately did not have time to read all
of the hundreds of letters from WSB's publishers, literary agents, and
the magazine editors who had written to him. The collection is now
owned by the International Center of Art and Communication in
Vaduz, Liechtenstein, where it is hoped that students will eventually
be able to come and study it. Among its papers there are undoubt-
edly clues to many items which are missing from this listing.

It is safe to say that the several months I spent working each day
with William Burroughs and Brion Gysin on their archives afforded
me a unique opportunity to fill in as much detail as possible and
correct errors in my existing manuscript. They told me of dozens of
items I had no knowledge of, and but for them this bibliography
would be nowhere near as complete as it presently is. To them go my
greatest thanks for their interest and patience.

William Burroughs's French-language translators and sometime
collaborators, Claude Pélieu and Mary Beach, also provided me with
invaluable information, enthusiasm, free access to their library and
archives, and much delightful company. I must also thank Richard
Aaron of Am Here Books in Val d'Illiez, Switzerland, who made his
checklist of WSB's periodical publications available to me, allowed
me to inspect his library, published the description I made of the
Burroughs/Gysin papers (*A Descriptive Catalogue of the William S.
Burroughs Archive*, complied by Miles Associates for William Burroughs and Brion Gysin [London, 1973]), and put me in touch with
my collaborator.

In addition I must thank all the many people who took the trouble
to reply to my letters, who allowed me to inspect their libraries, who
typed parts of the manuscript, were pestered, inconvenienced, and
otherwise troubled by the compilation of this bibliography. Among
them I must particularly thank Lilia Aaron, J. G. Ballard, Victor

Bockris, Archie Boyle, Christian Bourgois, Bobbie Bristol, Peter Broxton, Ann Buchanan, Bill Butler, John Calder, Jean Fanchette, Sarah Fenwick, Gaît Frogé, Allen Ginsberg, Urban Gwerder, Walter Hartmann, Jan Herman, Traudel Jansen, Pierre Joris, Graham Keen, Nick Kimberley, Susan Lewis at Northwestern University Library, Kenneth Lohf at Columbia University Library, the late Donatella Manganotti, Pearce Marchbank, Tom Maschler, Claudia Menza, Philippe Mikriammos, Susan Miles, Eric Mottram, Yuji Noguchi, Daniel Odier, Robert Palmer, Debra Pelletier, Michael Petree, Richard Phillips at Amherst College Library, Massimo Pini, Fernanda Pivano, David Prentice, Marguerite Schluter, the late Ian Sommerville, Bernard Stone, Emma Tennant, Simon Vinkenoog, Anne Waldman, Larry Wallrich, Ken Weaver, Carl Weissner, the staff of the British Museum Libraries, and the New York Public Library.

MILES

Some Notes on the Bibliography

Books

The books and pamphlets are arranged in chronological order. Each different book is numbered; under that number the first edition is lettered a and second or subsequent editions of the same book are assigned consecutive letters of the alphabet. Reprints are noted in the printing histories of the first edition. When the book has been re-released with revisions or even a new cover or when the same book has come from another publisher, the book has been considered another edition and is separately lettered. These minor editions have not been as fully described as their precursors as they usually—except for the new cover, publisher, etc.—are identical with the previous editions.

We must apologize to our readers for the occasional lack of information in the publishing histories. They are in many cases incomplete or not present at all because the publishers either did not cooperate with us or had no existing records. Therefore, some of the dates and quantities had to be approximated; but where no information at all was offered or was extant, it was thought better to leave a blank. It is hoped that later these figures may be retrieved as more information is made available to us, either by the publishers or our readers.

Berserk Machine, A Distant Hand Lifted, Johnny's So Long at the Fair, Mr. Bradley Mr. Martin, The Revised Boy Scout Manual, and *Vaudeville Voices* do not appear in this bibliography as they were working titles of books never published, incorporated into *The Soft Machine, The Ticket That Exploded,* and *The Wild Boys.*

Queer exists in manuscript but has not been published, and so is also not included. *The Third Mind,* announced by Grove Press for 1970, has not yet been published and is therefore not in the bibliography.

Port of Saints, planned for release in 1973, was not published by Am Here Books until 1975 due to the paper shortage in Great Britain, and so is not included.

WSB did not write the Akbar del Piombo books.

Anthologies

Rather less information than usual has been given here as virtually all of the anthology appearances are reprints from magazines or books and have little connection with the author.

Periodicals

Rather more details concerning WSB's magazine contributions have been included here than is usual. This is because WSB used the magazine format as a platform for most of his experimental work, his collaborations with other writers, and his experiments with newspaper formats. This listing, however, does not include full details of WSB's collaborations with other writers (notably with Brion Gysin, Claude Pélieu, Carl Weissner, and Jeff Nuttall) except where WSB's actual words appear as he wrote them. That is to say, cut-ups of WSB's words by others have not been included, nor have the original articles which WSB himself cut up. For example, if one of WSB's collaborators publishes a text in a magazine and WSB answers it in the next issue, then only WSB's answer will be entered here (though often a footnote records the circumstances of such a text). We hope to compile a full bibliography of these collaborations, and it may be possible to include it in a later edition.

All entries can be considered to be the first printing of a piece unless stated or unless its title describes its origin.

Foreign-language magazine contributions have been included as these are sometimes the first appearance of a piece.

Foreign Editions

It has not been possible to inspect all of the foreign editions, something which we hope to correct in a later edition. The French and some of the German and Italian translations were prepared with consultation with the author. It will be noted that the L'Herne texts and *Sterminatore!* represent hardback collections of short pieces which have not previously appeared in book form.

Interviews

Only those interviews which purport to print WSB's actual words have been listed. Those interviews describing a visit with only paraphrases of conversation have been excluded.

The most obvious omission is that of critical articles and book reviews. Preliminary investigations reveal that considerably more articles and reviews have been written about William Burroughs than he has himself written. As only a very small percentage of them are of interest and as the compilation of criticism would have delayed publication by several years, it was decided to exclude this material. It is noted however that the Burroughs/Gysin archives contain a large quantity of critical material in the form of clippings and Xerox copies of reviews supplied by WSB's publishers. Though not complete, this collection will form a good basis for some future catalogue of critical articles and reviews.

Finally, we recognize that the first edition of a bibliography can rarely hope to be much more than an introductory checklist and that it is its release into the world which provokes those librarians, scholars, and readers who have the missing information at their fingertips to write to us. We welcome corrections, additions, and any further information.

William S. Burroughs

A Bibliography

1953-73

ACE
DOUBLE
BOOKS
D-15

TWO BOOKS IN ONE 35c

JUNKIE

Confessions of an Unredeemed Drug Addict

An ACE
Original

WILLIAM LEE

A1a

A   Books and Pamphlets

A1   JUNKIE

a. Ace Books, Inc.   1953

JUNKIE | by William Lee | ACE BOOKS, INC. | 23 West 47th Street, New York 36, N.Y.

Collation: 16.3 × 10.6 cm. 160 leaves; pp. [1–4] 5–149 [150–151], [inverted:] 169–5 [4–1].

Note: The second pagination sequence is *Narcotic Agent* by Maurice Helbrant, bound with *Junkie* and printed upside down with the back cover of the volume as its front cover.

Pages 1–2: 'PUBLISHER'S NOTE'. p. 3: title. p. 4: 'JUNKIE | Copyright, 1953, by Ace Books, Inc. | All Rights Reserved | The names of all characters in this book are fictious. Any | similarity between these names and those of actual persons, | living or dead, is entirely coincidence. *To A. L. M.* | [heavy short rule] | NARCOTIC AGENT | Copyright, 1941, by the Vanguard Press, Inc. | [heavy short rule] | Printed in U.S.A.' pp. 5–10: 'Preface' by William Burroughs (hereafter referred to as WSB). pp. 11–16: '*Glossary*'. pp. 17–149: text of *Junkie*. pp. 150–151: publisher's advertisement. Paged backwards and printed upside down: pp. 169–5: text of *Narcotic Agent* by Maurice Helbrant. p. 4: 'NARCOTIC AGENT | Copyright, 1941, by the Vanguard Press, Inc. | Reprinted by arrangement with the Van-guard Press, Inc. | No portion of this book may be reprinted in any form without | the written permission of the publisher, except by a reviewer | who wishes to quote brief passages for inclusion in a news-|paper or magazine. | *To Anne, Of Course* | [heavy short rule] | JUNKIE | Copyright, 1953, by Ace Books, Inc. | [heavy short rule] | Printed in U.S.A.' p. 3: 'NARCOTIC | AGENT | by Maurice Helbrant | *Formerly of the Federal Bureau of Narcotics,* | *United States Treasury Department* | ACE BOOKS, INC. | 23 West 47th Street, New York 36, N.Y.' pp. 1–2: quotes from seven reviews of *Narcotic Agent*, headed: '"MORE THRILLING THAN ANY | FICTION STORY"'.

Contents: Publisher's note, preface by WSB, glossary, text of *Junkie*, and text of *Narcotic Agent.*

Paper: White wove paper.

Binding: Perfect-bound, no sigs. Stiff pictorial wrappers. Front cover: at top left, superimposed on and below red panel across top, publisher's device in a white panel, '[red, shadowed with black] ACE | [white, on the black spines of two stacked books with blue covers, red edges] DOUBLE | BOOKS | [black below] D–15'; within red panel across top, '[white] TWO BOOKS IN ONE 35¢'; below, superimposed on color illustration of a man and a woman struggling over a packet of heroin, '[yellow, outlined in green] JUNKIE | [white] *Confessions of an Unredeemed Drug Addict* | [at left center] An ACE | Original | [at right bottom] WILLIAM LEE'. Spine: divided into two panels, red and black, with publisher's device, as before, except 'D–15' is at top within panel instead of bottom, superimposed at top and at bottom; down the spine within the red panel, '[white, outlined in black] JUNKIE [white only] WILLIAM LEE'; reading up the spine within the black panel, '[yellow] NARCOTIC AGENT MAURICE | HELBRANT'. Back cover: at top left, superimposed on and below red panel, publisher's device, as on front cover; within red panel across top, '[white] TWO BOOKS IN ONE 35¢'; below, superimposed on color illustration of man putting cuffs on a busty brunette sitting in front of a table on which are her "works," '[yellow] Gripping True Adventures of a | T-Man's War Against the Dope Menace | [white] NARCOTIC AGENT | [yellow at left center] MAURICE | HELBRANT | [at left bottom] Abridged Edition'. All edges trimmed and light orange.

Publication: Of this edition, published in 1953, no printing records survive. But, in a letter to A. A. Wyn of Ace Books, April 25, 1954, Burroughs said that the publisher's statement showed that 113,170 copies were sold before December 30, 1953. The contract called for a royalty escalation after the sale of 150,000 copies, so that it would seem that the latter figure may well be the amount of the first printing.

b. Digit Books   1957

JUNKIE | CONFESSIONS OF AN UNREDEEMED | DRUG

ADDICT | By | William Lee | To | A. L. M. | DIGIT BOOKS | Brown, Watson Ltd. | London

Collation: 18.4 × 11.4 cm. A–E¹⁶, 80 leaves; pp. [1–4] 5–160. Page 1: 'JUNKIE | CONFESSIONS OF AN UNREDEEMED | DRUG ADDICT | Not since De Quincey's "The Confessions of | an English Opium Eater" has the finger of | light shone so glaringly on the wasteland of the | drug addict. | Yet, where De Quincey wrote in the vein of | dream-phantasy, "Junkie" is pitilessly factual | and hard-boiled. It strips down the addict | without shame or self-pity in all his nakedness.' p. 2: 'DIGIT BOOKS', publisher's advertisement: list of six titles. p. 3: title. p. 4: 'JUNKIE | A DIGIT BOOK | First publication in the United Kingdom. | American edition published by Ace Books Inc., New York. | The names of all characters in this book are fictitious. | Any similarity between these names and those of | actual persons, living or dead, is entirely coincidence. | *This book is copyright. No | portion of it may be repro-|duced without written permission.* | Digit Books are published by Brown, Watson Ltd., | 123 Kensal Road, London, W.10 | Made and printed in Great Britain by | Cole & Co. (Westminster), Ltd., Boscombe, Hants.' pp. 5–6: '*Publisher's Note*'. pp. 7–158: text. pp. 159–160: publisher's advertisements.

Contents: Publisher's note and text of *Junkie.*

Paper: White wove paper.

Binding: Bound in stiff pictorial wrappers. Front cover: all lettering superimposed over a color painting (in mostly red, black-brown, white, and green) based on the cover of **A1a**; at top, '[white] CONFESSIONS OF AN UNREDEEMED DRUG ADDICT | [yellow] JUNKIE | [white] WILLIAM LEE | [publisher's device: a yellow circle with a V opening at its top through which is seen four red lines; within the circle in red is] DIGIT | BOOKS'. Spine: on red, '[down, white] JUNKIE [black] CONFESSIONS OF AN UNREDEEMED DRUG ADDICT [white] WILLIAM LEE | [across, yellow and red publisher's device, as before]'. Back cover: left half is a drawing (in mostly red and white on black) of a woman giving herself a heroin injection in her right thigh; on the right half, on white, is '[orange] JUNKIE | [red] THE CONFESSIONS OF AN | UNREDEEMED DRUG ADDICT | [black] WILLIAM LEE | NEVER BEFORE |

HAS THE FINGER | OF LIGHT SHONE | SO GLARINGLY ON | THE WASTELAND | OF THE DRUG | ADDICT. . . . . | [red] JUNKIE [black] IS | PITILESSLY FACTUAL | AND HARD-BOILED. | IT STRIPS DOWN | THE ADDICT | WITHOUT SHAME | OR SELF-PITY IN | ALL HIS | NAKEDNESS. . . . . | [yellow and red publisher's device, as before]'. All edges trimmed and white.

Publication: Of this edition, published in 1957, probably no printing records survive.

A1b

c. Ace Books, Inc.   1964

William | Burroughs | Junkie | *(Originally published under the pen-name of William Lee)* | ACE BOOKS, INC. | 1120 Avenue of the Americas | New York, N.Y. 10036

Collation: 17.8 × 10.5 cm. 64 leaves; pp. [1–4] 5–11 [12] 13–17 [18] 19–126 [127–128].

Contents: First separate publication of *Junkie* in U.S.A. without Maurice Helbrant's *Narcotic Agent* (see **A1a**). The publisher's note has been expanded, and a foreword by Carl Solomon has been added (pp. 5–6). Pages 12 and 18 are blank, and pp. 127–128 are publisher's advertisements.

Paper: White wove paper.

Binding: Perfectbound, no sigs. Stiff pictorial wrappers. Front cover is a drawing (on black-brown ground) of a kneeling man, in brown pants and T-shirt, clawing at a wall. On the back cover at bottom is a reduction of the drawing and above it, the publisher's blurb. All edges trimmed and orange.

Publication: This edition, published in November 1964, consisted of 75,939 copies. It was reprinted in January 1970 (145,164 copies) and in December 1972 (86,056 copies). The 1972 printing has a slick color photocover showing a blue-jeaned, T-shirted youth "nodding out" on a doorstep.

d. The Olympia Press   1966

[Within a border of black ornaments] WILLIAM BURROUGHS | JUNKIE | Originally published under the | pen-name of William Lee | No. 114 | THE OLYMPIA PRESS | TRAVELLER'S COMPANION SERIES | GENERAL EDITOR: MAURICE GIRODIAS | PUBLISHED BY THE NEW ENGLISH LIBRARY LIMITED

Collation: 18 × 10.7 cm. 80 leaves; pp. [1–6] 7–11 [12] 13–152 [153–154] 155–159 [160].
    Note: At chapter endings pages are unnumbered: pp. 20, 31, 38, 48, 53, 64, 80, 91, 111, 117, 127, 140, and 147.

Contents: Preface by WSB, text of *Junkie* as in **A1a**, except that the editor's notes originally printed in the text are published here in a

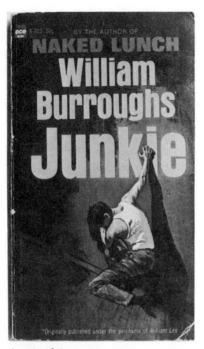

A1c (1964)

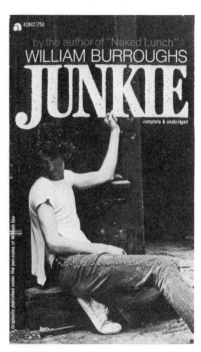

A1c (1972)

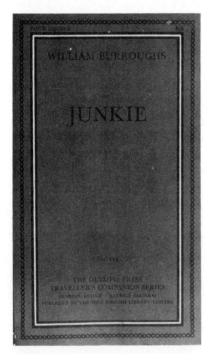

A1d

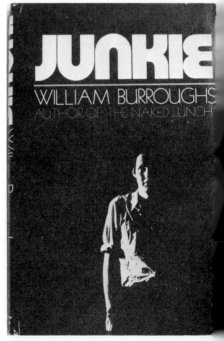

A1e

separate section on p. 154. The glossary is in a different location (pp. 155–160), and on p. 5 is a foreword concerning the history of The Olympia Press. Page 2 is the publisher's advertisement .

Paper: White wove paper.

Binding: Perfect-bound, no sigs. Stiff olive-green wrappers. Front cover: within a border rule consisting of a black chain-link rule enclosing a black-white-black rule, '[black, above the inner rule] FOUR SQUARE 8/6 | [within inner rule] WILLIAM BUR-ROUGHS | JUNKIE | No. 114 | THE OLYMPIA PRESS | TRAVELLER'S COMPANION SERIES | GENERAL EDITOR: MAURICE GIRODIAS | PUBLISHED BY THE NEW ENGLISH LIBRARY LIMITED'. Spine: '[black, down, on top three-quarters, on white ground within black-ruled rectangle] 114 JUNKIE [at bottom, outside rectangle] 1687'. Back cover: at top, '[black] PUB-LISHED BY THE NEW ENGLISH LIBRARY LIMITED [pub-lisher's device (numeral 4 in black square)]'. All edges trimmed.

Publication: This edition, published in July 1966, was reprinted in July 1969 with a new cover, and reprinted again in April 1972, again with a new cover. Probably 5,000 copies were issued each time.

e. David Bruce & Watson   1973

William | Burroughs | Junkie | *(Originally published under the pen-name of William Lee)* | [publisher's device (a spider hanging from a web)] | David Bruce & Watson | LONDON

Collation: 19.7 × 12.7 cm. [1–4]^{16}, 64 leaves, with last leaf glued to back cover; pp. [1–4] 5–11 [12] 13–17 [18] 19–126 [127–130].
   Note: The front free endpaper is included in the enumeration as pp. 1–2, and pp. 12, 18, and 127–130 are blank.

Contents: Identical to **A1c**, except without publisher's advertise-ments.

Paper: White wove paper. Endpapers white.

Binding: Bound in black cloth, spine lettered in gilt: '[down] Junkie | WILLIAM BURROUGHS [across, bottom, publisher's device, as above]'. Issued with a black dust jacket, the front of which is an early black-and-white photo of WSB above which appears the title and author's name in white and light orange lettering, and on the back is a full-face blowup from the same photo. All edges trimmed.

Publication: This edition, published in June 1973, consisted of 1,500 copies.

A2   THE NAKED LUNCH

a. The Olympia Press   1959

[Within a border of green ornaments] WILLIAM BURROUGHS | THE | NAKED | LUNCH | THE TRAVELLER'S COMPANION | *SERIES* | published by | THE OLYMPIA PRESS | 7 *rue Saint-Séverin, Paris 5*

Collation: 17.5 × 11.1 cm. 1–14^8 15^4, 116 leaves; pp. [1–6] 7–225 [226–232]. All gatherings signed '76'.
Pages 1–2: blank. p. 3: half title. p. 4: blank. p. 5: title. p. 6: 'PRINTED IN FRANCE | [line rule] | *Copyright by William Burroughs, 1959*'. pp. 7–208: text. pp. 209–226: '*Atrophied Preface* | WOULDN'T YOU?' by WSB. p. 227: 'Printed by S.I.P., Montreuil, France, in July 1959 | *Dépôt légal : 3e trimestre 1959*'. pp. 228–232: blank.

Contents: Text, *Naked Lunch*, and "Atrophied Preface, Wouldn't You?".

Paper: White wove paper.

Binding: Bound in stiff olive-green wrappers. Front cover: within a border rule consisting of a black chain-link rule enclosing a black-white-black rule, '[black] WILLIAM BURROUGHS | THE | NAKED | LUNCH | n° 76 | *THE* | TRAVELLER'S COMPANION | *SERIES*'. Spine: '[black, within black-ruled rectangle, across at bottom] 76 [up, within rectangle] THE NAKED LUNCH'. Back cover: bottom right corner, '[black] Francs: 1,500 | NOT TO BE SOLD IN | THE U.S.A. OR U.K.'; on some copies, 'NEW PRICE | NF 18' was stamped over in purple within purple rule border with old price canceled by two purple rules. Issued with a white ground dust jacket which reproduced a calligraphic drawing by WSB, on the front of which is printed within a vertical purple strip: '[white] WILLIAM | BURROUGHS | [yellow] THE | NAKED | LUNCH'. Jacket spine:

A2a (jacket)

A2a (cover)

'[across at bottom, black] THE | OLYMPIA | PRESS. | [up, purple] THE NAKED LUNCH | [up top, black] WILLIAM | BUR-ROUGHS'. The drawing by WSB continues on the back of the dust jacket. On the inside flaps are a photo of WSB and the publisher's blurb. All edges trimmed. Miles states that the very first issues were released without the dust jackets; they were added after a month or so.

Publication: This edition, published in July 1959, consisted of 5,000 copies. It was reprinted soon after the original publication in a printing of 5,000 copies, and reprinted again in June 1965 (5,000 copies). Both reprints are without the green ornament border on the title page and did not have the dust jacket. In the June 1965 reprint, the last signature (the 15th) has only two leaves, and the colophon reads: 'PRINTED IN FRANCE | [line rule] | by Imprimerie Crout-zet, June 1965 | First Printing 1959. Copyright © 1959, 1965 by William S. Burroughs. | Library of Congress catalogue card number 60–11097. | Depot legal 1959, 2ᵉ trimestre 1965.' On some 1965 copies over the original price is a light green, black-outlined sticker within which is: 'OLYMPIA PRESS | [short line rule] | 9 FRANCS'.

There also exist two sets of unbound sheets of the first edition intended for a special edition that was never issued. One of these is in the William Burroughs Archive, and the other in a private collection.

There is also a pirated edition (not examined), probably done in Formosa, copying the Traveler's Companion format.

b. Grove Press   1962

William S. Burroughs | NAKED LUNCH | [double-line rule enclosing slashes] | *Grove Press, Inc.* | *New York*

Collation: 20.2 × 13.5 cm. [1–6]¹⁶ [7]⁸ [8–9]¹⁶, 136 leaves; pp. [i–iv] v–xv [xvi] [1] 2–235 [236–239] 240–255 [256].
Page i: half title. p. ii: blank. p. iii: title. p. iv: '*Copyright © 1959 by William Burroughs* | All Rights Reserved | Library of Congress Catalog Card Number: 60–11097 | First Printing | *Manufactured in the United States of America*'. pp. v–xvi: 'Introduction | DEPOSI-TION: TESTIMONY CONCERNING | A SICKNESS' by WSB. pp. 1–217: text. pp. 218–235: 'ATROPHIED PREFACE | WOULDN'T YOU?' by William Burroughs; p. 235: signed '*Tangier, 1959.*' p. 236: blank. p. 237: 'APPENDIX'. p. 238: blank. pp.

239–255: 'LETTER FROM A MASTER ADDICT TO | DANGEROUS DRUGS'. p. 256: blank.

Contents: "Deposition: Testimony concerning a Sickness" (reprinted from *Evergreen Review,* 1960 [see **C12**]); text, *Naked Lunch*; "Atrophied Preface, Wouldn't You?"; "Appendix: 'Letter from a Master Addict to Dangerous Drugs'" (reprinted from *The British Journal of Addiction,* 1957 [see **C1**]).

Paper: White wove paper. Endpapers white.

Binding: Bound in half black cloth and boards. Front and back covers blank. Spine: '[in gilt] *Burroughs* | [publisher's device] | NAKED | LUNCH | [publisher's device] | *Grove Press*'. Issued in a dust jacket with a black and yellow photograph of some unidentified objects on the front and spine. Jacket front cover: superimposed over photograph at the top, '[white] | NAKED LUNCH | [red] By William Burroughs'. Jacket spine: '[red, across top] BURROUGHS | [down] NAKED LUNCH | [across at bottom], GROVE | PRESS'. Dust jacket back cover: white with Martha Rocher's photo of WSB in the top right corner; at top right, in red, 'Comments about | NAKED LUNCH'; following (in black) is a long quote from WSB regarding his work and four short quotes from Norman Mailer, Robert Lowell, E. S. Seldon, and Jack Kerouac regarding *Naked Lunch,* at the bottom of which is a long rule and 'GROVE PRESS, INC. 64 University Place, New York 3, N.Y.' Inside flaps have the publisher's blurb, a short biographical sketch of the author, and the price, '$6.00'. All edges trimmed, top edge stained black.

Publication: This edition, published March 21, 1962, consisted of 3,500 copies. Its Grove Press Catalogue number was GP244. It was reprinted perhaps a dozen times, but the printer and Grove Press could supply no information as to the dates and quantities printed since they had no existing records of those printings. Some copies of this edition are found with a wraparound band (7.6 cm. wide) on which is printed in black: 'Recommended for Sale | to Adults Only | $6.00'.

c. John Calder   1964

THE | NAKED | LUNCH | WILLIAM BURROUGHS | LONDON | JOHN CALDER | in association with | OLYMPIA PRESS

A2b, f

A2c, [e]

A2d

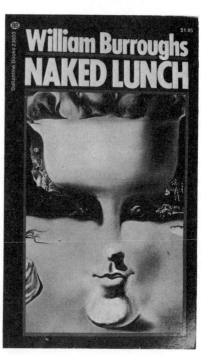

A2g

Collation: 20.4 × 13.3 cm. [1]⁸ 2–16⁸, 128 leaves; pp. [i–iv], [1] 2–232 [233–234] 235–251 [252]. All gatherings signed 'TNL' except 2, 3, 4, which are signed 'N.L.', and 1, which is unsigned. Page i: half title. p. ii: blank. p. iii: title. p. iv: *'Originally published in English by Olympia Press, Paris 1959 and | Subsequently by Grove Press, New York 1962, Sugar Editore, Milan | 1963, and Editions Gallimard, Paris 1964* | FIRST PUBLISHED IN GREAT BRITAIN 1964 | BY JOHN CALDER (PUBLISHERS) LIMITED | 17 SACKVILLE STREET, LONDON, W.1 | *Copyright © 1959 by William Burroughs* | *All Rights Reserved* | PRINTED IN GREAT BRITAIN BY | THE VILLAFIELD PRESS, BISHOP-BRIGGS, GLASGOW'. pp. 1–11: 'INTRODUCTION | *deposition: testimony concerning a sickness*' by WSB. pp. 12–215: text. pp. 216–232: *'atrophied preface* | WOULDN'T YOU?' by WSB; p. 232 signed *'Tangier, 1959.'* p. 233: 'APPENDIX'. p. 234: blank. pp. 235–251: 'LETTER FROM A MASTER ADDICT TO DANGEROUS DRUGS' by WSB. p. 252: blank.

Contents: Identical to **A2b**.

Paper: White wove paper. Endpapers white.

Binding: Bound in beige cloth. Front and back covers blank. Spine: '[in gilt, across at top] BURROUGHS | [down, in fancy lettering] The Naked Lunch | [across at bottom, publisher's device (a tree)] | CALDER'. Issued in a white ground dust jacket. Jacket front cover: at top, '[black] WILLIAM [red] BURROUGHS | [black] THE | [red] NAKED | [black] LUNCH'; the rest is given to a black and white photo (Ian Sommerville's) of WSB's head with the eyes cut out and replaced with two red dots. Jacket spine: '[black] WILLIAM | [red] BURROUGHS | [black] THE | [red] NAKED | [black] LUNCH | CALDER'. Jacket back cover: book title across the top in large red letters and the author's name in black under it; following is the publisher's blurb and six short quotes from Norman Mailer, Robert Lowell, E. S. Seldon, Jack Kerouac, Herbert Gold, and Mary McCarthy regarding *Naked Lunch*, headed *'From the American Reviews'*; at the bottom: '[black] JOHN CALDER (PUBLISHERS) LTD. | 17 SACKVILLE STREET, LONDON, W.1.' On inside flaps are the publisher's advertisement and, on flap 1, the book's price: '42S.' and, on flap 2, the credit: *'Photograph of William Burroughs | by Ian Sommerville'*.

Publication: This edition, published Nov. 19, 1964, consisted of 4,000 copies. The edition was reprinted in 1965, 1966, and 1970, but publisher would supply no dates or quantities printed, declaring that information to be confidential.

d. Grove Press, Inc.   1966

William S. Burroughs | NAKED | LUNCH | [double-line rule enclosing slashes] | *Grove Press, Inc.* | *New York*

Collation: 17.8 × 10.7 cm. 152 leaves; pp. [i–vi] vii–xlvii [xlviii], [1] 2–235 [236–239] 240–255 [256].
Pages i-ii: quotes from six reviews, headed: 'Acclaim for *Naked Lunch*'. p. iii: title. p. iv: 'Copyright © 1959 by William Burroughs | All Rights Reserved | Caution: No part of this book may be reproduced, for any reason, by any means, including any method of photographic | reproduction, without the permission of the publisher. | First Evergreen Black Cat Edition 1966 | First Printing | MANUFACTURED IN THE UNITED STATES OF AMERICA'. p. v: 'Contents'. p. vi: blank. pp. vii–xxxvi: '*Naked Lunch* on Trial'. pp. xxxvii–xlviii: 'Introduction | DEPOSITION: TESTIMONY CONCERNING | A SICKNESS' by WSB. pp. 1–217: text. pp. 218–235: 'ATROPHIED PREFACE | WOULDN'T YOU?' by WSB; p. 235 signed '*Tangier, 1959.*' p. 236: blank. p. 237: 'APPENDIX'. p. 238: blank. pp. 239–255: 'LETTER FROM A MASTER ADDICT TO | DANGEROUS DRUGS' by WSB. p. 256: blank. A two-leaf (4-page) card advertisement for *Evergreen Review* is inserted between pp. 104 and 105.

Contents: Identical to **A2b**, except for addition of "Naked Lunch on Trial," an expanded version (more prefatory remarks) of an article, "The Boston Trial of *Naked Lunch*," which appeared in *Evergreen Review*, 1965 (see **C118**).

Paper: White wove paper.

Binding: Perfect-bound, no sigs. Stiff white wrappers. Front cover: at top, '[red and black] BC–115 [publisher's device (head of a black cat with white eyes)] $1.25'; rest of lettering is within a tilted black-lined rectangle, '[black] FIRST PAPERBACK EDITION OF THE COM-|PLETE $6 GROVE PRESS BEST-SELLER | [long red rule] | [large red caps] NAKED | LUNCH | [long red rule] | [black] BY WILLIAM S. BURROUGHS | [purple] "THE ONLY AMERI-

CAN NOVELIST LIVING | TODAY WHO MAY CONCEIVA-BLY BE POS-|SESSED BY GENIUS." —NORMAN MAILER | [in black at bottom on purple circle outlined in white and red with red triangles] WITH | MASSACHUSETTS | SUPREME COURT DE-CISION | AND EXCERPTS FROM | THE BOSTON | TRIAL'. Spine: '[down, in black, purple, and red] NAKED LUNCH BY WILLIAM S. BURROUGHS | [across at bottom, publisher's device in black (as before)] | [red] BC–115 | GROVE | PRESS'. Back cover: at top, '[red and black] AN EVERGREEN BLACK CAT BOOK —BC–115 [publisher's device (as before)] $1.25'; the remainder of the back cover is given to short quotes (separated by long purple rules) from five reviews of the book, headed [red] "A savagely funny . . . | terrifying | masterpiece."' All edges are red and trimmed.

Publication: This edition, published in October 1966, consisted of 25,000* copies. It was reprinted in November 1966 (25,000* copies), February 1969 (24,339 copies), November 1969 (25,629 copies), July 1970 (22,746 copies), August 1971 (24,351 copies), May 1972 (11,995 copies), February 1973 (15,000 copies), September 1973 (10,000 copies), and April 1974 (20,000 copies). Later reprints do not have the Evergreen card advertisement, and have white edges.

e. Corgi Books   1968

William | Burroughs | THE | NAKED | LUNCH | [publisher's device (in a black circle, the white head of a wolf with a book in its mouth)] | CORGIBOOKS ['CORGI' in black; 'BOOKS' in white outlined in black] | A DIVISION OF TRANSWORLD PUB-LISHERS

Collation: 18.1 × 11 cm. [T.N.L.–1]¹², T.N.L.–2—T.N.L.–12¹², 144 leaves; pp. [1–6] 7–261 [262–264] 265–286 [287–288].
Page 1: publisher's blurb with two quotes on the work from Norman Mailer and the Oxford *Mail*. p. 2: blank. p. 3: title. p. 4: 'THE NAKED LUNCH | A CORGI BOOK 552 07938 3 | Originally published in Great Britain | by John Calder (Publishers) Limited. | PRINTING HISTORY | John Calder Edition published 1964 | Corgi Edition published 1968 | Copyright © 1959 by William Bur-roughs | Originally published in English by Olympia Press, Paris

---

*Quantity approximated.

1959, | and subsequently by Grove Press, New York 1962, | Sugar Editore, Milan 1963, and Editions Gallimard, Paris 1964 | Conditions of sale—This book is sold subject to the | condition that it shall not, by way of trade *or otherwise*, be lent, re-sold, hired out or otherwise *circulated* | without the publisher's prior consent in any form of | binding or cover other than that in which it is published | *and without a similar condition including this condition* | *being imposed on the subsequent purchaser.* | This book is set in 12 point Linotype Baskerville | Corgi Books are published by Transworld Publishers | Ltd., Bashley Road, London, N.W.10. | Made and printed in Great Britain by | Hazell Watson & Viney Limited, Aylesbury, Bucks.' p. 5: half title. p. 6: blank. pp. 7–18: 'INTRODUCTION | deposition: testimony concerning a sickness' by WSB. pp. 19–244: text. pp. 244–261: *'atrophied preface* | WOULDN'T YOU?' by WSB; p. 261 signed *'Tangier, 1959.'* p. 262: blank. p. 263: 'APPENDIX'. p. 264: blank. pp. 265–286: 'LETTER FROM A MASTER ADDICT TO | DANGEROUS DRUGS' by WSB. pp. 287–288: publisher's advertisement.

Contents: Identical to **A2b**.

Paper: White wove paper.

Binding: Stiff white pictorial wrappers. Front cover: a smaller reproduction of the front dust jacket of **A2c**, except at top right is '[black] CORGI | [white, outlined in black] BOOKS | [publisher's device (in white within a red circle, a wolf's head with a book in its mouth)]' and at bottom right is '[black] 552 07938 3'. Spine: '[across top, black] 552 | 07938 | 3 | NOVEL | [publisher's device as on front cover] | WILLIAM | BURROUGHS | [thin red rule] | [down, black] THE | [red] NAKED | [black] LUNCH'. The back cover has quotes from three reviews (Kenneth Allsop, *Daily Mail*; Anthony Burgess, *The Guardian*; and the *Sunday Times*) in red (signed in black), headed: '[black] THE | NAKED | LUNCH'; at the bottom is: '[black] 552 07938 3 U.K. 7s.6d. * AUSTRALIA $1.15 * NEW ZEALAND $1.5'. All edges trimmed.

Publication: The publisher would supply no information regarding the printing of this edition, published in 1968, declaring the information to be confidential. It was reprinted twice in 1969 and once in 1972.

f. Castle Books   1973

An authorized reprint (light brown cloth boards) of **A2b**. Collation (except for slightly larger leaf size) and contents are identical to **A2b**. Issued with a reproduction of the original dust jacket. All edges trimmed.

Publication: This edition, published in March 1973, consisted of 5,000 copies. Though priced $6.00, copies were remaindered at $1.98.

g. Ballantine Books   1973

An authorized reprint (with new, surrealistic wrappers) of **A2d**. Collation and contents are the same as **A2d**. Paperbound and priced $1.95. All edges trimmed and light orange.

Publication: This edition, published in November 1973, consisted of 35,500 copies. Edition reprinted in June 1974 (25,000 copies).

A3   **MINUTES TO GO**

a. Two Cities Editions   1960

MINUTES TO GO | SINCLAIR BEILES | WILLIAM BUR-ROUGHS | GREGORY CROSO | BRION GYSIN | "Not knowing what is and is not knowing | *I knew not.*" | Hassan Sabbah's "Razor". | TWO CITIES EDITIONS

Collation: 21 × 13.5 cm [1–4]⁸, 32 leaves; pp. [1–2] 3–63 [64]. Page 1: title. p. 2: 'The publication of this book has been rendered possible | by the cooperation of | THE ENGLISH BOOKSHOP | 42, rue de Seine, Paris (VIᵉ) | All rights reserved | *Copyright* Jean Franchette, 1960 | 189, rue Ordener, Paris–18ᵉ'. pp. 3–62: text. p. 63: 'Post-script from Gregory Corso:–'. p. 64: 'Acheve d'imprimer le 13 avril 1960 | par Techni-Press, PRO 51–77, pour | le compte de Jean Franchette et des | Editions de la Revue TWO CITIES | Depot legal: 2ᵉ trimestre 1960 | Il a été tire de | "MINUTES TO GO" | dix exemplaires numerotes de 1 à 10 | le tout constituant l'édition originale.'

Contents: Pages 3–5: 'MINUTES TO GO' by Brion Gysin. pp. 6–10: 'FIRST CUT-UPS' by Brion Gysin. pp. 11–12: 'OPEN LETTER

TO LIFE MAGAZINE' by WSB. pp. 12–13: 'CANCER MEN . . .
THESE INDIVIDUALS | ARE MARKED FOE . . . ' by WSB. pp.
13–14: 'FORMED IN THE STANCE' by WSB. p. 15: 'VIRUSES
WERE BY ACCIDENT?' by WSB. p. 16: 'THE ACTUAL MA
VIRUSES IN POLIO | PHOTO FOR FUR FUZZ?' by WSB. p. 17:
'DISH SOPRANO MADE THE NIGHT FOR SHE OVATION'
by WSB. p. 18: 'OTHERS KILL CELLS AND FUTURE | FOR
NEW CANCER HOLES' by WSB. p. 19: untitled cut-up by WSB.
p. 20: 'MAO TZE: TA TA KAN KAN. . . . KAN KAN TA TA . . . '
by WSB. p. 21: 'FROM SAN DIEGO UP TO MAINE' by WSB. p.
22: '"San Diego Up To Maine" Cut Up' by WSB. p. 23:
'EVERYWHERE MARCH YOUR HEAD' by WSB and Gregory
Corso. pp. 24–25: 'SONS OF YOUR IN' by WSB and Gregory
Corso. pp. 26–28: 'REACTIVE AGENT TAPE CUT BY LEE THE
AGENT | IN INTERZONE' by WSB. pp. 29–31: 'CALLING ALL
RE ACTIVE AGENTS' by Brion Gysin. p. 32: 'SPONTANEOUS
PIECE ON THE "50"S IN AMERICA' by Gregory Corso. p. 33:
'CUT UP of Eisenhower Speech & Mine Own Poem | gregory corso'.
p. 34: 'CUT UP of Ginsberg Letter & Herald Trib Paris Editorial |
gregory corso'. p. 35: 'CUT UP of one of my poems | gregory corso'.
p. 36: 'TINKLING DECIBEL OF MjQ' by WSB and Sinclair Beiles.
p. 37: untitled cut-up by Sinclair Beiles, p. 38: "TELEGRAM FROM
MEKNES' by Sinclair Beiles. pp. 39–41: 'UNITED EITHER
DARK AND LUGUBRIOUS WITH | NATIONS' by Sinclair
Beiles. pp. 42–46: 'CUT ME UP * BRION GYSIN * CUT ME UP *
BRION / GYSIN * CUT ME UP * BRION GYSIN * CUT ME
IN *' by Brion Gysin. p. 47: 'I THINK THEREFORE I AM' by Brion
Gysin. p. 48: 'THE NEW TESTAMENT | ST MATTHEW (from
chap 27)' by Sinclair Beiles. pp. 48–49: 'TACITUS (from Imperial
Rome)' by Sinclair Beiles. pp. 49–54: 'TO BE CUT UP BY YOU'
by Sinclair Beiles. pp. 55–58: 'THINGS TO CUT-UP, COL-
LECTED BY GREGORY CORSO'. pp. 59–60: 'Words Dealth by
William Lee Dealer', unsigned, probably by WSB. p. 61: 'MOVE
THE BONE WORDS OF THE IMMORTAL BARD | WILLIAM
SHAKESPEARE', unsigned, probably by WSB. p. 62: 'RUB OUT
THE WRITE WORD' by Brion Gysin. p. 63: 'Post-script from
Gregory Corso:—' by Gregory Corso. p. 64: Colophon as above.

Paper: White wove paper.

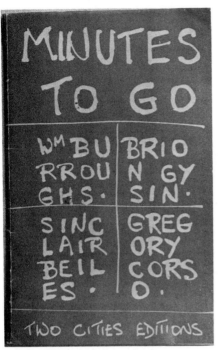

A3a (front cover)

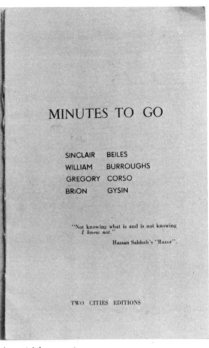

A3a (title page)

A3b

Binding: Stiff light blue pictorial wrappers. Front cover: in drawn white capital letters, at top 'MINUTES | TO GO'; in center, author's names in tic-tac-toe design; at bottom, 'TWO CITIES EDITIONS'. Spine: '[up, black] TWO CITIES MINUTES TO GO'. Back cover is a calligraph in white and blue by Brion Gysin. All edges trimmed.

Publication: This edition, published April 13, 1960, consisted of 1,000 copies priced at 7.20F. There was also a printing of 10 copies on fine paper, numbered 1–10. Some copies were issued with a white wraparound band, 5.7 cm. wide, reading: 'Un reglement de comptes | avec la litterature'.

b. Beach Books, Texts & Documents   1968

MINUTES TO GO | SINCLAIR BEILES | WILLIAM BUR-
ROUGHS | GREGORY CORSO | BRION GYSIN | "Not know-
ing what is and is not knowing | *I knew not*" | Hassan Sabbah's
"Razor". | [publisher's device (a white handstamp in a black circle,
outlined in white and black)] | BEACH BOOKS, TEXTS &
DOCUMENTS | Distributed by | City Lights Books, 1562 Grant
Avenue, San Francisco, California 94133

Collation: 21.5 × 13.5 cm. 34 leaves; pp. [i–ii], [1–2] 3–63 [64–66].
Page i: title. p. ii: '© 1968 BEACH BOOKS, TEXTS & DOCU-
MENTS'. p. 1: half title. p. 2: 'COLLAGE BY CLAUDE PÉLIEU'.
pp. 3–62: text. p. 63: 'Post-script from Gregory Corso:—'. p. 64:
blank. p. 65: publisher's advertisement. p. 66: blank.

Contents: Except for the collage by Claude Pélieu, the contents are identical to **A3a**.

Paper: White wove paper.

Binding: Perfect-bound, no sigs. Stiff light brown pictorial wrappers. Front cover: across the top, '[black] MINUTES TO GO'; below, the authors' names on baggage checks. Spine: '[down, black] MINUTES TO GO BEACH BOOKS'. Back cover is a calligraph by Brion Gysin, with price at top: '$1.25'. All edges trimmed.

Publication: This edition, published in 1968, consisted of 1,000*
copies.

*Publisher has no record, but remembers edition to be 1,000 copies.

A4   THE EXTERMINATOR

a. The Auerhahn Press   1960

THE EXTERMINATOR | "LET PETTY KINGS THE NAME OF
PARTY KNOW | WHERE I COME I KILL BOTH FRIEND
AND FOE." | *WILLIAM BURROUGHS* | *BRION GYSIN* | 1960 |
[swelled rule] | THE AUERHAHN PRESS

Collation: 23.3 × 15.7 cm. [1–4]⁸, 32 leaves; pp. [i–vi], [1–4] 5–45
[46] 47 [48] 49 [50] 51 [52–58].
Pages i–iv: blank. p. v: half-title. p. vi: blank. p. 1: title. p. 2:
'Copyright 1960 by William Burroughs'. pp. 3–4: blank. pp.
5–44: text. pp. 45, 47, 49, and 51: calligraphs by Brion Gysin, pp.
46, 48, 50, and 52: blank. p. 53: '[publisher's design (a florallike
ornament)] | This book was designed | and printed by Dave L. |
Hazelwood and James F. | McIlroy at the Auerhahn | Press, 1334
Franklin, San | Francisco, California.' pp. 54–58: blank.

Contents: "The Exterminator" by WSB; "Who Sends the Man?,"
"Kick That Habit Man," "Junk Is No Good Baby," "Can Mother Be
Wrong?," "Short Time to Go," "In the Beginning Was the Word,"
"Rub Out the Words," and "Proclaim Present Time Over" by Brion
Gysin; four calligraphs by Brion Gysin.

Paper: White wove paper.

Binding: Stiff white pictorial wrappers. Front cover: green callig-
raphy by Brion Gysin over which is printed '[red] THE | EXTER-
MINATOR'; then in black and reading down, the authors' names
separated by a swelled rule. Spine: the drawing of Brion Gysin
continues across the spine. Back cover: on the right a continuation of
Brion Gysin's calligraphy; on the left, '[at top, red] THE [publisher's
design (a rooster)] | EXTERMINATOR | [center, the publisher's
blurb in black] | [at bottom, red] The Auerhahn Press | 1334
Franklin, San Francisco, California'. All edges trimmed.

Publication: This edition, published in 1960, consisted of 1,000*
copies. Per copy price was $1.50.

---

* Quantity approximated.

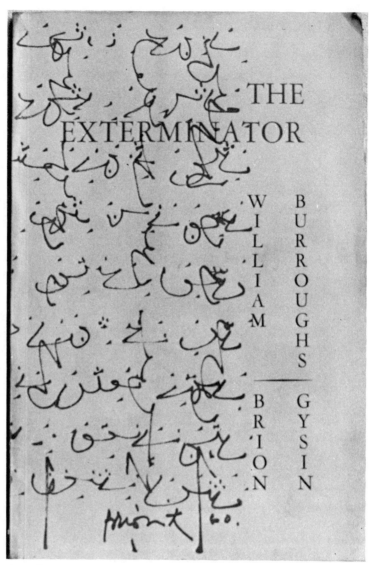

A4a, [b]

b. Dave Haselwood Books   1967

A second edition, slightly larger in size, with wrappers of white calligraphy over blue field. The collation (except for minor differences) and contents are identical to **A4a**. Published in 1967 in a run of 1,000* copies. Priced $1.50.

A5   **THE SOFT MACHINE**

a. The Olympia Press   1961
[Within a border of green ornaments] WILLIAM BURROUGHS | THE | SOFT | MACHINE | THE TRAVELLER'S COMPANION | SERIES | published by | THE OLYMPIA PRESS | 7 *rue Saint-Séverin, Paris 5*

Collation: 17.5 × 11 cm. 1–11⁸, 12⁴, 92 leaves; pp. [1–6] 7–43 [44] 45–147 [148] 149–181 [182–184]. All gatherings signed '88'. Pages 1–2: blank. p. 3: half title. p. 4: '*Jacket designed* | *by Brion Gysin* | PRINTED IN FRANCE | by Imprimerie S.I.P., Montreuil (Seine). June 1961 | [line rule] | *Copyright © by William S. Burroughs, 1961.* | Dépôt légal : 3ᵉ trimestre 1961.' p. 5: title. p. 6: blank. pp. 7–182: text. pp. 183–184: blank. Pages 44, and 148 are also blank.

Contents: Text of *The Soft Machine*, first version.

Paper: White wove paper.

Binding: Bound in stiff olive-green wrappers. Front cover: within a border rule consisting of a black chain-link rule enclosing a black-white-black rule, '[black] WILLIAM BURROUGHS | THE | SOFT | MACHINE | Nº 88 | *THE* | TRAVELLER'S COMPANION | SERIES'. Spine: '[black, within black-ruled rectangle, across at bottom] 88 [up] THE SOFT MACHINE'. Back cover: bottom right corner, '[black] 15 N.F. | NOT TO BE SOLD | IN U.S.A. & U.K.'; on some copies, 'NEW PRICE | NF 18' was stamped over in black within black rule border with old price canceled by two black rules. Issued with a gray-black dust jacket which reproduces a calligraphic drawing by Brion Gysin. On the front, the top 6/7 of the cover is the drawing in black, white, and gray; the remaining 1/7 is a deep purple panel within which is printed: '[white] William Burroughs | [red] THE SOFT MACHINE'. Jacket spine: the Brion Gysin drawing

* Quantity approximated.

continues over the top 6/7 of the spine; the bottom 1/7 is a continuation of the deep purple panel, within which is '[red] THE | SOFT | MACHINE'. Back jacket cover: a continuation of the drawing on the front occupies the top 6/7; below it is the deep purple panel within which is printed '[red] the olympia press | PARIS'. On inside flap 1 is the publisher's blurb; inside flap 2 is the publisher's advertisement. All edges trimmed.

Publication: This edition, published in June 1961, consisted of 5,000 copies.

The announced February 1963 revised edition of *The Soft Machine* was never published by The Olympia Press. It was published later (1966) by Grove Press (see **A5b**).

b. Grove Press, Inc.   1966

WILLIAM S. BURROUGHS | THE SOFT MACHINE | Grove Press, Inc., New York

Collation: 20.1 × 13.5 cm. [1–4]^{16}, 92 leaves; pp. [1–8] 9–29 [30] 31–35 [36] 37–55 [56] 57–97 [98] 99–117 [118] 119–123 [124] 125–129 [130] 131–149 [150] 151–175 [176] 177–182 [183–184].
Page 1: half title. p. 2: blank. p. 3: title. p. 4: 'Copyright © 1961, 1966 by William S. Burroughs | All Rights Reserved | Library of Congress Catalog Card Number: 66–14096 | First Printing | Manufactured in the United States of America | by The Book Press, Brattleboro, Vermont'. pp. 5–6: 'Contents'. p. 7: second half title. p. 8: blank. pp. 9–182: text. pp. 183–184: blank. Pages 30, 36, 56, 98, 118, 124, 130, 150, and 176 are also blank.

Contents: Text of *The Soft Machine*, second version; a rearrangement of the first Olympia text, with additions and expansions.

Paper: White wove paper. Endpapers white.

Binding: Bound in dark red cloth. Front and back covers blank. Spine: '[silver, down] THE SOFT MACHINE WILLIAM S. BURROUGHS | [across at bottom] GROVE | PRESS'. Issued with a white ground dust jacket, on the front of which is a calligraphic drawing by WSB in black, light brown, brown, and violet. Jacket front cover: at top, above drawing, '[black] The Soft Machine | [gray]

A5a

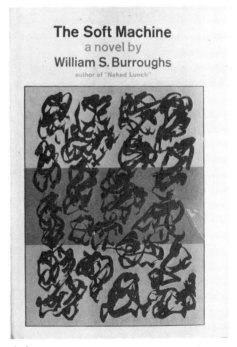

A5b

a novel by | [gray-black] William S. Burroughs | [violet] author of "Naked Lunch" '. Spine: '[down, in black, light brown, and violet] THE SOFT MACHINE BY WILLIAM S. BURROUGHS | [across at bottom, violet] GP–361 | [light brown] GROVE | PRESS'. On three-fourths of the back of the jacket, reproduced in sepia, is a photograph of WSB by Charles Henri Ford, below which is a short biographical sketch of the author in black, below which is: '[violet] GROVE PRESS, INC., 80 University Place, New York, N.Y. 10003'. Inside flaps are the publisher's blurb; at the bottom of flap 2 are three short quotes on WSB from Norman Mailer, Jack Kerouac, and John Ciardi followed by the credit: '[violet] Jacket design from a drawing by William S. Burroughs'; at the top of flap 1 is the book's price, '[black] $5.00'. All edges trimmed.

Publication: This edition, published March 21, 1966, consisted of 18,000 copies. At least two reprints were done, but The Book Press had no records of the dates or quantities printed and Grove Press could supply no further information. Later editions were bound in black cloth.

c. Grove Press, Inc.   1967

The title page is identical to **A5b**.

Collation: 17.8 × 10.5 cm. 96 leaves. Except for two extra leaves at the beginning and two more at the end, the pagination is identical to that of **A5b**.

Pages i–iii: short quotes from nine reviews plus a statement from WSB, headed: 'About William Burroughs | and The Soft Machine'. p. iv: blank. p. 1: half title. p. 2: blank. p. 3: title. p. 4: 'Copyright © 1961, 1966 by William S. Burroughs | All Rights Reserved | First Evergreen Black Cat Edition 1967 | First Printing | Manufactured in the United States of America'. pp. 5–6: 'Contents'. p. 7: second half title. p. 8: blank. pp. 9–182: text. p. 183: publisher's advertisement for *Evergreen Review.* p. 184: blank. pp. 185–188: publisher's advertisement. A two-leaf (four-page) card advertisement for *Evergreen Review* is inserted between pp. 92 and 93.

Contents: Text of *The Soft Machine,* second version, as in **A5b**.

Paper: White wove paper.

Binding: Perfect-bound, no signatures. Stiff black-and-white pictorial wrappers. Front cover: a black-and-white photo of WSB by Charles Henri Ford, cropped from the larger one on the reverse jacket of **A5b**; above the photo is '[at top right, red] BC–131 [publisher's device (head of a cat)] 95¢ | [flush left, white] The Soft Machine | [red] a novel by | [orange] William S. Burroughs | The author of Naked Lunch'. Spine: '[down, orange] THE SOFT MACHINE [black] WILLIAM S. BURROUGHS | [across at bottom, orange, 'BC–131 | [publisher's design (as before)] | GROVE | PRESS'. Back cover: '[at top right, black] AN EVERGREEN BLACK CAT BOOK [publisher's design (as before)] 95¢ | BC–131 | [flush left, orange] The | Interstellar | War of the Sexes | [long heavy red rule] | [black] publisher's blurb. | [long heavy red rule] | [black] quote on WSB from Jack Kerouac | [long heavy red rule] | [bottom left, black] Photo: Charles Henri Ford | Printed in U.S.A.'. All edges are orange and trimmed.

Publication: This edition, published in March 1967, consisted of 25,000* copies. It was reprinted in April 1967 in a printing of 24,052 copies. Also reprinted in July 1973 (5,000 copies) and May 1974 (5,000 copies). Reprint does not have the card advertisement and has white edges.

d. Calder and Boyars   1968

THE SOFT | MACHINE | a novel | William Burroughs | CALDER AND BOYARS | LONDON

Collation: 19.7 × 12.7 cm. [1–6]¹⁶, 96 leaves; pp. [1–4] 5–187 [188–192].
Page 1: half title. p. 2: '*By the same author* | DEAD FINGERS TALK | THE NAKED LUNCH | THE TICKET THAT EXPLODED'. p. 3: title. p. 4: 'This revised edition first published in Great Britain 1968 | by Calder and Boyars Ltd, 18, Brewer Street, London, W.1. | First version published by The Olympia Press, Paris 1961. | Second version published by Grove Press Inc., New York, 1966 | © William Burroughs, 1961, 1966, 1968 | ALL RIGHTS RESERVED | Set by C. Nicholls & Company Ltd and | Printed in England by | Latimer Trend & Co. Ltd'. pp. 5–169: text; p. 169 signed 'Jan. 25, Gibraltar.' p. 170: 'APPENDIX TO THE SOFT MACHINE'. pp. 171–176: 'A TREATMENT THAT CANCELS ADDICTION'. p. 177: 'PLAN

*Quantity approximated.

DRUG ADDICTION'. pp. 178–188: 'JAIL MAY BE BEST RX FOR ADDICTS MD SAYS', all by WSB.

Contents: Text of *The Soft Machine*, third version (the second version with additions to and expansions of text), and "Appendix to *The Soft Machine*," "A Treatment That Cancels Addiction," "Plan Drug Addiction," and "Jail May Be Best RX for Addicts MD Says."

Paper: White wove paper. Endpapers white.

Binding: Bound in light brown cloth. Front and back covers blank. Spine: '[in gilt, down] THE SOFT MACHINE | William Burroughs | [across at bottom] CALDER | [line rule] | BOYARS'. Issued with a bown-and-white dust jacket designed by Kaye Bellman, the front of which is a brown field on which is, in swirling white letters within a stylistic white line-enclosure: 'THE | SOFT | MACHINE | a novel by | william | burroughs'. Jacket spine: '[down, in swirling white letters] THE | SOFT MACHINE william burroughs | [across at bottom, in white caps] CALDER | BOYARS'. On the reverse of the jacket (in brown on white field) is, at top: 'THE SOFT MACHINE | William Burroughs'; the publisher's blurb occupies the next 5/8 of the jacket; at the bottom (within a rectangle) is the publisher's advertisements, underneath which is: 'CALDER & BOYARS LTD | 18 Brewer Street London W1'. Inner flaps are both given to the publisher's advertisement. At the bottom of flap 1 is the price, '42s'. All edges trimmed.

Publication: This edition was published July 25, 1968. The publisher would give no number of copies printed, declaring this information to be confidential.

e. Calder and Boyars 1968

The title page is identical to **A5d**.

Collation: Except for slight difference in size (this edition is 19.5 × 13 cm.) the collation is identical to **A5d**.

Contents: Identical to **A5d**.

Paper: White wove paper.

Binding: Bound in stiff yellowish-green-and-white wrappers. Front cover (except for coloration) is the same as the front dust jacket of **A5d**. Spine: '[yellowish-green, down] THE SOFT MACHINE

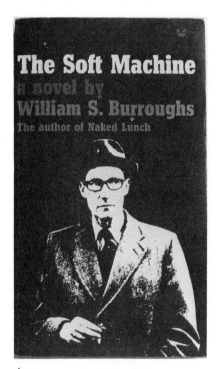

A5c

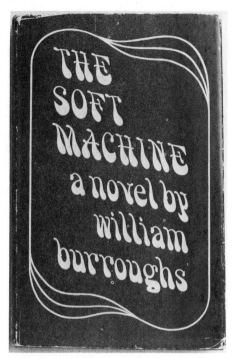

A5d, [e]

A5f

A5g

William Burroughs | [across at bottom] CB | 223'. Back cover: all in yellowish green on white; at top, 'A Calder book CB 223 15s [and directly below] 75p | THE SOFT MACHINE | William Burroughs'; directly underneath is the publisher's blurb and two short quotes from reviews of the work, headed: '*Some Press Opinions*'; at the bottom is a small publisher's advertisements, and at the extreme bottom: 'CALDER & BOYARS LTD | 18 BREWER STREET LONDON W1 | ISBN 0 7145 0732 6'. All edges trimmed.

Publication: This edition was published simultaneously with **A5d** (July 25, 1968). The number of copies printed could not be obtained from the publisher as that information is confidential.

f. Corgi Books   1970

The second UK paperback of **A5**, with white wrappers and the title in large red-orange letters outlined and shadowed in yellow and black to give 3-D effect. Collation (except for minor differences) and contents are the same as **A5d**. Priced at 35p.

Publication: The publisher would give no information on this edition except that it was published in 1970; all other data are confidential.

g. Ballantine Books   1973

An authorized reprint (with new, surrealistic wrappers) of **A5c**. Collation (with minor differences) and contents are the same as **A5c**. Paperbound and priced $1.50. All edges trimmed.

Publication: This edition, published in November 1973, consisted of 37,000 copies.

A6   **THE TICKET THAT EXPLODED**

a. The Olympia Press   1962

[Within a border of green ornaments]WILLIAM BURROUGHS | THE TICKET | THAT | EXPLODED | THE TRAVELLER'S COMPANION | *SERIES* | published by | THE OLYMPIA PRESS | 7 *rue Saint-Séverin, Paris 5*

Collation: 17.4 × 11 cm. 1^4, 2–12^{16}, 92 leaves; pp. [1–6] 7–182 [183–184].

Pages 1–2: blank. p. 3: half title. p. 4: 'ACKNOWLEDGMENT |
The sections entitled *In A Strange* | *Bed* and *The Black Fruit* were |
written in collaboration with | Michael Portman. | The design on p.
183 is by | Brion Gysin. | *Other works by William Burroughs* | *published
by The Olympia Press:* | THE NAKED LUNCH : 1959. | THE SOFT
MACHINE | First edition: 1961. | New and revised and augmented |
edition: February 1963.' p. 5: title. p. 6: 'PRINTED IN FRANCE |
by Imprimerie Desgrandchamps, Paris, December 1962. | [line rule]
| *Copyright by William Burroughs, 1962.* | *Dépôt légal : 4ᵉ trimestre
1962.*' pp. 7–183: text. p. 184: blank. Page 183 of text fades into
calligraphy of Brion Gysin.

Contents: Text of *The Ticket That Exploded*, first version.

Paper: White wove paper.

Binding: Bound in stiff olive-green wrappers. Front cover: within a
border rule consisting of black chain-link rule enclosing a black-
white-black rule, '[black] WILLIAM BURROUGHS | THE
TICKET | THAT | EXPLODED | n° 91 | *THE* TRAVELLER'S
COMPANION | *SERIES*'. Spine: '[black, within black-ruled white
rectangle, across at bottom] 91 [up] THE TICKET THAT
EXPLODED'. Back cover: bottom right corner, '[black] 18 N.F. |
NOT TO BE SOLD | IN U.S.A. & U.K.' Issued with a dust jacket
which is a black-and-gray photo collage by Ian Sommerville torn at
bottom to reveal on a white field, on front of jacket: '[red script] the
ticket | that exploded. | [black type] BY WILLIAM BUR-
ROUGHS'. The torn collage continues on the jacket spine, which
reads: '[up, red] THE TICKET THAT | EXPLODED | [black]
WILLIAM BURROUGHS'. The jacket back is a continuation of the
collage, also torn at the bottom to reveal a white field, wherein is
printed: '[black] THE OLYMPIA PRESS'. Both inside flaps carry
the publisher's blurb. All edges trimmed.

Publication: This edition, published in December 1962, consisted of
5,000 copies. There was no February 1963 Olympia Press revised
edition. It was issued (1967) by Grove Press (see **A6b**).

b. Grove Press, Inc.   1967

William S. Burroughs | The Ticket That Exploded | [line rule] | *posed
little time* | *so I'll say* | *"good night"* | [line rule] | Grove Press, Inc. |
New York

A6a

Collation: 20.3 × 13.4 cm. [1–7]¹⁶, 112 leaves; pp. [i-vi], 1–202 [203–204] 205–217 [218].

Page i: half title. p. ii: blank. p. iii: title. p. iv: 'Copyright © 1962, 1964, 1966, 1967 by William S. Burroughs | All Rights Reserved | Library of Congress Catalog Card Number: 66–28732 | An earlier version of this novel was first published in 1962 by | The Olympia Press, Paris. Part of the section entitled *silence* | *to say good bye* appeared in *The Insect Trust Gazette*, No. 1, | Summer, 1964; a portion of the Appendix was published in *The* | *International Times*, London. | First Printing | Manufactured in the United States of America'. p. v: '*Acknowledgment*' by WSB. p. vi: blank. pp. 1–202: text. p. 203: calligraphy of Brion Gysin. p. 204: blank. pp. 205–217: '*the invisible* | *generation*' by WSB. p. 218: blank.

Contents: Text of *The Ticket That Exploded*, second version (a rear-rangement of the first Olympia text, with additions and expansions); plus "The Invisible Generation," a piece incorporating two earlier articles from *International Times*, 1966 and 1967 (**C157** and **C162**).

Paper: White wove paper. Endpapers white.

Binding: Bound in orange cloth. Front and back covers blank. Spine: '[black, down] The Ticket That Exploded Burroughs | [across at bottom] Grove | Press'. Issued with a white dust jacket designed by Kuhlman Associates, on the front of which is, at top: '[orange] THE TICKET THAT EXPLODED | [brown] BY WILLIAM S. BUR-ROUGHS'; below is a drawing in black and white of a Chaplinesque character with a word collage exploding out the top of his top hat. Jacket spine: '[down, black] THE TICKET THAT EXPLODED [brown] BY WILLIAM S. BURROUGHS | [across at bottom, orange] GP–388 | GROVE | PRESS'. On the back of the dust jacket is a large black and white photo of WSB by Martha Rocher, with credit to the right: '[black] Photograph © Martha Rocher'; below it in black is a short biographical sketch, underneath which is a long heavy black rule beneath which is: '[orange] GROVE PRESS, INC., 80 University Place, New York, N.Y. 10003'. Inside flaps 1 and 2 have the publisher's blurb. At top of flap 1 is: '[orange] $5.00 | GP–388'. At bottom of flap 2 is a heavy black line rule beneath which is: '[orange] DESIGN: KUHLMAN ASSOCIATES'. All edges trimmed.

Publication: This edition, published June 19, 1967, consisted of 10,000 copies.

c. Grove Press, Inc.   1968

William S. Burroughs | The Ticket That Exploded | [line rule] | *posed little time* | *so I'll say* | *"good night"* | [line rule] | Grove Press, Inc. | New York

Collation: 17.7 × 10.6 cm. 112 leaves; [i–vi], 1–202 [203–204] 205–217 [218].
Page i: short biography of WSB. p. ii: blank. p. iii: title. p. iv: 'Copyright © 1962, 1964, 1966, 1967 by William S. Burroughs | All Rights Reserved | Library of Congress Catalogue Card Number: 66–28732 | An earlier version of this novel was first published in 1962 by The Olympia Press, Paris. Part of the section entitled *silence* | *to say good bye* appeared in *The Insect Trust Gazette*, No. 1, Summer, 1964; a portion of the Appendix was published in *The International Times*, London. | First Evergreen Black Cat Edition 1968 | First Printing | Manufactured in the United States of America'. p. v: 'Acknowledgment' by WSB. p. vi: blank. pp. 1–202: text. p. 203: calligraph by Brion Gysin. p. 204: blank. pp. 205–217: '*the invisible* | *generation*' by WSB. p. 218: blank. Two-leaf (four-page) advertisement for *Evergreen Review* inserted between pp. 106 and 107.

Contents: text of *The Ticket That Exploded* as in **A6b** with "The Invisible Generation" (see **C157**).

Paper: White wove paper.

Binding: Perfect-bound, no sigs. Bound in stiff white wrappers. Front cover: '[at top right, blue] B–164 [publisher's device (a cat's head)] $1.25 | [center, black] THE TICKET THAT EXPLODED | [gray] BY WILLIAM S. BURROUGHS | [light-gray] AUTHOR OF NAKED LUNCH | [at bottom, in exploding red, blue, green, and purple letters] TICKET'. Spine: '[down, black] THE TICKET THAT EXPLODED [blue] WILLIAM S. BURROUGHS | [across at bottom, in blue, publisher's device, as before] | B–164 | GROVE | PRESS'. Back cover: across top, '[blue] AN EVERGREEN BLACK CAT BOOK [publisher's device, as above] $1.25 | B–164'; following is a quote from *Playboy* magazine on WSB and the publisher's blurb,

A6b

A6c

A6d, e

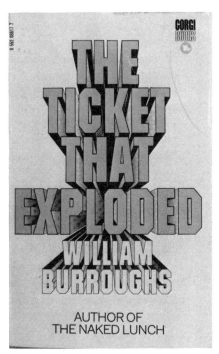

A6f

separated from the quote by a heavy blue line rule; at the bottom is '[blue] Printed in U.S.A.' All edges trimmed and light blue.

Publication: This edition, published in March 1968,* consisted of 15,000† copies. It was reprinted in July 1968* in a run of 15,000† copies. Also reprinted in September 1968* (10,000 copies)† and December 1973 (5,000) copies).

d. Calder and Boyars   1968

William S. Burroughs | The Ticket That Exploded | [line rule] | *posed little time | so I'll say | "good night"* | [line rule] | CALDER AND BOYARS | LONDON

Collation: 19.5 × 12.7 cm. [1–7]^{16}, 112 leaves; pp. [i–vi], 1–202 [203–204] 205–217 [218].
Page i: half title. p. ii: blank. p. iii: title. p. iv: 'First published in Great Britain 1968 | by Calder and Boyars Ltd. | 18, Brewer Street, London, W.1. | An earlier version of this novel was first published in 1962 by | The Olympia Press, Paris. Part of the section entitled *silence to say goodbye* appeared in *The | Insect Trust Gazette*, No. 1, Summer 1964; a portion of the Appendix was published in *The | International Times*, London. This version first published in 1967 by Grove Press, Inc., New York. | © William S. Burroughs, 1962, 1964, 1966, 1967, 1968 | All Rights Reserved'. p. v: 'Acknowledgment' by WSB. p. vi: blank. pp. 1–202: text. p. 203: calligraph by Brion Gysin. p. 204: blank. pp. 205–217: '*the* invisible generation' by WSB. p. 218: blank.

Contents: Identical to **A6b**.

Paper: White wove paper.

Binding: Bound in light blue cloth. Front and back covers blank. Spine: '[in gilt, down] THE TICKET THAT EXPLODED William Burroughs | [across at bottom] CALDER | [line rule] | BOYARS'. Issued with a white dust jacket designed by John Sewell, on the front of which is a collage in black, white, blue, and orange; above which is: '[black] THE | TICKET | THAT EXPLODED | [bold orange line rule] | [black] WILLIAM | BURROUGHS'. Jacket spine: '[down, blue] The TICKET | That Exploded | [orange] William Burroughs |

[at bottom, blue] CALDER | AND | BOYARS'. Back of dust jacket: at top, '[black] THE TICKET THAT EXPLODED | William Burroughs'; top to past center, publisher's blurb; near bottom, publisher's advertisement; at bottom, 'CALDER & BOYARS LTD | 18 Brewer Street London WIR 4AS'. Inside flaps 1 and 2 are given to the publisher's advertisement. At bottom of flap 1 is: 'Jacket design by John Sewell | 42s'. All edges trimmed.

Publication: This edition was published November 7, 1968. The publisher would give no other information.

e. Calder and Boyars   1968

The title page is identical to **A6d**.

Collation: Except for slight difference in size (this edition is 19.6 × 12.8 cm.), the collation is identical to **A6d**.

Contents: Identical to **A6d**.

Paper: White wove paper.

Binding: Bound in stiff white wrappers. Front cover is same as the front dust jacket of **A6d**. Spine: '[down, orange] William Burroughs | [blue] The TICKET | That Exploded | [at bottom, black] CB | 222'. Back cover: all lettering in black; across top, 'A Calderbook CB222 15s [and directly below] 75p | THE TICKET THAT EXPLODED | William Burroughs'; top to middle of cover, publisher's blurb and 'This book is also available in hardcover at 42s (£2.10).'; to near bottom, quotes from three reviews of the work headed '*Some press opinions*' and publisher's advertisement; at bottom,'CALDER & BOYARS LTD | 18 BREWER STREET LONDON W1'; at extreme bottom 'ISBN 0 7145 0733 4'. All edges trimmed.

Publication: This edition was published simultaneously with **A6d** (Nov. 7, 1968); the number of copies printed could not be obtained from the publisher as that information was confidential.

f. Corgi Books   1971

The second UK paperback of **A6**, with pale-yellow wrappers and the title in large red letters, outlined and shadowed in black and gray to give exploding 3-D effect. Collation (except for minor differences) and contents are the same as **A6d**. Priced at 35p.

Publication: The publisher would give no information on this edition except that it was published in 1971; all other data were considered confidential.

A7 DEAD FINGERS TALK

a. John Calder 1963

DEAD | FINGERS | TALK | WILLIAM BURROUGHS | [publisher's device (a tree)] | LONDON | JOHN CALDER | in association with | OLYMPIA PRESS

Collation: 20.2 × 13.2 cm. [1]–13⁸ 14² [15]⁶, 112 leaves, with last leaf glued to back cover; pp. [i–vi], [1] 2–215 [216–220]. All gatherings signed 'D.F.T.', except 1 and 15. The second leaf of gathering 14 is signed 'D.F.T.' and marked '14*'.
Page i: half title. p. ii: blank. p. iii: title. p. iv: 'FIRST PUBLISHED IN GREAT BRITAIN IN 1963 | BY JOHN CALDER (PUBLISHERS) LTD., | 17 SACKVILLE STREET, LONDON, W.1 | © COPYRIGHT WILLIAM BURROUGHS 1963 | PRINTED IN GREAT BRITAIN BY | BLACKIE & SON LTD.' pp. 1–215: text. pp. 216–220: blank.

Contents: Text, *Dead Fingers Talk*.

Paper: White wove paper. Endpapers white.

Binding: Bound in light gray cloth. Front and back covers blank. Spine: '[in gilt, across top] BURROUGHS | [down in scriptlike lettering] Dead Fingers Talk | [across at bottom, publisher's device (a tree)] | CALDER'. Issued with a black-and-white dust jacket using photographs of Ian Sommerville; the front is a collage photo of the Olympia editions of WSB's books with a ghostly hand superimposed; on the palm, '[red] WILLIAM | BURROUGHS', on three of the fingers, '[black] DEAD | FINGERS | TALK'. Jacket spine: '[across at top, red] WILLIAM | BURROUGHS | [down, black] DEAD FINGERS TALK | [at bottom, red] CALDER'. Back of dust jacket is the front photo (without the hand) over which is superimposed a full-face black-and-white photo of WSB. Inside flap 1 is the publisher's blurb, at the bottom of which is 'JOHN CALDER (PUBLISHERS) LIMITED | 17 SACKVILLE STREET · LONDON, W1 | *Photos by Ian Sommerville* | [thin slanted rule | 25s.' All edges trimmed.

Publication: This edition, published Nov. 15, 1963, consisted of 4,000 copies.

b. Tandem Books Limited   1966

DEAD FINGERS | TALK | WILLIAM BURROUGHS | [publisher's device (two black-outlined commas in tandem)] | TANDEM BOOKS LIMITED | 33 Beauchamp Place, London, S.W.3

Collation: 18.1 × 11.1 cm. [A]¹⁶ B-G¹⁶, 112 leaves; pp. [1–6] 7–223 [224].

Page 1: half title. p. 2: *'Photograph of the Author | by Brion Gysin'.* p. 3: publisher's blurb, headed: 'DEAD FINGERS TALK | William Burroughs'. p. 4: blank. p. 5: title. p. 6: 'First published in Great Britain by Calder and Boyars Ltd. | Copyright © William Burroughs 1963 | Tandem Edition 1966 | Made and printed in Great Britain by Love & Malcomson Ltd. | Brighton Road, Redhill, Surrey. | This book is sold subject to the condition that it shall not by way of | trade, be lent, re-sold, hired out, or otherwise disposed of without the | consent of the publisher in any form of binding or cover other than | that in which it is published'. pp. 7–224: text.

Contents: Text, *Dead Fingers Talk,* as in **A7a.**

Paper: White wove paper.

Binding: Bound in stiff pictorial wrappers. Front cover: a color painting (blue and blue-black ground) of a sleeved hand giving an arm a mainline injection, with blood running down the arm; over the painting is superimposed '[at top right, white] A [publisher's device (two commas in tandem)] | TANDEM | BOOK | 3/6 | [at left, green] WILLIAM | BURROUGHS; [red] DEAD | [white] FINGERS | [red] TALK | [white] The sensational | novel of the | nightmare world | of the junky | by the author of | [red] THE NAKED LUNCH'. Spine: '[black, across at top, publisher's device, as before] | [down] Dead Fingers Talk William Burroughs | [across at bottom] T55'. Back cover: '[black, publisher's device, as before] A TANDEM BOOK [inset, a small black-and-white photo of WSB] | [long rule] | [red and black, eight quotes from reviews of WSB's work, headed in red] What they say about | WILLIAM BURROUGHS'. All edges trimmed.

A7a

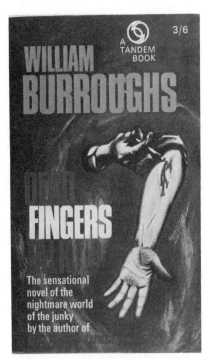

A7b

A7c

Publication: The publisher would give no information about this edition other than its year of publication, 1966, declaring such information to be confidential.

c. Tandem Books Limited   1970

A reprint of **A7b** with new wrappers (front cover is black with a round color photo of a young man in dark glasses at the bottom of a fire escape giving himself a mainline injection). Collation (with minor differences) and contents are the same as **A7b**. Paperbound and priced at 5/–25p.

Publication: The publisher would give no information about this edition other than its year of publication, 1970, declaring such information to be confidential.

A8   THE YAGE LETTERS

a. City Lights Books   1963

THE | YAGE | LETTERS | William Burroughs | & | Allen Ginsberg | [publisher's device (letter Y with a circle; Gothic symbol for man)] | CITY LIGHTS BOOKS

Collation: 18.3 × 12.4 cm. [1]¹⁰ [2–4]⁸, 34 leaves; pp. [1–6] 7–46 [47–48] 49 [50] 51–52 [53] 54–62 [63–64] 65–68.
Page 1: title. p. 2: 'Library of Congress Catalog Card Number: 62–12222 | ©1963 by William S. Burroughs & Allen Ginsberg | The cover photo of a *curandero* from the Vaupes region of | Columbia is reprinted by permission of the Botanical Museum | of Harvard University. The author's thanks must be given to | Aileen Lee and Alan Ansen who in 1953 helped type and | preserve Burroughs' letters and to Melville Hardiment who | later preserved Ginsberg's. The 1953 letters were subsquently | published in BIG TABLE and KULCHUR. Burroughs' | 1960 letter was in FLOATING BEAR No. 5. 'I Am Dying, | Meester?' was in CITY LIGHTS JOURNAL No. 1. Gins-|berg's 1960 letter and his note 'To Whom It May Concern' | have not been printed before. Drawings by Ginsberg were | included in his letter from Pucallpa. | Printed in England | *CITY LIGHTS BOOKS are published at the City Lights | Bookstore, Columbus & Broadway, San Francisco 11, California.'* p. 3: 'CON-

A8a

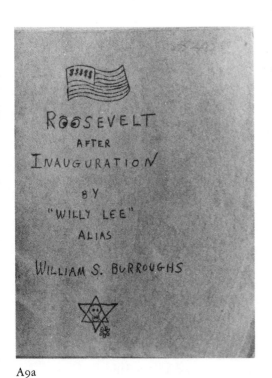

A9a

TENTS'. p. 4: blank. p. 5: 'IN SEARCH OF YAGE (1953)'. p. 6: blank. pp. 7–46: text of WSB's letters to Allen Ginsberg. p. 47: 'SEVEN YEARS LATER (1960)'. p. 48: blank. pp. 49–59: text of Allen Ginsberg's letters to WSB. pp. 60–62: WSB's 1960 letter to Allen Ginsberg. p. 63: 'EPILOGUE (1963)'. p. 64: blank. p. 65: note: 'To whom it may concern:' by Allen Ginsberg. pp. 66–68: 'I AM DYING, MEESTER?' by WSB (C66). On pp. 50 and 53 are drawings by Allen Ginsberg.

Contents: WSB's 1953 letters to Allen Ginsberg; Allen Ginsberg's 1960 letters to WSB; WSB's 1960 letter to Allen Ginsberg; Allen Ginsberg's note "To Whom It May Concern"; and WSB's "I Am Dying, Meester?" reprinted from *City Lights Journal*, 1963 (C66); and two drawings by Allen Ginsberg.

Paper: White wove paper.

Binding: Bound in stiff black-and-white pictorial wrappers. Front cover: a black-and-white photo of a *curandero* over which is lettered '[white] the | YAGE | letters | william | burroughs | & | allen | ginsberg'. Spine: '[down, black] the YAGE letters burroughs & ginsberg city lights'. Back cover: '[black on white, publisher's blurb | $1.25'. Inside front cover blank. Inside back cover is the publisher's advertisement. All edges trimmed.

Publication: This edition, published Nov. 31, 1963,* consisted of 3,000† copies. It was reprinted in August 1965 (4,000† copies), November 1966 (5,000 copies), May 1968 (3,000 copies), September 1969 (5,000 copies), and August 1971 (5,000 copies).
  Note on the Printings: The first two were done on letterpress by Villiers Publications, Ltd., London; the other printings were offsets printed by Edwards Brothers, Ann Arbor, Michigan, from photographed plates of the English original. The two English printings are thread-sewn; the American offsets are all perfect-bound.

*Date approximated.
†Quantity approximated.

A9   ROOSEVELT AFTER INAUGURATION

a. Fuck You Press   1964

[Cover title, hand-drawn and hand-lettered] [flag with dollar signs instead of stars] | ROOSEVELT [the 0s are two crossed eyes] | AFTER | INAUGURATION | BY | "WILLY LEE" | ALIAS | WILLIAM S. BURROUGHS | [a skull with a daisy in its teeth within a star of David]

Collation: 14.1 × 10.9 cm. One unsigned gathering of 14 leaves; pp. [1–28].
Page 1: cover title. p. 2: blank. p. 3: excerpt from May 23, 1953, letter of WSB to Allen Ginsberg from Lima, explaining origin of the Roosevelt routine; note by publisher, Ed Sanders: 'This routine was bricked out of | the City Lights Volume by | paranoid printers in England. | It was first stomped into print | in Floating Bear #9.' p. 4: blank. pp. 5–24: text. p. 25: blank. p. 26: '[underlined with wavy bold rule] ROOSEVELT AFTER INAUGURATION | by | [wavy caps] WILLIAM BURROUGHS | (covers by Allen Ginsberg, L.A.M.F.) | a / [next three words in cartouche] FUCK YOU / press ejaculation | printed, published, & zapped | at a secret location in | the lower east side, new york city | Jan 1964 | [underlined with bold rule] TOTAL ASSAULT ON THE CULTURE!! | [drawing of an ejaculating penis]'. p. 27: blank. p. 28: hand-lettered blurb. Pages 6, 8, 10, 12, 14, 15, 17, 19, 21, and 23 are blank.

Contents: Text of routine, *Roosevelt after Inauguration* (C33, C258).

Paper: six pink, four white, and four light blue leaves. Pink leaves are laid paper; white and blue leaves are wove paper.

Binding: A paper pamphlet of 14 pink, white, and blue leaves, staple-bound and mimeographed. Front cover is title page; back cover is hand-lettered blurb by Allen Ginsberg. All edges trimmed.

Publication: This edition, published in January 1964, consisted of 500* copies at 50¢ (later $1.00). The cases in which some copies are found were made by the book's retailers. The publisher did not issue the book in cases.

On the first printing, the mimeo machine destroyed all of the pages; therefore all extant copies are of the subsequent printing.

---

* Publisher's estimate.

A10 NOVA EXPRESS

a. Grove Press, Inc. 1964

William S. Burroughs | NOVA | EXPRESS | [wavy rule] | GROVE PRESS, INC. | NEW YORK

Collation: 20.1 × 13.4 cm. [1–6]¹⁶, 96 leaves; pp. [i–ii], [1–11] 12–23 [24–25] 26–42 [43] 44–75 [76–77] 78–98 [99] 100–125 [126–127] 128–140 [141] 142–154 [155] 156–187 [188–190]. Pages i–ii: blank. p. 1: half title. p. 2: blank. p. 3: title. p. 4: '*Copyright © 1964 by William S. Burroughs* | All Rights Reserved | Acknowledgement is due to Alfred A. | Knopf, Inc. for permission to quote from | *The Trial* by Franz Kafka, translated by | Willa and Edwin Muir, Copyright © 1937, | 1956, by Alfred A. Knopf, Inc. | Library of Congress Catalog Card Number: 64–10597 | First Printing | MANUFACTURED IN THE UNITED STATES OF AMERICA'. p. 5: 'FOREWORD NOTE' by WSB. p. 6: blank. p. 7 contents. p. 8: blank. p. 9: second half title. p. 10: blank. pp. 11–187: text; p. 187 signed '*July 21, 1964* | *Tangier, Morocco* | *William Burroughs*'. pp. 188–190: blank. Pages 24, 76, and 126 are also blank.

Contents: Text, *Nova Express*.

Paper: White wove paper. Endpapers white.

Binding: Bound in red-orange cloth. Front and back covers blank. Spine: '[black, down] NOVA EXPRESS WILLIAM S. BUR-ROUGHS | [across at bottom] GROVE | PRESS'. Issued with a dust jacket designed by Roy Kuhlman, the front of which is an orange sunburst design on black, over which is superimposed at bottom: '[white] NOVA EXPRESS | WILLIAM S. BURROUGHS | A NOVEL BY THE AUTHOR OF NAKED LUNCH'. Jacket spine: '[down, black] NOVA EXPRESS [orange] BY WILLIAM S. BUR-ROUGHS | [across at bottom, black] GP–307 | [orange] GROVE | PRESS'. The back of the dust jacket is white and reproduces a black-and-white photo of WSB by Martha Rocher. At top left of the photo (reading down) is the credit: 'Photo © Martha Rocher'. Underneath the photo is a short biographical sketch of WSB, at the bottom of which is '[orange] GROVE PRESS, INC., 64 University Place, New York 3, N.Y.' Inside flaps are the publisher's blurb. At top of

A10a, [b]

flap 1 is '[black] $5.00 | GP–307'. At bottom of flap 2 is '[orange] COVER DESIGN BY ROY KUHLMAN'. All edges trimmed.

Publication: This edition, published Nov. 9, 1964, consisted of 10,000 copies. Both Grove Press and its printer, The Book Press, could supply no further information as no records existed of any reprints.

b. Grove Press, Inc.   1965

Nova Express | [swelled rule] | WILLIAM S. BURROUGHS | *An Evergreen Black Cat* [publisher's design (stylized head of a black cat)] *Book* | GROVE PRESS, INC. NEW YORK

Collation: 17.9 × 10.7 cm. 80 leaves; pp. [1–10] 11–35 [36] 37–63 [64] 65–115 [116] 117–127 [128] 129–155 [156] 157–160.

Page 1: half title. p. 2: blank. p. 3: title. p. 4: 'Copyright © 1964 by William S. Burroughs | All Rights Reserved | First Evergreen Black Cat Edition 1965 | Acknowledgment is due to Alfred A. Knopf, Inc. | for permission to quote from *The Trial* by Franz | Kafka, translated by Willa and Edwin Muir, Copy-|right © 1937, 1956, by Alfred A. Knopf, Inc. | MANUFACTURED IN THE UNITED STATES OF AMERICA'. p. 5: 'FOREWORD NOTE' by WSB. p. 6: blank. p. 7: contents. p. 8: blank. p. 9: second half title. p. 10: blank. pp. 11–155: text; p. 155 signed *'July 21, 1964 | Tangier, Morocco | William Burroughs'.* p. 156: blank. pp. 157–160: publisher's advertisement. Pages 36, 64, 116, and 128 are also blank.

Contents: Text, *Nova Express.*

Paper: White wove paper.

Binding: Perfect-bound, no sigs. Stiff pictorial wrappers. Front cover: '[at top, orange on white] An Evergreen Black Cat Book [publisher's device in black, as before] 95¢ | BC–102'; then a reduced reproduction of the front dust jacket of **A10a**, the orange sunburst design on black, over which is lettered '[white] NOVA EXPRESS | WILLIAM S. BURROUGHS | A NOVEL BY THE AUTHOR OF NAKED LUNCH'. Spine: '[down, black] NOVA EXPRESS [orange] BY WILLIAM S. BURROUGHS BC–102 [across, publisher's design in black, as before] GROVE | PRESS'. Back cover: '[at top, orange] An Evergreen Black Cat Book [publisher's design in black, as before] 95¢ | BC–102 | [black] NOVA EXPRESS | [orange] BY WILLIAM

S. BURROUGHS'; then follow quotes from three reviews, separated by three orange rules. All edges trimmed and orange. Later
issues have white edges.

Publication: This edition, published Nov. 15, 1965, consisted of
15,000* copies. It was reprinted in October 1965 in a printing of
15,000* copies, in February 1970 in a printing of 7,563 copies, and in
August 1971 in a printing of 5,241 copies. Also reprinted June 1973
(5,000 copies) and January 1974 (5,000 copies).

c. Jonathan Cape   1966

William S. Burroughs | NOVA | EXPRESS | [long wavy rule] |
[publisher's device (an urn within two circles with fruit at top and 'J'
and 'C' at each side)] | JONATHAN CAPE | THIRTY BEDFORD
SQUARE | LONDON

Collation: 19.6 × 12.7 cm. [A]¹⁶ B-F¹⁶, 96 leaves, with last leaf glued
to back cover; except for this and the wording of page 4, the collation
is the same as **A10a**. Page 4 reads: 'First published in Great Britain
1966 | © 1964 by William S. Burroughs | Acknowledgement is due to
Alfred A. | Knopf, Inc. for permission to quote from | *The Trial* by
Franz Kafka, translated by | Willa and Edwin Muir, Copyright ©
1937, | 1956, by Alfred A. Knopf, Inc. | Printed in Great Britain by |
Lowe and Brydone (Printers) Ltd, London | on paper made by John
Dickinson & Co. | and bound by A. W. Bain & Co. Ltd, London'.

Contents: Text, *Nova Express*, as the American edition (**A10a, b**).

Paper: White wove paper. Endpapers white.

Binding: Bound in black cloth. Front and back covers blank. Spine:
'[in gilt] NOVA | EXPRESS | [publisher's design] | WILLIAM S. |
BURROUGHS | [publisher's device, as before]'. Issued with a red
dust jacket designed by Leigh Taylor which is (front, spine, and back)
a collage (in letters, texts, photo, and line drawing) of a black train on
a red field. On the front (superimposed at the top) is: '[black] NOVA
| EXPRESS | [white] WILLIAM | BURROUGHS'. Jacket spine: '[at
top, black] NOVA EXPRESS | [white] WILLIAM BURROUGHS';
at bottom in white is the publisher's device, as before. The back of the
dust jacket is a continuation of the collage. Inside flaps are the

---

*Publisher's estimate.

Aɪoc

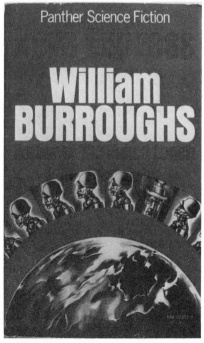

Aɪod

Aɪoe

Aɪof

publisher's blurb. At top of flap 1 is a black-and-white photo of WSB by John Hopkins; at bottom is price: '25s. net | in U.K. only'. At bottom of flap 2 is credit: 'Jacket design by Leigh Taylor | © Jonathan Cape 1966'. All edges trimmed, top edge light orange.

Publication: This edition, published Feb. 10, 1966, consisted of 10,000 copies.

d. Panther Books 1968

William Burroughs | *Nova Express* | *A Panther Book*

Collation: 17.8 × 11.1 cm. [NE–1]⁸, NE–2—NE–10⁸, 80 leaves; pp. [1–8] 9–156 [157–160].

Page 1: published blurb, at the bottom of which is a quote on WSB from *Books and Bookmen*. p. 2: blank. p. 3: title. p. 4: 'Nova Express | *A Panther Book* | First published in Great Britain | by Jonathan Cape Limited 1966 | Panther Edition published 1968 | Copyright © William Burroughs 1964 | Acknowledgment is due to Alfred A. Knopf | Inc, for permission to quote from *The Trial* | by Franz Kafka, translated by Willa and | Edwin Muir, copyright © 1937, 1956, by | Alfred A. Knopf Inc. | This book is sold subject to the | condition that it shall not, by way | of trade *or otherwise*, be lent, | re-sold, hired out or otherwise | *circulated* without the publisher's | prior consent in any form of binding | or cover other than that in which | it is published *and without a similar* | *condition including this condition* | *being imposed on the subsequent* | *purchaser.* | Printed in England by Hunt Barnard & Co. Ltd., | at the Sign of the Dolphin, Aylesburg, Bucks, and | published by Panther Books Ltd., | 3 Upper James Street, London, W.1.' p. 5: 'Foreword Note' by WSB. p. 6: blank. p. 7: contents. p. 8: blank. pp. 9–157: text; p. 157 signed *July 21, 1965* | *Tangier, Morocco* | *William Burroughs*'. pp. 158–160: publisher's advertisements.

Contents: Text, *Nova Express*, as the American edition (**A10a, b**).

Paper: White wove paper.

Binding: Bound in stiff black pictorial wrappers. Front cover: '[at top, pea green] WILLIAM BURROUGHS | [darker green] author of THE NAKED LUNCH | [dark green] NOVA EXPRESS | [at right, black within dark green oval] Panther | [white down] 23771'; rest of front cover is black and white, depicting an hypodermic syringe one-third full of a green substance being launched like a rocket. Spine: '[down, pea green] William Burroughs [white] Nova Express [yellow] Panther Books 23771'. Back cover is black on which is printed: '[at top, white] William Burroughs | sensational author of The Naked Lunch | takes off with interplanetary cops and | robbers in | Nova Express'; followed by quotes from four reviews of WSB's work and '[green] panther science fiction'; at bottom left, in black, within four different-colored rectangles stacked on each other and divided by black rules, '[in yellow rectangle] UNITED KINGDOM 5/- [in pink rectangle] AUSTRALIA 80c | [in pea-green rectangle] NEW ZEALAND (6/6) 65c | [in light blue rectangle] SOUTH AFRICA 60c'. All edges trimmed.

Publication: The publisher would give only the year date (1968) of this edition, declaring the other information to be confidential.

e. Panther Books Ltd.   1969

A reprint of **A10d** with new wrappers (front cover: a pink and green crayfish stoking a furnace with computer tape; out of the furnace is arising smoke in which is a specimen jar containing a blue head being strangled and some people in a lifeboat escaping a dinosaur). Collation (except for minor differences) and contents are the same as **A10d**. Paperbound and priced at 5s. (25p.).

Publication: The publisher would give only the year date (1969) of this edition, declaring the other information to be confidential.

f. Panther Books Ltd.   1972

Another reprint of **A10d** with new wrappers (front cover: a scarred planet with a large hole near its top and a series of portraits above it). Collation (with minor differences) and contents are the same as **A10d**. Paperbound and priced at 35p.

Publication: The publisher would give only the year date (1972) of this edition, declaring the other information to be confidential.

A11   TIME

a. 'C' Press   1965

Note: Title occupies left third of p. 1 and is separated by a vertical line rule from the publisher's statement regarding the four editions of *Time* and the index.

TIME | · | BY WILLIAM | BURROUGHS | · | WITH 4 DRAW-INGS | BY BRION GYSIN | · | 'C' Press | 210 West 88 | NYC 10024 | · | General Editor: | Ted Berrigan | TIME Editor: | Ron Padgett | Art Director: | Joe Brainard | · | Copyright © 1965 by | William Burroughs | Printed in U.S.A.

Collation: 27.9 × 21.4 cm. One unsigned gathering of 16 leaves, pp. [1–32].
Page 1: title, publisher's statement, and index. pp. 2–31: text. p. 32: blank. Page 14, 15, 16, and 17 are calligrams by Brion Gysin.

Paper: White wove paper.

Binding: Staple-bound, stiff gray pictorial wrappers. Front cover: in gray and black and white, a collage by WSB of a *Time* magazine cover, dated Nov. 30, 1962, which serves as the title. The top half of the magazine cover is reproduced, and pasted over the bottom half is a drawing of a landscape in the foreground of which is a man-figure; at the top of the drawing is superimposed: [black] 'WILLIAM BUR-ROUGHS'. At the bottom of the cover are prices of *Time* in countries of the world. Back cover blank. All edges trimmed.

Publication: This edition, published in 1965, consisted of 1,000 copies. Of these, 886 copies constituted the trade edition. Another 100 copies were numbered and signed by WSB and Brion Gysin, and 10 of these copies were numbered A–J, were hardbound in special floral cloth, and each contained an original manuscript page by WSB and an original colored drawing by Brion Gysin. The remaining 4 copies were *hors commerce*. Some copies were issued in a case. Trade paper edition was priced at $1.50; signed paper edition was $10; and A–J hardcover signed was $25.

b. Urgency Press Rip-Off   1972

An admitted piracy by Roy Pennington of the American edition. Sixteen photo-offset leaves (33 × 20.4 cm.) printed on both sides,

A11a, b

unpaginated, and stapled at the top. Reproduces contents of **A11a**, though in slightly different order, leaving out p. 9 of the original.

Publication: This edition, published in May 1972 for the Bickershaw Festival, consisted of 495 copies; at least 20 were given away, and the remaining copies were sold at 30p. each.

A12   HEALTH BULLETIN: APO–33,
               A METABOLIC REGULATOR

a. Fuck You Press   1965

HEALTH BULLETIN:AP0–33 | WILLIAM BURROUGHS | [within an oval] CHLORHYDRATE | [also within the oval] D'APOMORPHINE | FACTEUR DE REGULATION EMOTIO-NELLE | INDICATIONS—ANGOISSE—|—ANXIETE—EMOTIVITE—|INSOMNIES—FUCKED UP—|INTOXICA-TIONS—TOXICOMANIES—|published by the FUCK YOU/ press: | Prof. Elaine Solow, Textual & Sexual Consultant; | Chairman of the Headcopping and | Manuscript Preparation Division. | Dr.'s Ken Weaver & Peter Orlovsky, Collating Consultants. | Ed Sanders, Scat.D., Imperial Lotus Freak, Designing & | Printing Departments | TOTAL ASSAULT ON THE CULTURE! | [a drawing by Sanders built on the Egyptian hieroglyph for the Eye of Horus; at the top is the ankh, the hieroglyph for life, and at the bottom a mimeo machine, a hookah, and an ejaculating movie camera] | [within an oval] fug-press | peace pussy perversion

Collation: 27.9 × 21.5 cm. 27 single leaves (including covers); mimeographed, electrostenciled, and hand-lettered on one side only; pp. [i-vii], [1] 2–16 [17] 18–19 [20].
Page i: front cover. p. ii: title. p. iii: colophon: 'HEALTH BULLE-TIN: APO–33 | copyright © 1965 | by William S. Burroughs | First Printing | published by | The FUCK YOU/® press | Secret Location | Lower East Side | New York City | U.S.A. | Ed Sanders, | Chairman of the Board | copies may be purchased | from the | PEACE EYE BOOKSTORE | 383 East 10th Street | New York, New York 10009 | U.S.A. | Bookstores, book dealers | given full trade discount.' p. iv: 'Table of Contents'. p. v: 'LOCKED OUT OF TIME' (Apomorphine Statement 1) by WSB. p. vi: 'ARTICLE Sunday Times LONDON

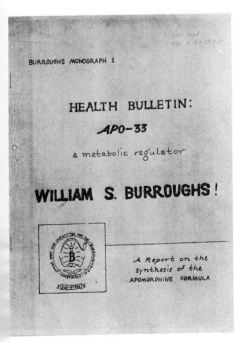

A12a

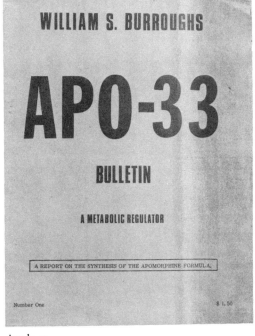

A12b, c

15/11/64'. p. vii: Apomorphine Statement 2 by WSB. pp. 1–19: text. p. 20: back cover.

Contents: Text, *Health Bulletin: APO–33*; "Locked Out of Time" (Apomorphine Statement 1); reprint of *Sunday Times* (London) article, Nov. 15, 1964; Apomorphine Statement 2.

Note: Six items listed in the table of contents are not included: (1) text of WSB letter to the editor of the *Sunday Times*; (2) text of letter from editorial department, *Sunday Times*, in reply to letter of WSB; (3) text of letter containing WSB's reply to letter from editor, *Sunday Times*; (4) text of letter by WSB in response to a letter by former Commissioner of Narcotics Anslinger in the *Herald Tribune*; (5) appendix, index, credits; and (6) bibliography. Regarding the omissions, Sanders, in a letter to Miles dated Nov. 29, 1974, stated, "Burroughs never sent that, or he was waiting for copies to arrive at which time he would have sent them for printing."

Papers: Front and back sheets and pp. ii–iv, 3, 4, and 5 are buff-colored, laid mimeo stock, watermarked 'Laid | Gilbert Bond'. Page vi is Xeroxed, on white wove paper. Page v is stiff gray wove paper. Page vii is white wove paper, watermarked 'DECISION LEDGER | VALLEY PAPER CO.' The remaining pages are all white mimeo stock.

Binding: A pamphlet of 27 leaves, printed on buff, gray, and white papers and bound together with two staples on the extreme left side. Front cover (p. i): hand-lettered and drawn by Sanders, '[black, top left] BURROUGHS MONOGRAPH 1 | [center] HEALTH BULLETIN: | APO–33 | a metabolic regulator | WILLIAM S. BURROUGHS! | [at bottom left, within a black-ruled square, lettered around a circle enclosing a snake, a mushroom, an eye, two ejaculating penises, and a glowing letter B, reading clockwise] · LOWER EAST SIDE COMMITTEE FOR THE BURROUGHSIAN· CONSPIRACY | [on a banner below circle] Fug-press | [at bottom right, line rule] | A Report on the | synthesis of the | APOMORPHINE FORMULA'. Back cover: '[black, at top] HEALTH BULLETIN: APO–33!! | $1.25 | [center] WILLIAM S. BURROUGHS | works for the NOVA POLICE. | In his brilliant & beautiful | poetic tales of states, nations, | drugs, mores, morons, creeps | & junk monsters, Mr. Burroughs | takes his place beside Swift, | Blake, Paine & Pindar. | Freak out his classics!: NAKED | LUNCH, NOVA

EXPRESS, TICKET | THAT EXPLODED, DEAD FINGERS | TALK, & TIME. These books are | published in heaven. | [bottom, Sanders's drawing of a mushroom within a circle, at the top of which are two ejaculating penises between which is the peace sign] | THE FUCK YOU/Press | Secret Location | LOWER EAST SIDE | NEW YORK | U.S.A.' All edges trimmed.

Publication: According to Miles a print run of 5,000 copies was projected for this edition. Since the mimeo would not print the full width of WSB's columns before it faded, the columns were typed down the page and a new column was started at the top again, which resulted in the columns changing a bit from WSB's manuscript. Also the illustrations, done on the electrostencil, did not turn out too well and were glued in the finished text at places different from where they were in the original manuscript (one was glued over some text). A copy was sent to WSB and he thought it was a "pasteup dummy," which disappointed Sanders. Burroughs also expressed his nervousness about the column changes, which further disappointed Sanders, making him so embarrassed that he abandoned the project; but the ones he had already collated (Sanders said "maybe as many as ten or twenty") had been distributed beforehand. Phoenix Bookshop obtained some, and a good early copy was secured by Bill Beckman. The copy described here is in the Special Collections Department of Northwestern University Library, Evanston, Illinois. Miles also owns a copy, which appeared in Sanders's catalogue number 4 as item 287, priced at $5.00.

After the project was abandoned, WSB gave the manuscript to Mary Beach to publish. The result was the second edition which follows.

b. Beach Books, Texts & Documents   c. 1966

The second edition (27.5 × 21.3 cm.), in stiff light brown wrappers, of which the front one is the title page. The title here is given as *APO–33: Bulletin, a Metabolic Regulator.* 24 pp. This printing is a photo-offset of WSB's manuscript. It was the complete text of *Health Bulletin: APO–33*, but it does not have "Locked Out of Time" or Apomorphine Statement 2, which were in **A12a**. It also is missing the six items that were missing in **A12a**.

Publication: This edition, published c. 1966, consisted of 3,000*
copies. Edition reprinted in 1967 in a run of 3,000* copies.

c. Beach Books, Texts & Documents   1968

Third edition of *Health Bulletin: APO–33*. Identical in collation and
contents to **A12b**, except for inside front cover, which reads: ' © by
William S. Burroughs | 1966, 1967, 1968 | Second Printing | [pub-
lisher's device (a handstamp in black circle ringed in light brown)] |
BEACH BOOKS TEXTS & DOCUMENTS | [publisher's adver-
tisement]'. Price was $1.25.

Publication: This edition, published in 1968, consisted of 3,000*
copies.

A13   **SO WHO OWNS DEATH TV?**

a. Beach Books, Texts & Documents   1967

[Cover title][black] William S. Burroughs | Claude Pélieu | Carl
Weissner | [red] SO WHO OWNS DEATH TV? | [black] BEACH
BOOKS TEXTS & DOCUMENTS | "a black bag pamphlet" |
DISTRIBUTED BY CITY LIGHTS BOOKS

Collation: 21.6 × 14.2 cm. One unsigned gathering of eight leaves;
pp. [1–16].
Page 1: cover title. p. 2 (inside front wrapper): '50¢ | © 1967 BEACH
BOOKS, TEXTS & DOCUMENTS'. pp. 3–13: text. p. 14: blank.
p. 15 (inside back cover): 'VORTEX PRINTERS | CHARLEY D.
PLYMELL–PAMELA PLYMELL | 2180 BRYANT | SAN FRAN-
CISCO, CALIFORNIA 94110'. p. 16 (back cover); '[publisher's
device (a red dot inside which is a handstamp surrounded by a white
circle)] | [publisher's advertisement] | "TOTAL BUGGERY ON
THE CULTURE"'. Page 10 is blank.

Contents: Text, *So Who Owns Death TV?* (Reprinted in *ppH0069
Intercontinental* [**C248**]).

Paper: White wove paper.

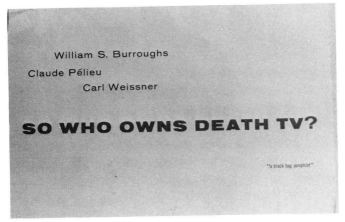

A13[a], b

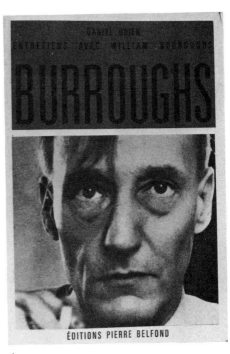

A14a   A15a

Binding: A pamphlet of eight leaves, staple-bound at top. Slick white wrappers. Front cover: title page. Back cover: transcribed above as p. 16. All edges trimmed.

Publication: This edition, published in 1967, consisted of 3,000* copies. There is a variant issue (21.5 × 14.3 cm.) in black with white printing and without '50¢' on inside front cover. The publisher estimates that 200 of these variants were issued.

b. Beach Books, Texts & Documents   1967

Second edition of **A13a**, expanded to 20 pages (counting front and back wrappers) to include illustrations (a photograph of Pélieu, a photo-collage by Jean-Jacques Lebel, a photo-collage by Liam O'Gallagher, and a photo-collage by Jean-Jacques Lebel and Claude Pélieu). Text is same as **A13a**. Slick white wrappers; front cover is title page. Inside front cover is price: '75¢'. All edges trimmed.

Publication: This edition, published in 1967, consisted of 3,000* copies.

A14   **THE DEAD STAR**

a. The Nova Broadcast Press   1969

Note: Title occupies bottom sixth of p. 2, remainder of which is text.

THE DEAD STAR | William Burroughs | The Nova Broadcast Press | San Francisco: 1969

Collation: One unsigned leaf (66.6 × 20 cm.), which folds to 20 × 11.8 cm.; pp. 1–2.
Page 1: text, in newspaper format (3 columns), headed: 'THE DEAD STAR | Dutch Schultz Machine Gunned | in Newark Bar | 3 Aides Die | October 23, 1935'. p. 2: continuation of text with title page (transcribed above) at bottom.

Contents: Text, *The Dead Star.*

Paper: White wove paper.

Binding: A one-leaf pamphlet, staple-bound to stiff white wrappers.

---

* Publisher's estimate.

Front cover: '[at top, in white in light purple band] NOVA broadcast | [below band, at right, black] 5 | [at bottom, gray] The dead star | [dark purple band] | [gray] william burrouGhs'. Back cover: '[at top, in white in light purple band] Nova Broadcast Series Number 5 | $1.25'; at bottom, in white within dark purple band, publisher's advertisement. Inside front cover blank. Inside back cover: 'Copyright 1969 by William Burroughs | The Nova Broadcast series is published and edited by Jan Jacob Herman. | Distributed in the USA by City Lights Books, 1562 Grant Avenue, | San Francisco, California 94133, and in England by McBride | Brothers & Broadley, Bucks, England. | *The Dead Star* is published here for the first time in the United States. | Acknowledgements to Jess Nuttall who published it for the first | time *in a different format* in my own mag, in England.' (see **C122**).

Publication: This edition, published in November 1969, consisted of 2,000 copies.

A15 ENTRETIENS AVEC WILLIAM BURROUGHS

a. *Éditions Pierre Belfond 1969*

daniel odier | entretiens | avec | william | burroughs | éditions pierre belfond | 4, rue guisarde, paris

Collation: 18 × 12.5 cm. 104 leaves; pp. [1–8] 9–13 [14–16] 17–45 [46–48] 49–100 [101–102] 103–120 [121–122] 123–201 [202] 203 [204] 205 [206] 207 [208].

Pages 1–2: blank. p. 3: half title. p. 4: blank. p. 5: title. p. 6: ' © William Burroughs et Daniel Odier, 1969 | © Editions Pierre Belfond, 1969'. p. 7: '*ne marchez pas | sur les indiens*'. p. 8: blank. pp. 9–13: preface by Daniel Odier. p. 14: blank. p. 15: '*voyage | dans l'espace–temps*'. p. 16: blank. pp. 17–201: text. p. 202: blank. p. 203: '*index des nomes cities*'. p. 204: blank. p. 205: '*table*'. p. 206: blank. p. 207: publisher's advertisement. p. 208: 'ACHEVE D'IMPRIMER LE | 17 JANVIER 1969 SUR LES | PRESSES DE L'IMPRIMERIE | CH. GUYET, 224, RUE DE | COURCELLES, PARIS | Dépôt légal : 1er trimestre 1969 | *Imprimé en France*'. Pages 46, 48, 102, and 122 are blank.

Contents: Original French text of *The Job: Interviews with William Burroughs* (**A**16).

Paper: White wove paper.

Binding: Perfect-bound, no sigs. Stiff white pictorial wrappers. Front cover: '[at top, in black within red panel] DANIEL ODIER | EN-TRETIENS AVEC WILLIAM BURROUGHS | [in large black capitals] BURROUGHS | [large black-and-white photograph of WSB] | [at bottom, black] ÉDITIONS PIERRE BELFOND'. Spine: '[across at top, black] daniel | odier | [up, red] *entretiens avec william burroughs* | [across at bottom, black] pierre | belfond'. Back cover: '[at top, red] *collection "entretiens"* | [the front cover photo of WSB with a short biographical sketch and a photograph of Odier with a short biographical sketch, all in black on white] | [at bottom, black] H59.0767.0 | 13,50 [and, directly below, rule and] 14,00'. All edges trimmed.

Publication: This edition, published Jan. 17, 1969. Quantity printed is not known.

A16   THE JOB

a. Grove Press, Inc.   1970

The Job | *interviews with* | William S. Burroughs | *by Daniel Odier* | *revised and enlarged edition* | GROVE PRESS, INC. New York

Collation: 20.2 × 13.3 cm. [1–6]^{16}, 96 leaves; pp. [1–12] 13–48 [49–50] 51–102 [103–104] 105–116 [117–118] 119–189 [190–192].

Page 1: half title. p. 2: blank. p. 3: title. p. 4: 'Copyright © 1969, 1970 by William S. Burroughs and Daniel Odier | All Rights Reserved | An earlier edition of this book appeared in a French translation as | *Entretiens avec William Burroughs*, copyright © 1969 by William | Burroughs, Daniel Odier, and Editions Pierre Belfond, Paris, | France. | No part of this book may be reproduced, for any reason, by any | means, including any method of photographic reproduction, with-|out the permission of the publisher. | Portions of this book were originally published in *Books and* | *Bookmen* and *Mayfair*. | Library of Congress Catalog Card Number: 72–101387 | First Print-ing | Manufactured in the United States of America'. p. 5: 'From the diary of a six year old boy at the American | School in Tangier Morocco: "I get up at 8:30. I eat my | breakfast. Then I go to the job." | When asked what he meant by the job he said, "school | of course." ' p. 6: blank. p. 7: epigraph, ' *"Navigare necesse es. Vivare no es necesse."* ' by WSB. p. 8: blank. p. 9: *'Author's Foreword'* by WSB. p. 10: blank pp. 11–189: text; p. 189 signed *'William S. Burroughs/October 15, 1968 / London'*. pp. 190–192: blank. Pages 12, 50, 104, and 118 are also blank.

Contents: English translation of French text, *Interviews with William Burroughs* without Odier's preface. Added in this edition are the Tangier schoolboy quote, WSB's "Foreword," and "The Invisible Generation." Also the chapter titled "Le Truc orgasme-mort" is retitled "A New Frog" in this edition and the chapter "N'entrez pas dans le jardin des delices" is retitled "Academy 23." The division of these two chapters varies by a few pages in this edition.

Paper: White wove paper. Endpapers white.

Binding: Bound in black cloth. Front and back covers blank. Spine: '[bright green] Burroughs | *Odier* | The Job GROVE PRESS'. Issued with a white dust jacket designed by Kuhlman Associates, the front of which is a black-and-white photograph of WSB from Bennett Studio, London, over which is superimposed: '[at top left, white] The Job | [blue-green] Interviews with | [light blue] William S. Burroughs | [green] by Daniel Odier'. Spine: '[down, black] The Job [green] by William S. Burroughs and Daniel Odier | [across at bottom, black] GP–596 | GROVE | PRESS'. The back of the dust jacket is given to short quotes from four reviews of the work, headed: '[black] Some comments on William S. Burroughs work:'. The reviews are separated by alternating green and light blue line rules. At the end of the reviews is a green rule beneath which is '[black] Grove Press, Inc., 214 Mercer Street, New York, N.Y. 10012'. Inside flaps are mainly the publisher's blurb. At top of flap 1 is: '[black] GP 596 | $5.95'. At bottom of flap 2 are short biographical sketches of the authors divided from the blurb and from each other by green, blue, green line rules. At the extreme bottom of flap 2 are the credits: '[black] DESIGN: KUHLMAN ASSOCIATES | Jacket photo: Bennett Studio, London'. All edges trimmed.

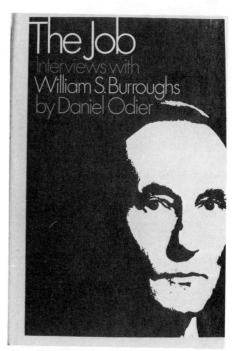

A16a

A16b

Publication: This edition, published May 15, 1970, consisted of 5,000 copies. Reprinted Aug. 20, 1971, in a quantity of 1,500 copies.

b. Jonathan Cape 1970

THE JOB | [line rule] | INTERVIEW WITH | *William Burroughs* | BY | DANIEL ODIER | [publisher's device (an urn within two circles, with fruit at top and 'J' and 'C' at each side)] | JONATHAN CAPE | THIRTY BEDFORD SQUARE | LONDON

Collation: 19.6 × 12.8 cm. [A]⁸ B–M⁸, 96 leaves; pp. [1–10] 11–48 [49–50] 51–104 [105–106] 107–119 [120–122] 123–192. Page 1: 'Also by William Burroughs | DEAD FINGERS TALK | NAKED LUNCH | JUNKIE | NOVA EXPRESS | THE SOFT MACHINE | THE TICKET THAT EXPLODED | THE EXTER-MINATOR | APO-33 | THE YAGE LETTERS (with Allen Ginsberg)'. p. 3: title. p. 4: 'FIRST PUBLISHED IN A FRENCH TRANSLATION BY | EDITIONS PIERRE BELFOND, PARIS 1969 | FIRST PUBLISHED IN GREAT BRITAIN 1970 | © 1969 BY WILLIAM BURROUGHS AND DANIEL ODIER | JONATHAN CAPE LTD | 30 BEDFORD SQUARE, LONDON, WC1 | SBN 224 61811 3 | PRINTED IN GREAT BRITAIN | BY EBENEZER BAYLIS AND SON, LIMITED | ON PAPER MADE BY JOHN DICKINSON AND CO. LTD | BOUND BY A. W. BAIN AND CO. LTD, LONDON'. p. 5: 'CONTENTS'. p. 6: blank. p. 7: '*Navigare necesse es. Vivare no es necesse.*' by WSB. p. 8: 'From the diary of a seven-year-old boy at the American | School in Tangier: | 'I get up at 8:30. I eat my breakfast. Then I go to the | job.' | When asked what he meant by 'the job' he said: 'School | of course.'' pp. 9–192: text; p. 192 signed '*October 15th, 1968* | *London*'. Pages 10, 50, 106, 120, and 122 are blank.

Contents: Same as **A16a**, except for some corrections and minor deletions (a few questions from the American edition are deleted and "The Invisible Generation" shortened). The "Author's Foreword" is also deleted.

Paper: White wove paper. Endpapers white.

Binding: Bound in black cloth. Front and back covers blank. Spine: '[in gilt down,] THE JOB | INTERVIEW WITH | WILLIAM BUR-ROUGHS | [across] DANIEL | ODIER | [at bottom, publisher's device, as before]'. Issued in a white dust jacket designed by Bill

Botten, the front of which is a drawing in shades of green and black of
police quelling a riot; in the foreground is the face of WSB; at the top
left is: [green] INTERVIEW WITH | [black] WILLIAM BUR-
ROUGHS | [green] BY DANIEL ODIER | [in tall green letters
partially outlined in black] THE JOB'. The drawing continues over
the spine, down which is: '[in tall green letters partially outlined in
black]THE JOB | [green] INTERVIEW WITH | [black] WILLIAM
BURROUGHS | [green] BY DANIEL ODIER | [in black], pub-
lisher's device, as before]'. The back of the dust jacket reproduces:
'*Navigare necesse es. Vivare no es necesse*', signed 'WILLIAM BUR-
ROUGHS'. Inside flap 1 is the publisher's blurb, at the bottom of
which is: '35^s net | [line rule] | IN UK ONLY | [line rule] | £1.75 net'.
Flap 2 is given to short biographical sketches of the authors; at the
bottom is: 'SBN 224 61811 3 | Jacket design by Bill Botten | ©
Jonathan Cape Ltd, 1970'. All edges trimmed.

Publication: This edition was published in 1970. The publisher would
give no other information.

A17   THE LAST WORDS OF DUTCH SCHULTZ

a. Cape Goliard Press   1970

THE LAST | WORDS | OF | DUTCH SCHULTZ | WILLIAM
BURROUGHS | CAPE GOLIARD PRESS | LONDON 1970

Collation: 24.8 × 16.4 cm. [1]^4 [2–6]^8 [7]^4, 48 leaves; pp. [i–viii],
[1–4] 5–7 [8] 9–67 [68] 69–73 [74] 75–81 [82–88].
Page i: sepia photo-collage of a man screaming. p. ii: blank. p. iii:
same photo as before (in sepia) but with background of building. p.
iv: blank. p. v: same sepia photo as before, but man's head is farther
to the right side and a man is entering the facade of the building. p. vi:
blank. p. vii: sepia photo of background building of the previous
photos, but without the screaming-man head; instead, at bottom is
lettered the half title. p. viii: blank. p. 1: title. p. 2: 'COVER
ILLUSTRATION (DUTCH SCHULTZ) | BY R. B. KITAJ | ©
copyright William Burroughs 1970. | SBN paper 206 61765 8; cloth
206 61764 X | This first edition has been designed, printed & |
published by Cape Goliard Press, 10a Fairhazel | Gardens, London
N.W.6; of this edition 100 copies | have been numbered and signed
by the author. | Printed in Great Britain.' p. 3: 'THIS IS NOT JUST

A FILM ABOUT DUTCH SCHULTZ. IT IS A FILM ABOUT | DUTCH SCHULTZ AND THE SETS IN WHICH HE LIVED AND OPERATED ... THERE IS NO REASON TO BELIEVE HE EVER SHOT ANYBODY BUT | HIMSELF. THE SETS ARE THE MEDIUM IN WHICH THE CHARACTERS | LIVE THAT INEXORABLY MOULD THEIR ACTIONS. WHEN A CHARACTER | IS NO LONGER ON SET HE IS FINISHED.' by WSB. p. 4: blank. pp. 5–7: 'SPECIAL FEATURES OF THIS FILM' by WSB. p. 8: blank. pp. 9–73: text. p. 74: blank. pp. 75–81: 'TRANSCRIPT OF DUTCH SCHULTZ'S LAST WORDS'. pp. 82–88: blank. Page 68 is also blank.

Contents: Foreword, "This Is Not Just a Film . . . "; "Special Features of This Film"; text, *The Last Words of Dutch Schultz*; and "Transcript of Dutch Schultz's Last Words."

Paper: White wove paper. Endpapers black.

Binding: Bound in light blue cloth. Front and back covers blank. Spine: '[down, bright red] THE LAST WORDS OF DUTCH SCHULTZ WILLIAM BURROUGHS CAPE GOLIARD'. Issued in a white dust jacket, on the front of which is a drawing by R. B. Kitaj (in shades of orange and black) of Dutch Schultz; underneath the drawing is: '[black letters shaded in orange] THE LAST WORDS | OF | DUTCH SCHULTZ | WILLIAM BURROUGHS'. Spine: '[down, black] THE LAST WORDS OF DUTCH SCHULTZ [brown] WILLIAM BURROUGHS [black] CAPE GOLIARD PRESS'. Back of dust jacket reproduces in black capitals the preface by WSB on p. 3. Inside flap 1 is blank, except at bottom is: 'CAPE GOLIARD PRESS | 35s. (1.75) net U.K. only'. Inside flap 2 is blank. All edges trimmed.

Publication: This edition was published May 28, 1970. The publisher would give no other publication information. The 100 numbered and signed copies were in a gray-green buckram binding and were issued without the dust jacket; they were in tissue wraps instead. The spine lettering on these special copies is in gold and the word 'PRESS' is included after 'CAPE GOLIARD'.

b. Cape Goliard Press 1970

A paperbound edition of **A17** issued simultaneously with the hardcover. Collation and contents are identical to **A17a**. The stiff

A17a, b

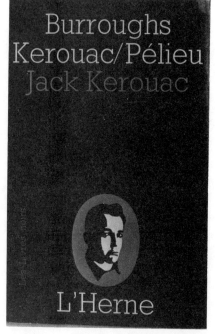

A18a

white wrappers reproduce the dust jacket of **A17a**. At bottom of back cover is: '[black] CAPE GOLIARD PRESS | 16s. (80p.) net U.K. only'.

Publication: This edition was published May 28, 1970. The publisher would give no other information.

A18   JACK KEROUAC

a. L'Herne   1971

Burroughs—Kerouac | Pélieu | Jack Kerouac | L'Herne

Collation: 21 × 13.6 cm. [1–6]⁸, 48 leaves; pp. [1–8] 9–15 [16] 17–21 [22] 23–51 [52] 53–64 [65–66] 67–87 [88] 89–91 [92] 93–95 [96].

Pages 1–2: blank. p. 3: half title. p. 4: '© 1971 by William S. Burroughs and Claude Pélieu'. p. 5: title. p. 6: '*Les textes de William Burroughs, Allen Ginsberg et* | *A. G. Aranowitz ont été traduits par Mary Beach.* | *L'interview avec Jack Kerouac est extraite de la revue* | *americaine «U.S.», Bantam Books, New York.* | *Le poéme d'Allen Ginsberg est extrait de la* | *revue amé*|*ricaine « Countdown ».* *New York.* Courtesy Allen Gin-s|berg. | *Le texte de William Burroughs a été publié dans le* Nou|vel Observateur *après la mort de Jack Kerouac.* Courtesy | William Bur-roughs. | *La note de Claude Pélieu est extraite du Notebook et est* | *publiée sous une autre forme dans « Les Transistors de* | *l'Innocence ». (Chris-tian Bourgois.).*' p. 7: 'In memoriam | Jack Kerouac | 1922–1969'. p. 8: blank. p. 9: '*When you went on the road looking for America you found* | *only what you put there and a man seeking gold* | *finds the only America there is to find; and his* | *investment and a poet's investment . . . the same* | *when comes the crash, and it's crashing, yet the* | *windows are tight, are not for jumping; from hell* | *none e'er fell* | Gregory Corso *from* « Elegiac Feelings American » | New Directions. N.Y.'. p. 10: '*Pull my daisy,* | *Tip my cups,* | *Cut my thoughts* | *for coconuts, and so on for three more stanzas.* | Allen Ginsberg *from I Beg You Come Back & Be Cheerful* | The Beat Scene | Corinth Book. N.Y. | *No one owns life, but anyone who can pick up a fryingpan* | *owns death.* | William Burroughs'. p. 11: a drawing, 'Roue de la vie tibetaine.' p. 12: a photograph of WSB by Brion Gysin. pp. 13–20: 'Jack Kerouac | par William S. Burroughs.' (p. 16 appears to be an American Civil War photograph). p. 21: a photograph of Jack Kerouac by William Eichel. p. 22: blank. pp.

23–51: 'Interview | avec Jack Kerouac | par Alfred G. Aranowitz'. p. 52: blank. pp. 53–61: 'Notes | par Jack Kerouac'. p. 62: photograph of Allen Ginsberg and Neal Cassady by Charles Plymell. p. 63: photograph of Claude Pélieu and Gregory Corso at Cherry Valley (uncredited). p. 64: photograph of Mary Beach (uncredited). p. 65: photograph of Claude Pélieu (uncredited). p. 66: blank. pp. 67–80: '*mosaïques electriques | indigo off soft zoom | Jack Kerouac et la radio-nuit-de-|l'enfance |* par Claude Pélieu'. pp. 81–86: 'chun | cromlrech moruah! | *notes |* par Claude Pélieu. p. 88: a reproduction of a newsclipping from the *Daily News* for Wednesday, Oct. 22, 1969, announcing the death of Jack Kerouac. pp. 89–90: 'Epilogue' by Claude Pélieu. p. 91: a reproduction of a piece headed '*Épitaphe pour un beatnik*' contained a quote from WSB, signed 'Londres, le 23 Octobre 1969.' and photos of WSB and Kerouac, credited to David Lardner and U.S.I.S. respectively, underneath which is '*Le Même peur*'. p. 92: blank. pp. 93–95: 'Jack Kerouac | est mort | le 21 octobre 1969' by Allen Ginsberg. p. 96: '[long rule] | 7900— Imprimerie Laboureur et Cie, 113, rue Oberkampf, Paris (11ᵉ) | Dépôt légal 3ᵉ trimestre 1971 | Numéro d'éditeur: 5 107'.

Contents: Three quotes from Gregory Corso, Allen Ginsberg, and WSB: "Jack Kerouac" by WSB (**C349**); interview with Jack Kerouac by A. G. Aranowitz; "Notes" by Jack Kerouac (from Ann Charter's *A Bibliography of Works by Jack Kerouac*); "Mosaïques electriques indigo off soft zoom Jack Kerouac et la radio-nuit-de-l'enfance" by Claude Pélieu; "Chun cromlrech moruah! Notes" by Claude Pélieu; reproduction of newspaper article, "Jack Kerouac, Beat Novelist Is Dead at 47," from N.Y. *Daily News*, Wednesday, Oct. 22, 1969; epilogue ("Jack Kerouac est mort") by Claude Pélieu; piece headed "*Épitaphe pour un beatnik*" (**C252**); and "Jack Kerouac est mort le 21 octobre 1969" by Allen Ginsberg, plus photos and illustrations.

Paper: White wove paper.

Binding: Bound in stiff black pictorial wrappers which fold to make inside flaps. Front cover: '[at top, white] Burroughs | Kerouac/Pélieu | [blue] Jack Kerouac | [at bottom, within blue oval, a black-and-white drawing of Jack Kerouac] | [in white] L'Herne | [to the left of the drawing and reading up, blue] Les Livres noirs'. Spine: '[up, white] L'Herne Burroughs, Kerouac, Pélieu [blue] Jack Kerouac'. Back cover: at top in white is a quote from WSB in French; at bottom is: '[white] Couverture de Pierre Bernard'. Inside flaps 1 and 2 are given to the publisher's advertisements. All edges trimmed.

Publication: This edition was published in 1971. Quantity printed and price are unknown.

A19 ALI'S SMILE

a. Unicorn Books 1971

[within thin brown rectangle with rounded sides] [a black-and-white drawing of a kris] | ALI'S SMILE | WILLIAM BURROUGHS | UNICORN BOOKS 1971

Collation: 20.2 × 15.6 cm. [1]⁴ [2]⁶ [3–5]⁴, 22 leaves; pp. [1–44]. Page 1: drawing of a kris by John Anderson. p. 2: blank. p. 3: this page has the issue number and the author's signature. p. 4: blank. p. 5: half title with kris drawing. p. 6: blank. p. 7: another half title with kris drawing. p. 8: blank. p. 9: another half title with kris drawing and title three times. p. 10: blank. p. 11: title. p. 12: 'Drawing of kris by John Anderson | Engraving of Constantinople from a 19th century travel book | Papers by G. F. Smith | Bound by F. H. Knight & Son'. pp. 13–39: text. p. 40: blank. p. 41: © William Burroughs 1971 | This first publication in any form of *Ali's Smile* is issued in an edition of 99 | numbered and signed copies of which numbers 1 to 90 are for sale and | numbers 1 to 99 are hors commerce. This book has been printed by Richard | Moseley/Graphic Workshop/Brighton in Univers/Perpetua/Palace Script types | and is published by Unicorn Books/50 Gloucester Road/Brighton England.' pp. 42–44: blank. Page 38 is also blank.

Contents: Text, *Ali's Smile*. (Reprinted complete in *Sixpack 2* [C337].)

Papers: G. B. Smith's Buckler and Tranby. First gathering is brownish-red wove paper. The second, third, and fourth gatherings are cream-colored wove paper. The fifth gathering is white wove paper. Endpapers are gray laid paper. All edges trimmed.

Binding: Bound in light brown buckram. The front cover has in its center a kris stamped in gilt. The spine and back cover are blank. The book was issued without a dust jacket.

Note: The book was issued in a light brown cardboard carton 39.9

A19a

cm. square which also contained a 12-inch LP phonorecord (mx.UB LP 1 A S/S), side A of which is WSB reading the second draft of the text. Side B is at 78 r.p.m. and contains what seems to be technical data of the recording process. Side A has a blank white label, while side B is unlabeled. The recording is enclosed in a soft white paper sleeve lined with transparent material with a center hole, then is packaged in a thin white cardboard container which opens at one side. Side B of the recording was intended to be blank.

Publication: This edition, published in October 1971, consisted of 99 copies.

A20　　　　　THE WILD BOYS

a. GROVE PRESS, INC.　　1971

The | Wild | Boys | [line rule] | *A Book of the Dead* | [line rule] | William S. Burroughs | Grove Press, Inc. | New York

Collation: 20.2 × 13 cm. 96 leaves; pp. [i–iv] v [vi], [1–2] 3–184 [185–186].
Page i: half title, p. ii: blank. p. iii: title. p. iv: 'Copyright © 1969, 1970, 1971 by William S. Burroughs | All Rights Reserved | "Mother and I Would Like to Know" was first pub-|lished in *Evergreen Review* No. 67; an earlier version | appeared in *Mayfair* and was reprinted in *The Job*. No part of this book may be reproduced, for any reason, | by any means, including any method of photographic | reproduction, without the permission of the publisher. | Library of Congress Catalog Card Number: 78–155133 | ISBN: 0–394–47586–0 | First Printing | Distributed by Random House, Inc., New York | Manufactured in the United States of America'. p. v: 'Contents'. p. vi: blank. p. 1: second half title. p. 2: blank. pp. 3–184: text; p. 184 signed '*William S. Burroughs* | *August 17, 1969* | *London*'. pp. 185–186: blank.

Contents: Text, *The Wild Boys*.

Paper: White wove paper. Endpapers white.

Binding: Perfect-bound, no sigs. Bound in black cloth, with the title blindstamped into the front cover. Spine: '[in gilt, down] The Wild Boys by William S. Burroughs | [across at bottom] GROVE |

PRESS'. Back cover blank. Issued with a dust jacket on the front of which is a color photograph by George Adams of a science-fiction-like guerilla warrior pointing a rifle off which the sun is glinting; at the bottom, on a black band is: '[white] The Wild Boys | a Book of the Dead | by William S. Burroughs'. Jacket spine: '[down, black] The Wild Boys [blue] by William S. Burroughs | [across at bottom, black] GROVE | PRESS'. The back of the dust jacket is a large black-and-white photograph of WSB by Bennett Studio, London, that was reproduced on the front of the jacket of **A16a**; to the right of the photo is: '[up, black] Photo: Bennett Studio, London'; underneath the photo is a short biographical sketch of WSB at the bottom of which is a long blue line rule, and underneath that is: '[black] 394–47586–0'. Inside flaps 1 and 2 are given to the publisher's blurb. At top of inside flap 1 is: 'GP–697 | $6.95'. At bottom of flap 2 is: '[blue line rule] | [black] Photo: George Adams'. All edges trimmed.

Publication: This edition, published Oct. 26, 1971, consisted of 5,619 copies.

b. Calder & Boyars   1972

The | Wild | Boys | [line rule] | *A Book of the Dead* | [line rule] | William S. Burroughs | Calder & Boyars | London

Collation: 19.7 × 12.5 cm. [1–6]¹⁶; pagination is same as **A20a**. Page iv: 'First published in Great Britain in 1972 | by Calder & Boyars Ltd | 18 Brewer Street London W1 | © William Burroughs, 1969, 1970, 1971 | ALL RIGHTS RESERVED | ISBN 0 7145 8093 4 | 'Mother and I Would Like to Know' was first | published in *Evergreen Review* No. 67; an earlier | version appeared in *Mayfair* and was reprinted in | *The Job.* | Any paperback edition of this book whether pub-|lished simultaneously with, or subsequent to the | case bound edition is sold subject to the condition | that it shall not, by way of trade, be lent, resold, | hired out, or otherwise disposed of, without the | publisher's consent, in any form of binding or cover | other than that in which it is published. | Printed in Great Britain by | Morrison & Gibb Ltd, London & Edinburgh'.

Contents: Text, *The Wild Boys,* as in the American edition.

Paper: White wove paper. Endpapers white.

A20a

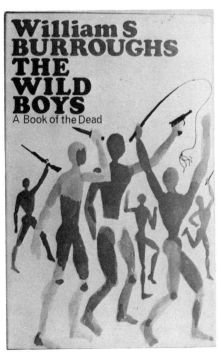

A20b, c

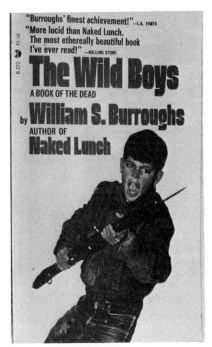

A20d (later printing)

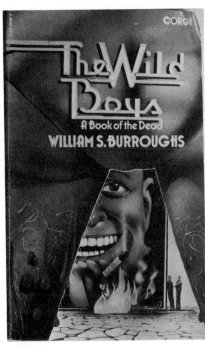

A20e

Binding: Bound in light red cloth. Front and back covers blank.
Spine: '[down, in gilt] BURROUGHS THE WILD BOYS CAL-
DER & BOYARS'. Issued in a white dust jacket designed by John
Sewell on the front of which in black, white, and shades of brown is a
drawing of a band of wild boys; above the drawing is: '[dark brown]
William S | BURROUGHS | [black] THE | WILD | BOYS | A Book
of the Dead'. Jacket spine: '[down, black] BURROUGHS [dark
brown] THE WILD BOYS [black] Calder & Boyars'. On the back of
the dust jacket is '[brown on white] THE WILD BOYS | A Book of
the Dead | [black] William Burroughs | [publisher's blurb and short
biographical sketch of WSB] | [brown] *From the same publishers:* | [in
brown rectangle, publisher's advertisement of five WSB books with
prices (all in black on white)] | [brown] CALDER & BOYARS LTD |
18 Brewer Street London W1'. Inside flaps 1 and 2 are given to the
publisher's advertisement. At the bottom of flap 1 is '[black] *Jacket
design by John Sewell* | [brown] ISBN 0 7145 0893 4 £2.50'. All edges
trimmed.

Publication: This edition was published May 25, 1972. The publisher
would give no other information.

c. Calder & Boyars   1972

The title page is identical to **A20b**.

Collation: Except for slightly different size (this edition is 19.8 × 12.8
cm.), the collation is identical to **A20b**.

Contents: Identical to **A20b**.

Paper: White wove paper.

Binding: Bound in stiff white pictorial wrappers. The front cover is a
reproduction of the front of the dust jacket of **A20b**. Spine: '[down,
black] BURROUGHS [brown] THE WILD BOYS [across at bot-
tom, black] C | [down] B | [across] 258'. Back cover: '[black] A
Calderbook CB 285 £1.00 | [brown] THE WILD BOYS | A Book of
the Dead | [black] William S. Burroughs | [quotes from 5 reviews of
the book] | Also available in hardcover at £2.50. | ISBN 0 7145
08942 | [publisher's advertisement as on reverse jacket of **A20b**] |
CALDER & BOYARS LTD | 18 Brewer Street London W1'. Inside
the front and back covers is the publisher's advertisement. At the

bottom of inside back cover: *'Cover design by John Sewell'*. All edges trimmed.

Publication: This edition was published simultaneously with **A20b** (May 25, 1972). Publisher would give no other information.

d. Grove Press, Inc.   1972

The title page is identical to **A20a**.

Collation: Except for smaller size (this edition is 17.8 × 10.6 cm), the collation of this edition is the same as **A20a**. Page i is the publisher's blurb.

Contents: Identical to **A20a**.

Paper: White wove paper.

Binding: Perfect-bound, no sigs. Bound in stiff white pictorial wrappers. Front cover: a color photograph of a guerilla warrior-boy, above which is '[in black, quotes from L.A. *Times* and *Rolling Stone* reviews of the book] | [red] The Wild Boys | [black] A BOOK OF THE DEAD | [black] by [red] William S. Burroughs | [black] AUTHOR OF | [red] Naked Lunch'; at top left is '[up, black] 9734 · 1.25'. Spine: 'at top, black] DELL | [line rule] | FIC | [down, red] The Wild Boys [black] William S. Burroughs | 440–9734–125'. Back cover is given to a quote from Norman Mailer on WSB and 2 quotes from reviews of the book (quotes in black, sources in red); at the right is: '[up, black] PRINTED IN USA COVER PHOTO: MAGNUM'. All edges trimmed and yellow.

Publication: This edition, published Aug. 12, 1972, consisted of 100,000 copies. Later printings of this edition had the Grove Press / Evergreen Black Cat publisher's design and number (B–370] and were priced at $1.50.

e. Corgi Books   1973

The second UK paperback of **A20**, with full-color wrappers (mostly red-pink and violet). The title is in white neon-type letters over a color illustration by Philip Castle of three wild boys in front of a picture of "the boy" smoking a cigarette and smiling. 144 pp. Priced at 35p.

Publication: The publisher would give no information on this edition other than the year of publication, 1973.

A21 ELECTRONIC REVOLUTION

a. Blackmoor Head Press 1971.

WILLIAM BURROUGHS | ELECTRONIC | REVOLUTION | 1970–71

Collation: 25.9 × 20.1 cm. 40 leaves; pp. 1–39 [40] 41– [77–80]. Page 1: blank. p. 2: title. p. 3: blank. p. 4: 'cover | original drawings by | BRION GYSIN | lay-out henri chopin'. p. 5: blank. p. 6: blank. pp. 7–39: text. p. 40: layout by Henri Chopin p. 41: 'version francaise | par jean chopin'. p. 42: blank. pp. 43–75: same text as on pp. 7–39, in French. pp. 76–77: blank. p. 78: 'La Révolution Electronique | se limite á | 500 exemplaires | se décomposant comme suit: | [underlined] 50 exemplaires no. | 1 à 50 | sur papier "Hayle" | —white mediaeval laid demy 25 lbs— | de J. Barcham Green Ltd | chaque exemplaire sous étui | étant signé par son auteur et | enrichi de deux sérigraphies signées | de Brion Gysin | et en outre l'exemplaire no. A | ayant recueilli tous les | manuscrits | [underlined] 450 exemplaires no. | 51 à 500 | sur papier offset | le tout constituant l'édition originale | Achevé d'imprimer pour le compte | d'Henri Chopin et de sa collection | OU, le 30 octobre 1971, sur les | presses de I. Ormiston, "Blackmoor | Head Press", Cambridge. | Copyright William Burroughs | et h.c.' p. 79: 'Electronic Revolution | is limited to | 500 | copies | numbered as follows: | [underlined] | 1 to 50 | Printed on "Hayle" paper | —white mediaeval laid demy 25 lbs— | made by J. Barcham Green Ltd | each copy is presented | in a cardboard wallet | and signed by the author | each contains two silkscreens | signed by Brion Gysin | the copy no. A also contains all the manuscripts | [underlined] 450 copies no. | 51 to 500 | on offset paper | all of this constitutes the original edition | Printed for Henri Chopin and his | Collection OU by Ian Ormiston | at the Blackmoor Head Press | Cambridge | 30th October 1971'. p. 80: blank. Pages 13, 14, 23, 24, 31, 32, 35, 36, 49, 50, 59, 60, 67, 68, 71, and 72 are also blank.

Contents: Electronic Revolution text in English and French, plus illustrations.

Paper: White wove paper.

Binding: Perfect-bound, no sigs. Stiff white pictorial wrappers, front, spine, and one-fourth of back cover of which are two graphlike drawings by Brion Gysin, one on top of the other. The top drawing on the front cover contains: '[red] ELECTRON | I | C REVOL | TI N'; the bottom one: ' ILLIAM | B   GHS'. The drawing continues over the spine and onto a fourth of the back cover, where beneath it is: '[black] DRAWINGS: BRION GYSIN'. All edges trimmed.

Publication: This edition, published Oct. 30, 1971, consisted of 500 copies, the first 50 of which were on special paper, signed by the author, and issued in a cardboard case which also contained two silkscreens by Brion Gysin, signed by the artist. The first copy contained all the manuscripts as well.

A22   BRION GYSIN LET THE MICE IN

a. Something Else Press, Inc.   1973

BRION GYSIN | [a calligraphic drawing by Gysin] | LET THE MICE IN |at left] By | Brion | Gysin | [down, at center Edited by | Jan | Herman | [down, at right] with Texts By | William | Burroughs | & | Ian | Sommerville | [across bottom, long rule] | [heavy long rule] | SOMETHING ELSE PRESS, *Inc.* | [long rule] | [heavy long rule]

Collation: 22.8 × 15.2 cm. [1–5]^8, leaves; pp. [i–vi], [1–2] 3–22 [23–24] 25–30 [31–32] 33–35 [36] 37–47 [48–50] 51–64 [65–74].

Page i: blank. p. ii: sepia photograph of Gysin painting. p. iii: title. p. iv: 'ISBN: 0–87110–105-X (cloth) and 0–87110–106–8 (paper) | Library of Congress Catalog Card No.: 72–96737 | Copyright © 1973 by Jan Herman. Published by Something Else Press, Inc., | P.O. Box 26, West Glover, VT 05875. All rights reserved. No portion whatever | of this text may be reproduced in any form except for brief passages quoted | for inclusion in a review written for a magazine or a newspaper or a radio or | television broadcast. | ACKNOWL-EDGEMENTS | Photo opposite title page by Christian Taillandier. Brion Gysin painting to | poetry in an appearance of "Le Domaine Poetizue" at the *Paris Biennale,* | 1961. | "CUT-UPS: A Project for Disastrous Success", © 1964, 1973 by Brion Gysin, | appeared for the

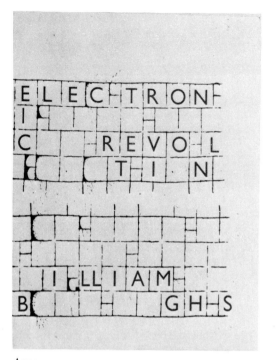

A21a

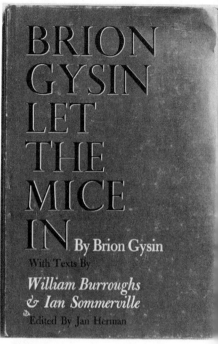

A22a, b

A23a

first time in *Evergreen Review*, No. 32, (April-May) 1964. It is |
reprinted by permission of the author and *Evergreen Review*. | "Brion
Gysin Let The Mice recorded | and played for the first time at the
Institute for Contemporary Arts (ICA) in | London, December,
1960. | "Dream Machine", © 1962, 1973 by Brion Gysin, appeared
for the first time in | *Olympia Magazine*, No. 2, 1962. It is reprinted
by permission of the author. | "Flicker", © 1962, 1973 by Ian Som-
merville, appeared for the first time in | *Olympia Magazine*, No. 2,
1962. It is reprinted by permission of the author. | "The Invisible
Generation", © 1969, 1973 by William S. Burroughs, appeared | for
the first time in *Klacto International* 23, 1969 (ed. Carl Weissner) [see
C241]. It is re-|printed by permission of the author and editor. |
"Word Authority More Habit Forming Than Heroin", © 1967, 1973
by Wil-|liam S. Burroughs, appeared for the first time in *The San
Francisco EARTH-|QUAKE*, No. 1, 1967 (ed. Jan Herman) [see
C175]. It is reprinted by permission of the | author. | "The Permu-
tated Poems of Brion Gysin" (as put through a computer by Ian |
Sommerville), © 1960, 1963, 1973 by Brion Gysin, have made
several appear-|ances. "Pistol Poem" was used as the leitmotiv of all
performances by "Le | Domaine Poetique" in Paris from 1960 on. It
also appeared in the *Biennale de Paris*, 1963, and it has been recorded
for OU (ed. Henri Chopin). Two | performances of this piece at the
ICA were Domaine Poetic activities which | included early sound
and light shows with the help of William Burroughs and | the techni-
cal assistance of Ian Sommerville. It was originally recorded by the |
British Broadcasting Company sound effects studio and broadcast in
| England by the BBC as part of a program entitled "The Permutated
Poems of | Brion Gysin" produced by Douglas Cleverdon. "I Am
That I Am" (The | Divine Tautology), "Junk Is No Good Baby7" and
"Kick That Habit Man" | were also recorded as mentioned above. All
of these peoms have been broad-|cast by Radio-Television Francaise
(RTF) in France, Czechoslovakia, Sweden, | Italy, and Switzerland. |
MANUFACTURED IN THE UNITED STATES OF AMERICA'.
Note: The editor mistakenly omitted the credit for "Parenthetically 7
Hertz," © 1967, 1973 by William S. Burroughs; it appeared for the
first time in *Klacto/23*, 1967 (C174). p. v: 'CONTENTS'. p. vi:
'EDITOR'S NOTE' by Jan Herman. p. 1: half title. pp. 2–74: texts
and photographs.

Contents: "Cut-ups: A Project for Disastrous Success," "Cut-ups Self-explained," and "Brion Gysin Let the Mice In" by Brion Gysin; "Flicker" by Ian Sommerville; "Dreamachine" by Brion Gysin; "The Invisible Generation," "Word Authority More Habit Forming than Heroin," and "Parenthetically 7 Hertz" by WSB: "Permutated Poems of Brion Gysin as Put through a Computer by Ian Sommerville: 'Pistol Poem,' 'I Am That I Am,' 'Junk Is No Good Baby,' and 'Kick That Habit Man.'" Included are numerous sepia photographs.

Paper: White wove paper. Endpapers pale green laid paper.

Binding: Bound in light green-blue cloth. Printed in silver across bottom front cover: 'Brion Gysin Let The Mice In *Brion Gysin*'. Spine: '[down, in silver] Brion Gysin Let The Mice In *Brion Gysin* | [across at bottom, publisher's device (the press name in a circle around a question mark)]'. Back cover blank. Issued with a light brown dust jacket on the front of which is: '[black outlined in white] BRION | GYSIN | LET | THE | MICE | IN [white] By Brion Gysin | [black] With Texts By | [white] *William Burroughs* | *& Ian Sommerville* | [black] Edited By Jan Herman'. Jacket spine: '[down, white] Brion Gysin Let The Mice In *Brion Gysin* | [across at bottom, black, publisher's device, as before]'. On the back of the dust jacket, at the top right is: '[black] ISBN: 0–87110–105-X'; following is a black-and-white photograph of Gysin by WSB with credit and title: '[black] Wm. Burroughs | Brion Gysin in Earl's Court, London, 1966'; then (also in black) a short biographical sketch of Gysin. Inside flap 1 at top is the price, '7.95', and the title, 'BRION | GYSIN | LET | THE | MICE | IN'; the rest of the flap is an excerpt from "Brion Gysin Let the Mice In." Inside flap 2 (at bottom) is: 'SOMETHING ELSE PRESS, *Inc.* | POST OFFICE BOX 26 | West Grover, Vermont 05875'. All edges trimmed. On the back endpaper pastedown is the colophon: 'Designed & printed by Graham Macintosh | at Noel Young Press in Santa Barbara, | in an edition limited to 1000 copies in softcover | and 500 copies in hardcover, February, 1973.'

Publication: This edition, published in February 1973, consisted of 500 copies.

b. Something Else Press, Inc.   1973

First paperbound edition of **A22**, issued simultaneously with the hardcover. Collation and contents are identical to **A22a**. The stiff light brown wrappers reproduce the dust jacket of **A22a** with some minor differences: the photograph of Gysin on the back is in sepia instead of black and white and at the bottom of the cover is the publisher's device; the lettering down the spine is all in black with logo, '*SOMETHING ELSE PRESS*', added; at the top of the back cover is: '[black] ISBN: 0–87110–106–8 $3.95'. The endpapers are present, but are cream-colored wove paper.

Publication: This edition, published in February 1973, consisted of 1,000 copies.

A23   EXTERMINATOR!

a. The Viking Press, Inc.   1973

Note: title page is a gray-toned black-and-white photograph of a dead roach-bug. The bug is at the bottom, the title and publisher's imprint are at the top in the gray field.

EXTERMINATOR! | A NOVEL BY | WILLIAM S. BUR-ROUGHS | A Richard Seaver Book | The Viking Press New York

Collation: 20.1 × 13.3 cm. [1–4]¹⁶ [5]⁸ [6]¹⁶, 88 leaves; pp. [i–vi], [1–2] 3–168 [169–170].
Page i: half title. p. ii: 'Also by William S. Burroughs | *Junkie* | *Naked Lunch* | *Nova Express* | *The Soft Machine* | *The Ticket That Exploded* | *The Wild Boys* | *Yage Letters (with Allen Ginsberg)*'. p. iii: title. p. iv: 'Copyright © 1966, 1967, 1968, 1969, 1973, by William Burroughs | All Rights Reserved | No part of this book may be reproduced, in any form or by any | means, without the prior written permission of the publisher, | excepting brief quotes used in connection with reviews written | specifically for inclusion in magazines or newspapers. | A Richard Seaver Book | The Viking Press | First published in 1973 by The Viking Press, Inc. | 625 Madison Avenue, New York, N.Y. 10022 | Published simultaneously in Canada by | The Macmillan Company of Canada Limited | SBN 670-30281-3 | Library of Congress catalogue card number: 72-9736 | First Printing | Manufactured in the United States of America | Portions of this volume have been previously published, in somewhat different form, in the following places: *Antaeus, Atlantic Monthly, Cavalier, Daily Telegraph* (London), | *Esquire, Evergreen Review, Mayfair, Rolling Stone, The*

A24a (back cover)

A24a (front cover)

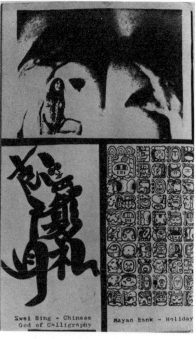

A25a (front cover)

A25a (back cover)

Village Voice. | Acknowledgment is made to Warner Bros. Music for lyrics from | "Ain't She Sweet." © 1927 Advanced Music Corporation. | Copyright renewed. All rights reserved. Used by permission of Warner Bros. Music.' pp. v-vi: 'CONTENTS'. p. 1: second half title. p. 2: blank. pp. 3–168: text. pp. 169–170: blank.

Contents: Text, *Exterminator!* (not related to **A4**).

Paper: White wove paper. Endpapers black.

Binding: Dull brown cloth. Front cover bears a silhouette of a roach-bug within a bold black rectangle at bottom right. Spine: '[down, white] William S. Burroughs | Exterminator! | [across at bottom, black] VIKING'. Back cover blank. Issued with a white dust jacket, on the front of which is: '[at top, black] Exterminator! | by William S. Burroughs | [at bottom right, bluish-green] a novel | [a cropped sepia-toned photograph of a live roach-bug]'. Jacket spine: '[black, down] Exterminator! | by William S. Burroughs | [across bottom] Viking'. The inside flaps are the publisher's blurb. At the top of flap 1 is: '$6.95'. At the end of the publisher's blurb on flap 2 is a small black-and-white photograph of WSB, to the right of which is the credit: '[black] Brion Gysin'. Beneath the photo is a short biographical sketch of the author, underneath which is a long thin black rule, beneath which is: '[blue] A RICHARD SEAVER BOOK | THE VIKING PRESS | *Publishers of The Viking Portable Library* | and Viking Compass paperbacks | 625 Madison Avenue, New York, N.Y. 10022'. All edges trimmed; top edge is reddish-brown.

Publication: This edition, published in August 1973, consisted of 7,500 copies. In WSB's collection there is a leather-bound (quarter morocco, gold-stamped), gilt-topped copy. It is not known how many other such deluxe copies exist.

A24   **WHITE SUBWAY**

a. Aloes seolA   1973

WHITE SUBWAY | [publisher's design (a square turning in on itself)] | William Burroughs | aloes seolA | [publisher's device (a thick book with a bite taken out of the right side)]. | Aloes seolA London

Collation: 20.8 × 15.9 cm. 38 leaves; pp. [i-ii], 1–73 [74].
Page i: title. p. ii: 'Today was like an old, worn-out film being run off—dim, | jerky, flickering, full of cuts, and with a plot he could | not seize. | It was hard to pay attention to it. | "Let it come down" by Paul Bowles, Tangier.' At the top of this quote is the front/back cover photograph; at the bottom is a collage photo of Bowles. Photos credited to, consecutively, 'Blagg' and 'McKay'. pp. 1–73, text. p. 74: 'CONTENTS [19 lines; see *Contents* below] | [long bold line rule] | This is an edition of 1000 copies of which | twenty five, perfect bound, have been | signed and numbered by the author. | [underlined twice, once heavy then light] Aloes Books and Aloes seolA | [underneath the logo are two addresses: '21, Carleton Road | London N7' and '18, Hayes Court | New Park Road | London SW2'; to the right of the logo and addresses is the publisher's device, as on title page, except reversed] | FORTHCOMING PUBLICATIONS include | "The He Expression" by Eric Mottram | "The Fox's Lair" by Jeff Nuttal'.

Contents: "Unfinished Cigarette" (**C63**); "Distant Hand Lifted" (**C74**); "The Conspiracy" (**C19**); "The Danish Operation" (**C85**); "The Cut" (**C86**); "Ancient Face Gone Out" (**C70**); "Who Is the 3rd. . . . ?" (**C82**); "The Last Post Danger" (**C128**); "Palm Sunday Tape" (**C123**); "The Beginning Is Also the End" (**C64**); "The Cold-spring News" (**C124**); "Who Is the 3rd. . . . ?" (**B16**); "St. Louis Return" (**C127**); and "Composite Text" (**C117**), all by WSB. "Anyone Who Can Pick Up a Frying Pan Owns Death" (*Big Table*, no. 2, Summer 1959) by Alan Ansen; "Burroughs in Tangier" (*Big Table*, no. 2, Summer, 1959) by Paul Bowles. Plus photographs and illustrations.

Paper: White wove paper, except for pp. 1–4 and 69–72, which are gray-white.

Binding: Perfect-bound, no sigs. Stiff black-and-white pictorial wrappers. On the front cover, spine, and back cover is a black-and-white photograph of an office building (at the corner of Allen and Canal streets, New York) on which is a big sign reading 'LICENSED EXTERMINATORS'; on the front cover, in an alleyway to the right of the shop, is: '[white] WHITE | SUBWAY | [publisher's design (a square turning in on itself)] | [each name lettered down, forming two columns] william burroughs'. All edges trimmed. Priced at 75p.

Publication: This edition, published in September 1973, consisted of 1,000 copies of which 25 were numbered and signed by the author.

A25 MAYFAIR ACADAMY SERIES MORE OR LESS

a. Urgency Press Rip-Off 1973

[Pink cover title] [black] WILLIAM S. | BURROUGHS | [long heavy rule] | [center left, photograph of WSB; center right, skin-mag photo, at the top of which is] Mayfair [Pink in black rectangle] 30 p. | [at bottom, pink in black rectangle] ACADAMY | [black] SERIES. <[Pink in black rectangle] MORE | or LESS [black] >

Collation: 21.2 × 12.6 cm. One unsigned gathering of 52 leaves; pp. 1–8 [9] 10–20 [21] 22–40 [41] 42–95 [96] 97–103 [104].
Front cover: title page. p. 1: '[underlined] CONTENTS:' [18 lines] | [line of hyphens] | Acadamy Series by William S. Burroughs | Appendage Two by William S. Burroughs | Appendage Three by R. Pennington | Illustrations by Caroline Turner | Richard Mahoney | Roy Pennington | [line of hyphens] | This edition of 650 run, typed on offset | paper plates. | [line of hyphens] | Urgency Press Rip Off, Brighton, Sussex. | [line of hyphens] | [in script] Dedication: To [underlined] HER: | "Rearrange the following into a well-known | phrase or saying: | Perhaps our bodies is it only us apart that | keeps?". p. 2: '[underlined] INTRODUCTION' by Roy Pennington. pp. 3–103: text. pages 96 and 104 are illustrations.

Contents: Introduction by Roy Pennington: "The Last Broadcast," "Do You Remember Tomorrow?," "Oh God Get Me Out of This," "Wind Die, You Die, We Die," "Man, You Voted for a Goddam Ape," "The Voracious Aliens," "The Transplant Apocalypse," "D.E. My Super-Efficiency System," "Without Your Name Who Are You?," and "Twilights Last Gleamings," all by WSB and all reprinted from *Mayfair* (**C189, C201, C204, C211, C219, C234, C267, C270, C279**, and **C299**); "Appendage One: Bibliography" (of *Mayfair* articles) by Roy Pennington; "Appendage Two: 'Distant Heels' [from *Adventures in Poetry*, 1972 (**C327**)], 'Pages from Chaos' [from *Antaeus 2*, 1971 (**C304**)], *Electricals*' [from *Antaeus 6*, 1972 (**C334**)]," all by WSB, "Appendage Three [wrongly listed as Appendage Two in text]: 'Some Disparate Mentionables'" by Roy Pennington. Plus illustrations.

Paper: 16 light orange leaves, 16 light green leaves, and 20 light blue leaves, all wove paper.

Binding: Staple-bound, stiff pink pictorial wrappers. Front cover: title page, transcribed above. No spine. Back cover has three illustrations, divided by a heavy T-rule: at top, a photo-collage; at left, an ideogram captioned at bottom, '[black] Kwei Sing—Chinese | God of Calligraphy'; and at right, an illustration captioned by bottom, '[black] Mayan Bank—Holidays'. All edges trimmed, but uneven at bottom.

Publication: This edition, published in 1973, consisted of 650 copies.

B Contributions to Books and Anthologies

1958

B1 *The Beat Generation and the Angry Young Men*
"My First Days on Junk"

a. Pp. 156–170 in *The Beat Generation and the Angry Young Men*. Ed. Gene Feldman and Max Gartenberg. New York: Citadel Press, 1958. 384 pp.
  Taken from *Junkie* and printed under the pseudonym of William Lee.

b. Pp. 156–170 in a paperback edition of **B1a** published by Dell Books, New York, in September 1959 (416 pp.) at 50¢.

1959

B2 *Protest*
"My First Days on Junk"

a. Pp. 139–152 in *Protest*. Ed. Gene Feldman and Max Gartenberg. London: Souvenir Press, 1959. 384 pp. 25s. A reprint of **B1a** under a new title.
  The piece is taken from *Junkie* and printed under the pseudonym of William Lee.

b. Pp. 121–132 in a paperback edition of **B2a** published by Panther Books, London, June 1960 (320 pp.) at 5s. Also pp. 121–133 in a second paperback edition issued by Quartet Books, London, Autumn 1973 (342 pp.) at 60p.

1960

B3 *The Beats*
"Two Episodes from *The Naked Lunch*"

a. Pp. 125–130 in *The Beats*. Ed. Seymour Krim. Greenwich,
Conn.: Gold Medal Books, Fawcett Publications, March 1960.
224 pp. Paperback. 35¢ (a second state has the price raised to 50¢).
Taken from *The Naked Lunch*.

1961

B4 *International Literary Annual*
"Thing Police Keep All Board Room Reports"

a. Pp. 65–72 in *International Literary Annual*, vol. 3. Ed. Arthur
Boyars and Pamela Lyon. London: John Calder, 1961. 230 pp.
Issued as a hardback with dust jacket at 25s.
   A photograph of WSB by Brion Gysin faces p. 116.

b. B4a issued as Calderbook CB–27 in paperback at 15s.

B5   *A Casebook on the Beat*
"Deposition: Testimony concerning a Sickness"
"The Cut-Up Method of Brion Gysin"
"A Newspeak Précis of the Article Made in Its Image with Its
Materials"

a. Pp. 98–105, 105–106, and 106–107 in *A Casebook on the Beat*,
Ed. Thomas Parkinson. New York: Thomas Y. Crowell Company,
Jan. 18, 1961. 326 pp. Paperback textbook. $3.00. A second
edition was published in July 1961 and a third edition in March
1965.
   "Deposition" and "A Newspeak Précis" are taken from *Ever-
green Review*, 1960 (**C12, C14**). The first magazine appearance of
"The Cut Up Method" did not occur until 1962 when it was in
Yugen (**C50**). It seems likely that this is the first publication of this
essay.

B6   *The Drug Experience*
"I Went into Pushing with Bill Gains Who Handled the Uptown
Business"
"I Saw the Apomorphine Treatment Really Work"

a. Pp. 167–175 and 207–214 in *The Drug Experience*. Ed. David Ebin. New York: Orion Press, 1961. 385 pp. $5.95.

The first selection was taken from *Junkie*, and the second is a reprint of the articles "Newspeak Précis" and "Deposition: Testimony concerning a Sickness," both from *Evergreen Review*, 1960 (**C14** and **C12**).

b. Pp. 167–175 and 207–214 in a paperback edition of **B6a** published by Grove Press as Evergreen Black Cat Book BC–62, New York, 1965 (385 pp.) at 95¢.

B7 *Banned*
"Selection from *The Naked Lunch*"

a. Pp. 269–278 in *Banned*. Ed. Max Gartenberg. New York: Berkeley Medallion Books, 1961.

1962

B8 *Beat: Eine Anthologie*
"Naked Lunch"

a. Pp. 191–199 in *Beat: Eine Anthologie*. Ed. Karl O'Paetal. Hamburg: Rowalt Paperbacks, November 1962. 304 pp. A second edition was published in June 1968.

The piece comes from the extracts from *The Naked Lunch* published in *Big Table 1* (Chicago, 1959), translated by Willi Anders. A bibliography of WSB appears on pp. 254–255.

B9 *Writers in Revolt*
"From *Naked Lunch*"

a. Pp. 328–337 in *Writers in Revolt: An Anthology*. Ed. Richard Seaver, Terry Southern, and Alexander Trocchi. New York: Frederick Fell, 1963. 366 pp. $7.50.

b. Pp. 345–354 in a paperback edition of **B9a** published as Berkeley Medallion Book N1092, New York, June 1965 (384 pp.) at 95¢.

B10   *The Moderns*
"Vaudeville Voices"
"Berserk Machine"
"The Ticket That Exploded"
"Note on Vaudeville Voices"
"The Cut Up Method"

a. Pp. 278–283, 284–286, 287–289, 345, 345–348 in *The Moderns: An Anthology of New Writing in America*. Ed. LeRoi Jones. New York: Corinth Books, 1963. 351 pp. $5.95.
    The first item is from *The Ticket That Exploded* and the third is from the "Silence to Say Goodbye" section of the same book. The second item is from *The Soft Machine*. The fourth and fifth items appear in the Appendix. The fifth item is from *Yugen*, 1962 (**C50**).

b. Pp. 278–283, 284–286, 287–289, 345, 345–348 in a paperback edition of **B10a** published "a year or two later," using the same sheets only paperbound, at $1.95. There was a price change to $3.50 at the third paperback edition.

c. Pp. 278–283, 284–286, 287–289, 345, 345–348 in hardcover U.K. reprint of **B10a**, issued by MacGibbon & Kee, London, 1965 (351pp.) at 30s.

d. Pp. 256–260, 261–263, 287–289, 314, 314–317 in a paperback edition of **B10c**, published by Mayflower-Dell Books as no. 5780–8, London, 1967 (320 pp.).

B11   *The Addict*
"Feeding the Monkey"

a. Pp. 80–97 in *The Addict*. Ed. Dan Wakefield. Greenwich, Conn.: Fawcett Publications, 1963. A Fawcett Premier Book. 192 pp. Paperback. 95¢.
    Taken from *Junkie* and printed under the pseudonym of William Lee.

1964

B12 *T.L.S. 2: Essays and Reviews from the* Times Literary Supplement, *1963 Letter*

a. P. 225 in *T.L.S.2: Essays and Reviews from the* Times Literary Supplement, *1963.* London: Oxford University Press, 1964. 246 pp. 30s.
Reprinted from the "Ugh!" correspondence in *T.L.S.* in 1963 (**C67**).

B13 *Alienation*
"Naked Lunch"

a. Pp. 190–199 in *Alienation.* Ed. Gerald Sykes. New York: George Braziller, Publisher, 1964. 1,237 pp. 2 vols. boxed. $15.00. Published simultaneously in Canada by Ambassador Books.

B14 *Rules of Duel* by Graham T. Masterton
"Foreword"
"Last Autumn. . . . over the Last Skyscrapers a Silent Kite. Sept 17, 1899, over New York"

a. Pp. i–ii and iii in *Rules of Duel* by Graham T. Masterton. London: Privately printed by the author, n.d. [1964]. Pp. i-iii + 1–10 mimeo in stiff card wrappers. Page 10 constitutes the recto of back wrapper. Front cover shows dual authorship but title page shows Masterton to be the author.
The second piece is a cut-up of WSB's foreword to the book; it is in the three-column style and dated Tangier, June 7, 1964.

B15 *LSD: The Consciousness-expanding Drug*
"Points of Distinction between Sedative and Consciousness-expanding Drugs"

a. Pp. 168–173 in *LSD: The Consciousness–expanding Drug.* Ed. David Solomon. New York: G. P. Putnam's Sons, 1964. 273 pp. $5.95.

b. Pp. 170–174 in a paperback edition of **B15a** published by Putnam's in their Berkeley Medallion series as no. N1277, New York, June 1966 (268 pp.) at 95¢.

1965

B16 *Darazt*
"Who Is the Walks beside You Written 3rd?"

a. Pp. 4–8 in *Darazt*. Ed. Miles. London: Lovebooks, July 1965. 24 pp. 10s. One of 500 numbered copies issued as a companion to Lee Harwood's magazine *Tzarad* (*Darazt* is *Tzarad* backwards). A Tangier 3-column style piece.

B17   *The Award Avant-Garde Reader*
"Proclaim Present Time Over"

a. Pp. 11–23 in *The Award Avant-Garde Reader*. Ed. Gil Orlovitz. New York: Award Books, March 1965. 256 pp. Paperback. 95¢.

B18   *New American Story*
"Ordinary Men and Women"
"Censorship"

a. Pp. 13–31 and 254–262 in *New American Story*. Ed. Donald M. Allen and Robert Creeley. New York: Grove Press, 1965. Grove Book no. GP–345. 278 pp. $3.95.
    The first piece is from *The Naked Lunch* and the second from *Transatlantic Review*, 1962 (**C51**).

b. Pp. 13–31 and 254–262 in a paperback edition of **B18a** published simultaneously as Evergreen Black Cat Book BC–77 at $1.45

B19   *The Olympia Reader*
Selections from The Naked Lunch, The Ticket That Exploded, and The Soft Machine

a. Pp. 449–455, 570–583, and 625–640 in *The Olympia Reader*. Ed. Marucie Girodias. New York: Grove Press, 1965. Grove Book no. GP–340. 725 pp. $12.50. Reprinted New York: Black Watch, c. 1973 at $5.98.

b. Pp. 435–442, 554–566, and 604–619 in a paperback edition of **B19a** published as Ballentine Book no. U 8601 in April 1967 (704 pp.) at $1.67, rising to $2.25 by the eighth printing in 1973. First printing, April 1967; second printing, April 1967; third printing, June 1967; fourth printing, October 1967; fifth printing,

THE AWARD
AVANT-GARDE
READER

Edited by GIL ORLOVITZ

AWARD BOOKS • NEW YORK CITY

B17 (title page)

February 1968; sixth printing, June 1968; seventh printing, August 1970; eighth printing, February 1973. The first Canadian printing was in May 1967 followed by a second printing in June 1967.

B20   *Le Poésie de la Beat Generation*
"La Machine molle (extraits)"

a. Pp. 46–49 in *La Poésie de la Beat Generation*. Ed. Jean-Jacques Lebel. Paris: Denoël, Jan. 4, 1965. 192 pp. Paperback. 12.50Fr.
Translated into French by Jean-Jacques Lebel.

B21   *Briefe an einen Verleger*
Letter dated January 24, 1961, Paris
Letter dated April 20, 1961, Tangier

a. Pp. 269, 272 in *Briefe an einen Verleger: Max Niedermayer zum 60. Geburtstag*. Ed. Marguerite Valerie Schluter. Wiesbaden: Limes Verlag, 1965. 379 pp.
Printed in the original English, the letters are from WSB to Max Niedermayer.

1966

B22   *The Marihuana Papers*
"Points of Distinction between Sedative and Consciousness-expanding Drugs"

a. Pp. 388–393 in *The Marihuana Papers*. Ed. David Solomon. Indianapolis: Bobbs-Merrill Company, 1966. 488 pp. $10.00.
Two long quotes from "Deposition: Testimony concerning a Sickness" (**C12**) appear in the editor's introduction to this piece.

b. Pp. 440–446 in a paperback edition of **B22a** published by Signet Books as no. W3442, New York, April 1968 (512 pp.) at $1.50.

c. Pp. 428–434 in a revised edition of **B22a** published as a paperback by Panther Modern Society, London, 1969 (480 pp.). A second edition was published in 1970 at 12s.

B23 *Harvard Advocate Centennial Anthology*
"Who Him, Don't Let Him Out of There"

a. Pp. 399–403 in *Harvard Advocate Centennial Anthology*. Ed. Jonathan D. Culler. Cambridge, Mass.: Schenkman Publishing Co., 1966. 460 pp. $11.25.
First published in *Harvard Advocate*, 1963 (see **C59**).

B24 *Astronauts of Inner Space*
"The Literary Techniques of Lady Sutton-Smith"

a. Pp. 28–29 in *Astronauts of Inner Space: An International Collection of Avant-Garde Activity*. San Francisco: Stolen Paper Review Editions, 1966. 68 pp. Paperback. $1.50.
An offset reproduction in book form from the *Times Literary Supplement*, Aug. 6, 1964 (**C81**).

B25 *The Best of Olympia*
"The Ticket That Exploded"

a. Pp. 140–145 in *The Best of Olympia*. Ed. Maurice Girodias. London: New English Library, October 1966. Traveller's Companion no. 107 and Four Square Illustrated no. 1645. 240 pp. 12s. 6d.
An anthology of material taken from *Olympia Magazine*.

B26 *Les U.S.A. á la recherche de leur identitié*
Quote from *Paris Review*
"La Peine de mort"
"L'Hallucination comique" (quotes)

a. Pp. 82, 229, and 306–317 in *Les U.S.A. á la recherche de leur identité* by Pierre Dommergues. Paris: Editions Bernard Grasset, Feb. 25, 1967. 448 pp. Paperback. 28.70Fr. 29.50Fr.
All selections are in French. The first item is quoted from *Paris Review*, 1965 (**E3**). The third item, the whole of chapter 4, consists of quotes from "Deposition: Testimony concerning a Sickness"; the Conrad Knickerbocker interview in *Paris Review*, 1965 (**E3**); "The Beginning Is Also the End" from *Transatlantic Review*, 1963 (**C64**); "Declaration" from *Transatlantic Review*, 1962 (**C51**); the Eric Mottram text from *Les Langues Modernes*, 1964 (**C77a**); and the Allen Ginsberg, Gregory Corso interview from *Journal for the Protection of All Beings*, 1961 (**E1**).

B27   *The New Writing in the U.S.A.*
"I Can Feel the Heat Closing In"
Untitled quote

a. Pp. 39–51 and 321 in *The New Writing in the U.S.A.* Ed.
Donald Allen and Robert Creeley. Harmondsworth: Penguin
Books, 1967. 336 pp. Paperback. 7s. 6d.
   The first item is taken from *The Naked Lunch*. The second is
included in the biographical notes section.

B28   *The Book of Grass*
"Cannabis and Opiates"

a. Pp. 207–208 in *The Book of Grass*. Ed. George Andrews and
Simon Vinkenoog. London: Peter Owen, 1967. 242 pp. 37s 6d.
   This piece is "Points of Distinction between Sedative and
Consciousness-expanding Drugs," which first appeared in **B23**.

b. Pp. 207–208 in a hardcover American edition offset from
B28a published by Grove Press, New York, 1967 (242 pp.) as
Grove Book no. GP–423 at $5.00.

c. Pp. 207–208 in a paperback edition of **B28b** published as
Evergreen Black Cat Book B–166, New York, 1968 (242 pp.) at
$1.25. At the fourth paperback printing the cover was changed
and the book's number became B–166Z.

d. Pp. 276–277 in a revised paperback edition of **B28a** published
by Penguin Books, Harmondsworth, 1972 (384 pp.) at 45p.

e. P. 283 as "La Cannabis et les opiacés," in French translation of
B28a, published as *Le Livre de chanure* by Fayard, Paris, July 20,
1970 (336 pp.) in L'Experience Psychique Collection edited by
Jacques Brosse.
   A translation in French by Eric Delorme.

B29   *With Revolvers Aimed. . . . Finger Bowls*, by Claude Pélieu
"Two Counterscripts"

a. Pp. i–iv and 3–6 in *With Revolvers Aimed. . . . Finger Bowls* by
Claude Pélieu. San Francisco: Beach Books, Texts & Documents,
1967. 92 pp. Paperback. $1.50.
   These items constitute the foreword to the book.

B30 *Dossier LSD*
"Apomorphine"

a. Pp. 35–39 in *Dossier LSD*. Ed. Pierre Bernard. Paris: Le Soleil Noir, Summer 1967. Les Cahiers Noirs du Soleil 1. 144 pp. Paperback. 8.50 Fr.
Translated into French by Claude Pélieu and Mary Beach.

B31 *Best Detective Stories of the Year*
"They Do Not Always Remember"

a. Pp. 173–176 in *Best Detective Stories of the Year*. Ed. Anthony Boucher. New York: E. P. Dutton and Co., 1967. 284 pp. $4.50
Reprinted from *Esquire*, 1966 (**C143**).

B32 *Authors Take Sides on Vietnam*
Untitled reply to two question on the Vietnam war

a. P. 25 in *Authors Take Sides on Vietnam: Two Questions on the War in Vietnam Answered by the Authors of Several Nations*. Ed. Cecil Woolf and John Bagguley. New York: Simon and Schuster, 1967. 96 pp. Paperback. $1.95.

B33 *Writers at Work: Third Series*
Facsimile manuscript of "St. Louis Journal"

a. Pp. 151–152 and 155 in *Writers at Work: Third Series*. Prepared by George Plimpton. New York: Viking Press, 1967. 368 pp. $7.95.
Reprints in facsimile the pages from WSB's "St. Louis Journal," which first appeared in *Paris Review*, 1965 (**C127**).

b. Pp. 151–152, 155 in the U.K. reprint of **B33a** issued by Secker and Warburg, London, 1968 (368 pp.) at 42s. It either uses original sheets or is reproduced in offset from them.

B34 *Rauschgiftesser erzählen*
"Was ist Sucht?"
"Entziehung in der Zelle"

a. Pp. 7–14, 185–195 in *Rauschgiftesser erzählen: Eine Dokumentation von Edward Reavis*. Frankfurt am Main: Verlag Bärmeier & Nikel, 1967. 322 pp.
The first item is a German translation of "Points of Distinction

between Sedative and Consciousness-expanding Drugs," first published in **B15a** (title is taken from the opening of the second
paragraph, "What Is Addiction?"); translated by Peter Behrens.
The second item is a German translation of a section from *Junkie*
taken from **D21**, translated by Katharina Behrens.

1968

B35 *Collection U/U2 les Etats-Unis d'aujourd'hui par les textes.*
"The Algebra of Need"

a. Pp. 234–238 in *Collection U/U2 les Etats-Unis d'aujourd'hui par
les textes*, vol. 5. Ed. Pierre Dommergues, Marianne Debouzy, and
Hélène Cixous. Paris: Libraire Armand Colin, Summer 1968.
In English.

B36 *S.F. 12*
"They Do Not Always Remember"

a. Pp. 271–274 in *S.F. 12*. Ed. Judith Merril. New York: De-
lacorte Press, 1968. 384 pp. $5.95.

b. Pp. 271–274 in a paperback edition of **B36a** published as Dell
7815 in June 1969 (384 pp.) at 75¢.
Reprinted from *Esquire*, 1966 (**C142**).

B37 *In Their Own Behalf: Voices from the Margin*
"Deposition: Testimony concerning a Sickness"

a. Pp. 41–48 in *In Their Own Behalf: Voices from the Margin*. Ed.
Charles H. McCaghy, James K. Skipper, Jr., and Mark Lefton.
New York: Appleton-Century-Crofts, 1968. 230 pp.
Reprinted from *Evergreen Review*, 1960 (**C12**).

B38 *Weergaloos*
"Herover het heelali"

a. Pp. 274–275 in *Weergaloos*. Ed. Simon Vinkenoog. Amsterdam:
Paul Brand, 1968. 499 pp.
Taken from the "Prisoners Come Out" section of *Nova Express*.
Translated into Dutch by Simon Vinkenoog.

B39 *Le Livre rose du Hippy*
Quote

a. Pp. 64–65 in *Le Livre rose du Hippy*. Ed. Paul Muller. Paris: Union Generale d'Editions, 1968. 124 pp. 10.30Fr.

B40 *London Magazine Stories 3*
"The Perfect Servant"

a. Pp. 72–76 in *London Magazine Stories 3*. Ed. Alan Ross. London: Alan Ross Ltd., 1968. 156 pp.
Taken from *London Magazine*, 1967 (**C186**).

B41 *Notes from the New Underground*
"Academy 23: A Deconditioning"

a. Pp. 110–114 in *Notes from the New Underground*. Ed. Jesse Kornbluth. New York: Viking Press, 1968. 302 pp. $7.50.
Taken from *Village Voice*, 1967 (**C169**).

b. Pp. 129–134 in a paperback edition of **B41a** published as Ace Book 58875, New York, 1968 (320 pp.) at $1.25.

B42 *Way Out*
"Kicking Drugs: A Very Personal Story"

a. Pp. 118–122 in *Way Out: A Thematic Reader*. Ed. Lois A. Michel. New York: Holt, Rinehart and Winston, 1968. 358 pp. Paperback.
Taken from *Harpers Magazine*, 1967 (see **C170**). This anthology is designed for use as a school textbook.

b. Pp. 139–143 in the second edition of **B42a** published as *Another Way Out*. Same editor, same publisher, New York, January 1974 (368 pp.), paperback.

B43 *High Priest* by Timothy Leary
Letter dated May 6, 1961, Tangier
Letter, n.d. [winter 1960–61], Paris
Quotes from *Minutes to Go*

a. Pp. 214–216 and 216–232 in *High Priest* by Timothy Leary. Cleveland: New American Library, 1968. 353 pp. $7.95.
The whole of chapter 11 concerns WSB. Entitled "Trip 11: Bill Burroughs Drops Out of Our Clan," it describes Leary's early association with WSB in Tangier, Paris, and Harvard.

b. Pp. 214–216 and 216–232 in a paperback edition of **B43a** published by College Notes and Texts, New York, n.d. (450 pp.) at $2.95. The paperback edition is offset from the original edition but has an additional 96-page appendix added at the end. A second printing occurred sometime before 1972.

B44   *Evergreen Review Reader*
"Deposition: Testimony concerning a Sickness"
"From Naked Lunch"
"Comments on 'The Night before Thinking'"

a. Pp. 279–282, 377–383, and 406–408 in *Evergreen Review Reader.* Ed. Barney Rosset. New York: Grove Press, 1968, 792 pp. $20.00. Reprinted New York: Castle Books, 1973 at $7.98.

The first item is taken from *Evergreen Review*, 1960 (**C12**); the second is from *The Naked Lunch*; and the third, from *Evergreen Review*, 1961 (**C30**).

1969

B45 *Drugs from A to Z: A Dictionary* by Richard R. Lingeman. Quotes

a. In *Drugs from A to Z: A Dictionary* by Richard R. Lingeman. New York: McGraw-Hill Paperbacks, 1969. 277 pp. Paperback. $2.95.

B46   *Telling It Like It Was: The Chicago Riots*
"Public Statements Presented at the Chicago Coliseum August 27, 1968"

a. P. 106 in *Telling It Like It Was: The Chicago Riots.* Ed. Walter Schneir. New York: Signet Books, New American Library, T3856, February 1969. 159 pp. Paperback. 75¢.

B47 *Mandala essai sur l'expérience hallucinogène*
"Quelques points de distinction"

a. Pp. 146–151 in *Mandala essai sur l'expérience hallucinogène.* Ed. Pierre Belfond. Paris: Editions Pierre Belfond, June 25, 1969. 334 pp. Paperback.

A translation into French by A. Illion of "Points of Distinction between Sedative and Consciousness-expanding Drugs," which first appeared in **B23**.

B48 *Acid—Neue amerikanische Szene*
"Rückkehr nach St. Louis"
"Die unsichtbare Generation"
"Akademie 23—Eine Entwöhnug"

a. Pp. 55–62, 116–174, and 363–367 in *Acid—Neue amerikanische Szene*. Ed. R. D. Brinkmann and R. R. Rygulla. Darmstadt: März Verlag, 1969. 419 pp.

The first item is a German translation of "St. Louis Return" taken from *Paris Review*, 1965 (**C127**). The second item is a German translation of "The Invisible Generation," which first appeared in *International Times*, 1966 (**C157**). Within the German text, on p. 173, in facsimile appear the four pages of manuscript that were reproduced as four separate pages in *Bulletin from Nothing*, 1965, under the title of "Palm Sunday Tape" (**C123**). Page 168 reproduces a collage by Claude Pélieu also taken from *Bulletin from Nothing* which includes as its major feature a photograph of WSB. The third item is a German translation of "Academy 23: A Deconditioning," which first appeared in *Village Voice*, July 6, 1967 (**C169**), but appears here credited to the 1968 reprint in *Notes from the New Underground* (**B41**).

B49 *Khudharta*
"A Tape Recorder Experiment"

a. Pp. 125–128 in *Khudharta: An Anthology of the Hungry Generation Writers and Poets*. Calcutta, c. 1969. 168 pp. Rs5.00.

A reprint, in English, from *Klactoveedsedsteen*, 1966 (**C144**).

B50 *Cut Up*
"Martins Mag"
"The Moving Times. Feb 10, 1964., Jan 17, 1947., September 17, 1899"
"The Coldspring News"
"Die Zukunft des Romans"
"Die Ausstellung"
Untitled facsimile manuscript
"Die dänische Operation"

**DOSSIER
LSD**

Réalisé sous la direction de
Pierre Bernard
par « Mandala »
Organe international d'Echanges
hallucinatoires :
Jean-Claude Bailly, Dominique Boistel,
Jacques Le Nadan,
Bernard Nexon, Gérard Rutten.

Correspondants à l'étranger :
Amsterdam : Simon Vinkenoog
Londres : Miles, Gilly Smyth
New York : Linn House (Innerspace)
San Francisco : Lawrence Ferlinghetti.

B30 (title page)

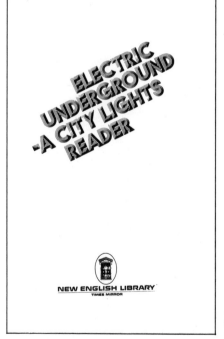

B49

Cut UP

Der sezierte Bildschirm der Worte
Herausgegeben und aus dem Amerikanischen übersetzt von
Carl Weissner

JOSEPH MELZER VERLAG · DARMSTADT

B50 (title page)

B71 (title page)

a. Pp. 10, 18, 19–23 , 24–32, 33, 34–36 in *Cut Up*. Ed. Carl Weissner. Darmstadt: Joseph Melzer Verlag, 1969. 108 pp. Paperback.

The first item is an offset facsimile reproduction, reversed out white on black and reduced in size to occupy one page, of the original which first appeared as a double-page spread in *Ambit*, 1964 (**C92**). The second item is an offset facsimile from the original which appeared in *My Own Mag*, 1964 (**C100**). This printing is reversed out, white on a black ground. The third item is an offset facsimile reproduction, reversed out white on black and reduced in size, of the original layout which first appeared in *Spero*, 1965 (**C124**). The fourth item is a German translation by Carl Weissner of "The Future of the Novel," which first appeared in *Transatlantic Review*, 1962 (**C51**). The fifth item is a German translation by Carl Weissner of "The Writing Machine" section of the Grove Press edition of *The Ticket That Exploded* (**A6b**). It lacks the first paragraph. The German title is "The Exhibition." The sixth item is a facsimile of p. 7 of *Time*, 1965 (see **A11**). The seventh item is a German translation by Carl Weissner of "The Danish Operation" from *Arcade*, 1964 (**C85**).

B51   *Who Am I?: Essays on the Alienated*
"Deposition: Testimony concerning a Sickness"

a. Pp. 256–263 in *Who Am I?: Essays on the Alienated*. Ed. Ned E. Hoopes. New York: Dell Books, August 1969. Laurel Leaf Library, no. 9572. 290 pp. 75¢. A second edition was published March 1970 and a third in August 1970.

B52   *Some of* IT
"The Function of the Underground Press"
"The Invisible Generation I"
"The Invisible Generation II"
"Towers Open Fire!"
"23 Skidoo Eristic Elite"

a. Pp. 11, 31–33, 34–36, 52, 114–115 in *Some of* IT. Ed. David Mairowitz. London: Knuller (P. P. & P.), 1969. 176 pp. 15s. First issued in card boards with a "Melonex" silver foil dust jacket on which was stuck a photographic design of a pair of eyes. This wrapper was protected by a further wrapper of thin tissue paper. The tissue outer wrapper was only on the very early copies and most copies of the silver wrapper edition lack it. The silver wrapper was also discontinued, and the third state has printed cards bearing a repeated pattern of the "*IT* -Girl" logo of the newspaper. This is the most common state found.

The first item is the introduction to an anthology of material which had appeared in *IT* (*International Times*). The second item first appeared in *International Times*, 1966 (**C157**). The third item first appeared on the *International Times* Christmas poster issue, 1966 (**C160**). The fourth item first appeared in *Film 37*, 1963 (**C65**). The last item was taken from *International Times*, 1967 (**C172**).

B53 *Pig* by Jeff Nuttall
"Preface"

a. P. 5 in *Pig* by Jeff Nuttall. London: Fulcrum Press, 1969. 96 pp. 28s. A special edition was also printed on amber Glastonbury antique laid paper, bound in buckram, and signed by Nuttall, in an edition of 75 numbered copies.

The piece is dated Nov. 28, 1968, and is also quoted on the inner flap of the dust jacket.

1970

B54 *Melzers Surf Rider 1970*
"M.O.B."

a. Pp. 83–84 in *Melzers Surf Rider 1970* (house catalogue of the Joseph Melzer Verlag). Darmstadt: Joseph Melzer Verlag, 1970. 120 pp.

Translation into German by Carl Weissner of "M.O.B.," which first appeared in *Contact*, 1970 (**C280**), though it was probably sent to the translator in manuscript form by WSB. Carl Weissner wrote to Richard Aaron: "Several hundred copies of *Surf Rider* were given away for free at Frankfurt International Book Fair 1970. Rest were confiscated by the cops."

B55 *The Braille Film* by Carl Weissner
"Braille Film Counterscript"
Letter dated April 21, 1966, to Carl Weissner

a. Pp. 4 and 30 in *The Braille Film* by Carl Weissner. San Francisco: Nova Broadcast Press, 1970. 112 pp. Paperback. $1.95.

The first item is a preface to the book which uses WSB material in some of its cup-ups. The second is a facsimile of the TLs, reduced out, white on black.

B56 *L'Internationale Hallucinex*
"La Generation invisible"

a. Pp. 1–5 in *L'Internationale Hallucinex*. Paris: Le Soleil Noir, 1970 (Spring). Les Cahiers Noirs du Soleil 3. 14 pp. A box containing 8 pamphlets. WSB appears in the one entitled "Manifestes de la generation grise et invisible."

A French translation of "The Invisible Generation," which first appeared in *International Times*, 1966 (**C157**).

B57 *Scenes along the Road* by Ann Charters
Quote

a. P. 35 in *Scenes along the Road: Photographs of the Desolation Angels, 1944–1960*. Comp. Ann Charters. New York: Portents/ Gotham Book Mart, 1970. 56 pp. The first edition consisted of 2,000 copies: 1,750 in wrappers, 200 hardbound, and 50 specially bound copies signed by Allen Ginsberg. By 1974 the paperback edition was in its fourth printing.

1971

B58 *Bamn: Outlaw Manifestos and Ephemera, 1965–1970*
"The Function of the Underground Press"

a. Pp. 44–45 in *Bamn: Outlaw Manifestos and Ephemera, 1965–1970*. Ed. Peter Stansill and David Mairowitz. Harmondsworth: Penguin Books, 1971. 280 pp. Paperback. 75p.

b. Pp. 44–45 in the American paperback edition of **B57a** published by Penguin Books, Baltimore, 1971, at $2.95. This edition has a different cover.

Piece is taken from **B51**.

B59 *The Youth Culture*
"The Drug Revolution"

a. Pp. 71–83 in *The Youth Culture*. Chicago: Playboy Press, 1971. 198 pp. $2.50.
Reprinted from *Playboy*, 1970 (**C226**).

B60 *A Reading Approach to College Writing*
"Kicking Drugs: A Very Personal Story"

a. In *A Reading Approach to College Writing*. Ed. Martha Heasley Cox. Scranton, N.J.: Chandler Publishing Co., 1971.
Reprinted from *Harpers Magazine*, 1967 (**C170**).

B61 *Questioning: A Thematic and Rhetorical Reader*
"The Cut-Up Method of Brion Gysin"

a. Pp. 588–589 in *Questioning: A Thematic and Rhetorical Reader*. Ed. Steven R. Carter and Mark Curran. Encino, Calif.: Dickenson Publishing Co., 1971. 659 pp. A textbook.
First appeared in *Yugen*, 1962 (**C50**), but this is probably reprinted from LeRoi Jones's anthology *The Moderns* (**B13**).

1972

B62 IT *Book of Drugs*
Quote from *The Naked Lunch*

a. P. 24 in IT *Book of Drugs* by Jonathan Green. London: International Times, 1972. 34 pp. 20p.

B63 *Cut Up or Shut Up*
". . . . Tickertape by William S. Burroughs . . . . "

a. P. 7 in *Cut Up or Shut Up* by Jan Herman, Jürgen Ploog, and Carl Weissner. Paris: Argentzia, 1972. Nouvelle Collection, 34. 80 pp.
The piece appears as a preface.

B64 *Man at Leisure* by Alexander Trocchi
"Introduction: 'Alex Trocchi Cosmonaut of Inner Space'"

a. Pp. 9–10 in *Man at Leisure* by Alexander Trocchi. London: Calder and Boyars, 1972. Signature series no. 15. 98 pp. £1.95. A paperback edition was issued simultaneously.

This introduction was originally intended for Trocchi's *Long Book* and probably dates to the mid-sixties.

B65   *First Reader of Contemporary American Short Fiction*
"From a Distant Hand Lifted"

a. Pp. 55–59 in *First Reader of Contemporary American Short Fiction*. Ed. Patrick Gleeson. Columbus, Ohio: Charles E. Merrill Publishing Co., 1972. 160 pp. A paperback textbook.

The piece is from *Transatlantic Review*, 1964 (**C72**).

B66   *The Underground Reader*
"Storm the Reality Studios"

a. Pp. 32–35 in *The Underground Reader*. Ed. Mel Howard and Thomas King Forcade. New York: Plume Books, New American Library, 1972. 326 pp. Paperback. $2.95.

From *Friends*, 1970 (**C287**).

B67   *Cnacarchives Takis*
"Paris 1960" (on Takis)
Untitled piece on Takis

a. Pp. 26–27, 51 in *Cnacarchives Takis*. Paris: Cnacarchives, Sept. 22, 1972. Cnacarchives series no. 6. 116 pp. 27.00Fr.

The text for item one was taken from the *Iris Clert presente l'impossible par Takis* exhibition catalogue, 1960 (**F1**), and opens: "Song cut along typographical magnetic lines. . . ." The text on p. 26 is in the original English. On p. 27 the text is translated into French by Anne Marie Lavagne. The text of the second item was taken from the Galleria Schwarz exhibition catalogue of April 14, 1962, Milan (**F5**), and it opens: "Takis is working with and expressing. . . ." French translation of the text is by Paulette Vielhomme.

B68   *Love & Napalm: Export U.S.A.* by J. G. Ballard
"Preface"

a. Pp. 7–8 in *Love & Napalm: Export U.S.A.* by J. G. Ballard. New York: Grove Press, 1972. 157 pp. $5.95.

This preface did not appear in the first edition of the book, published in London in 1970 as *The Atrocity Exhibition*.

1973

B69 *The Gay Liberation Handbook*
"Sexual Conditioning"

a. Pp. 194–195 in *The Gay Liberation Handbook*. Ed. Len
Richmond and Gary Noguera. San Francisco: Ramparts Press,
1973. 208 pp. $5.95. A paperback edition was published simul-
taneously at $3.95.

B70 *Whole Grains*
Quotes

a. Pp. 34, 39, 40, and 47 in *Whole Grains*. Ed. Art Spiegelman and
Bob Schneider. New York: Douglas Links, July 1973. 159 pp.
Paperback. $3.95.
    Taken from various books. *Whole Grains* is a compendium of
quotations.

B71 *Electric Underground—A City Lights Reader*
"I am Dying, Meester?"

a. Pp. 46–47 in *Electric Underground—A City Lights Reader*. Ed.
Laurence James. London: New English Library, 1973. 142 pp.
£1.75.
    Taken from *City Lights Journal*, 1963 (**C66**).

B72 *Breakthrough Fictioneers*
"Word Authority More Habit Forming than Heroin"

a. Pp. 198–202 in *Breakthrough Fictioneers*. Ed. Richard Kos-
telanetz. West Glover, Vt.: Something Else Press, 1973. 384 pp.
Issued in a clothbound and a paperback edition.
    First published in *San Francisco Earthquake*, 1967 (**C175**).

C   Contributions to Periodicals

1957

C1 "Letter from a Master Addict to Dangerous Drugs"

a. *British Journal of Addiction* 53, no. 2: 119–131. John Yerbury Dent. Shrewsbury, January 1957. 10s.

b. An offprint from C1a made at the request of the author, probably in an edition of 50 copies. The offprint is in every respect the same as the original magazine contribution and may have been a run-on of those pages when the magazine was printed. It is stapled.

C2 "From *Naked Lunch*, Book III: In Search of Yage"
Black Mountain Review 7:144–148. Black Mountain College, N.C., Autumn 1957 (actually issued in Spring 1958).
Burroughs uses the nom-de-plume of "William Lee."

1958

C3 "Have You Seen Pantapon Rose?"
Yugen 3:4–5. Ed. LeRoi Jones. New York, 1958. 50¢.

C4 "Excerpt: *Naked Lunch*"
Chicago Review 12, no. 1: 25–30. Ed. Irving Rosenthal. Chicago, Spring 1958. 75¢

C5 "Chapter 2 of *Naked Lunch*"
Chicago Review 12, no. 3: 3–12. Ed. Irving Rosenthal. Chicago, Autumn 1958. 75¢.

1959

C6 "Ten Episodes from *Naked Lunch*"
Big Table 1:79–137. Ed. Irving Rosenthal. Chicago, Spring 1959. $1.00.

C1a

C10

Constitutes the suppressed Winter 1958 issue of *Chicago Review*. Episode 2 was previously published in *Chicago Review*, Spring 1958, and episode 5 was previously published in *Chicago Review*, Autumn 1958, where it was called "Chapter 2 of *Naked Lunch*."

C7 "In Quest of Yage"
Big Table 2:44–64. Ed. Paul Carroll. Chicago, Summer 1959. $1.00.
Two uncredited photographs of WSB appear on pp. 34–35.

C8 "Two Scenes. 1: The Exterminator Does a Good Job. 2: Coke Bugs"
New Departures 1:25–28. Oxford, Summer 1959. 3s. 6d.

C9 "And Start West"
Jabberwock [1]:41–44. Edinburgh, 1959.

C10 "Open Letter to *Life* Magazine" (written with Brion Gysin, Sinclair Beiles, and Gregory Corso)
Nomad 5/6:22. Culver City, Calif., Winter 1959. $1.00.

C11 "Excerpt from Pantapon Rose"
Semina 4. Ed. Wally Berman. San Francisco, 1959.
Printed on yellow tissue and contained in a pocket located as p.3 of a folded card cover. The pocket contains 21 separate items in no specific order.

1960

C12 "Deposition: Testimony concerning a Sickness"
Evergreen Review 4, no. 11: 15–23. New York, Jan.–Feb. 1960. $1.00.
Written to help prepare the way for eventual publication of *Naked Lunch* in the U.S.A.

C13 "Temoignage à propos d'une maladie"
La Nouvelle Revue Francaise 85:82–92. Paris, Jan. 1, 1960.
A translation by Eric Kahane (brother of Maurice Girodias), of "Deposition: Testimony concerning a Sickness" (C12).

C14 "Newspeak Précis"
Evergreen Review 4, no. 11: 12–14. New York, Jan.–Feb. 1960.
$1.00.
Included in the "Notes on Contributors" section.

C15 "Quo Vadis?"
Mademoiselle, Jan. 1960:34, 17. New York. 50¢.
A symposium with WSB, Allen Ginsberg, Lorraine Hansberry,
Christopher Logue, Norman Podhoretz, François Truffaut, and
John Wain on "what they would like in the 60s."

C16 "But All Is Back Seat of Dreaming"
Big Table 4:13–19. Ed. Paul Carroll. Chicago, Spring 1960. $1.00.

C17 "Ten Age Future Time"
Between Worlds 1, no. 1: 121. San German, Puerto Rico, Summer
1960. $1.00.
A poem from the *Minutes to Go* material (see A3).

C18 "Nothing Is True, Everything Is Permitted"
Haute Société 1, no. 1. Paris, June 1960.
A one-shot magazine.

C19 "The Conspiracy"
Kulchur 1:5–8. New York, 1960. 75¢.
Described as a part of *The Naked Lunch* not available when the
book went to press. This is not true. This piece was never intended
to be included in *The Naked Lunch* but does come from the same
group of manuscripts which went to make up the book.

C20 "Have You Seen Slotless City?"
Sidewalk 2:48–53. Edinburgh, [1960]. 2s.

C21 Quote of five lines
Birth 3 (pt. 2): 46. New York, Autumn 1960. $2.00.
Taken from *British Journal of Addiction*, 1957 (**C1**).

C22 Quote on cocaine
Birth 3 (pt. 2): 48. New York, Autumn 1960. $2.00.
Taken from *The Naked Lunch*, Olympia Press edition (**A2a**).

C23 Quote on morphine
Birth 3 (pt. 2): 80. New York, Autumn 1960. $2.00.
Taken from *The Naked Lunch*, Olympia Press edition (**A2a**).

1961

C24 "From *Naked Lunch*"
Evergreen Review 5, no. 16: 18–31. New York, January 1961.
$1.00.
   From *The Naked Lunch*, Grove Press edition (**A2b**).

C25 "No Bueno, from *The Soft Machine*"
Metronome 78, no. 5: 18–19. New York, May 1961. 35¢.

C26 "Everywhere March Your Head" (written with Gregory Corso)
Locus Solus 2:148–149. Lans-en-Vercors (Isère), Summer 1961.
$1.00.
   A cut-up of Rimbaud's "To a Reason." Fifty copies were also
published in a numbered edition.

C27 "Sons of Your In" (written with Gregory Corso)
Locus Solus 2:150–151. Lans-en-Vercors (Isère), Summer 1961.
$1.00.
   A cut-up of Rimbaud's "To a Reason," Fifty copies were also
published in a numbered edition.

C28 "Transition Period"
Two Cities 6:43–46. Ed. Jean Fanchette, publisher of *Minutes to
Go*. Paris, Summer 1961. 3.50F. (**A3**)

C29 "This Is the Time of the Assassins"
Metronome 78, no. 8: 23–24. New York, August 1961. 35¢.

C30 "Comments on 'The Night before Thinking'"
Evergreen Review 5, no. 20: 31–36. New York, September 1961.
$1.00.
   "The Night before Thinking" is a story by Ahmed Yacoubi
which appears in the same issue.

C31 "Out Show Window and We're Proud of It"
Floating Bear 5:6. Ed. Diane di Prima and LeRoi Jones. New York,
1961. Distributed free to a mailing list.

C32 Letter: "Dear Allen . . . ," dated June 21, 1960
Floating Bear 5:7–8. Ed. Diane di Prima and LeRoi Jones. New
York, 1961. Distributed free to a mailing list.

C33 "Routine: Roosevelt after Inauguration"
Floating Bear 9:8–10. Ed. Diane di Prima and LeRoi Jones. New York, 1961. Distributed free to a mailing list.

An obscenity case resulted from the publication of this item in this issue of *Floating Bear,* and the same piece was also censored by the Villiers Press in London when they printed *The Yage Letters* for City Lights Books (**A8a**). It was eventually published separately by Ed Sanders (see **A 9**).

C34 "The Word"
Swank 8, no. 3: 51–55. New York, July 1961. 50¢.

C35 "Operation Soft Machine / Cut"
Outsider 1:74–77. New Orleans, Fall 1961. $1.00.

A three-column style arrangement. A photograph of WSB by Brion Gysin appears on p. 91.

C36 "In Search of Yage"
Kulchur 3:7–18. New York, 1961. $1.00.

Prints the cover letter which goes with "Routine: Roosevelt after Inauguration" (see **C33**).

C37 "Ten Episodes from *The Soft Machine*"
Olympia 1:4–15. Ed. Maurice Girodias. Paris, December 1961. 5F.

C38 "Wind Hand Caught in the Door"
Rhinozeros 5:24–25. Ed. Rolf-Gunter Dienst. Hamburg, 1961. DM1.50.

The item appears on p. 25. It is preceded by a German translation of the piece made by Anselm Hollo.

1962

C39 "Introduction to *Naked Lunch, The Soft Machine, Novia Express,* Episodes from *Novia Express*"
Evergreen Review 6, no. 22: 99–109. New York, January 1962. $1.00.

C40 "Take That Business to Wallgreens"
Nul 5: [unpaginated, 3 pp. of text]. Paradox Press, Jan. 2, 1962. 60F(Belgium).

C34

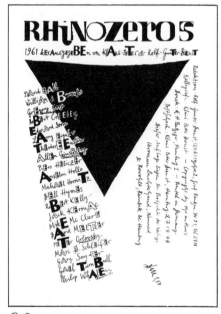

C37

C38

C41 "Routine: Roosevelt after Inauguration"
Nul 6: [unpaginated, 7 pp. of text]. Sint-Niklass: Paradox Press,
1962. 60F(Belgium).
    Reprinted from the *Floating Bear*, 1961 (**C33**).

C42 "One Chapter from the *Novia Express*"
Second Coming Magazine 3:44–45. New York, March 1962. 50¢.

C43 "Novia Express"
Rhinozeros 6:5. Ed. Rolf-Gunter Dienst. Hamburg, July 2, 1962.
DM1.50.

C44 "Outskirts of the City"
Evergreen Review 6, no. 25: 73–78. New York, July 1962. $1.00.

C45 "Be Cheerful, Sir Our Revels Touching Circumstance"
Rhinozeros 7:22. Ed. Rolf-Gunter Dienst. Hamburg, 1962.
DM1.50.

C46 "Wilt Caught in Time"
Outsider 2:3. New Orleans, Summer 1962. $1.00.

C47 "Spain & 42 St"
Floating Bear 24:1. New York, 1962. Distributed free to a mailing
list.
    A cut-up poem.

C48 "Dead Whistle Stop Already End"
Floating Bear 24:1. New York, 1962. Distributed free to a mailing
list.
    A cut-up poem.

C49 "Where Flesh Circulates"
Floating Bear 24:2. New York, 1962. Distributed free to a mailing
list.
    A cut-up poem.

C50 "The Cut-up Method of Brion Gysin"
Yugen 8:31–33. Ed. LeRoi Jones. New York, 1962. 75¢.

C51 "Censorship"
Transatlantic Review 11:5–10. London, Winter 1962. 4s.
    Subdivided into the following pieces: "Censorship," pp. 5–6;
"The Future of the Novel," pp. 6–7 (both of these were read at the

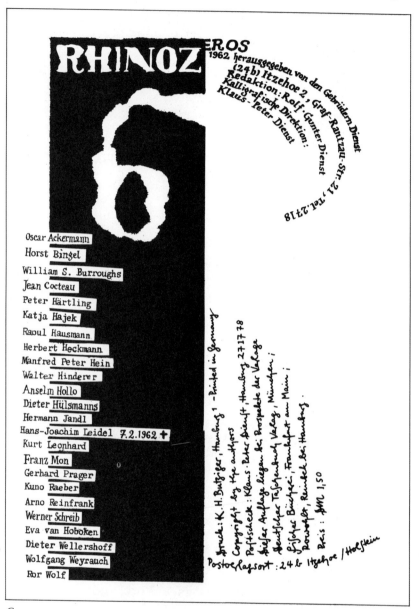

C45

1962 Edinburgh Writers Conference); "Notes on These Pages,"
pp. 7–8; "Nova Police Besieged McEwan Hall," pp. 8–10.

1963

C52 "Aan de rand van de stad Outskirts of the City"
Randstad 4:7–16. Amsterdam, January 1963. f4.50.
   Reprint of "Outskirts of the City" taken from *Evergreen Review*,
1962 (44) and translated by Cornelis Bastiaan Vaandrager and
Simon Vinkenoog into Dutch.

C53 "Two Episodes from *Nova Express*"
Evergreen Review 7, no. 29: 109–116. New York, March 1963.
$1.00.

C54 "The Ticket That Exploded"
Olympia 4:8–11. Ed. Maurice Girodias. Paris, April 1963. 2.50F.

C55 "Call the Old Doctor Twice?"
Yale Literary Magazine, Special Issue: New Poetry 1963, 131, nos.
3 & 4: 54–56. New Haven, April 1963. $1.00.

C56 Quote
Phantomas 38:17. Brussels, May 1963. 75F(Belgium).
   A "photo falling" section presented in the middle of a piece by
Brion Gysin. The manner of presentation qualifies it for inclusion
as it has Burroughs's name appended to it.

C57 "Take It to Cut City—U.S.A."
Outsider 3:35–39. New Orleans, Spring 1963. $1.45.

C58 "The Mayan Caper"
Gambit, Spring 1963:26–31. Edinburgh. 1s 6d.

C59 " 'Who Him? Don't Let Him Out There.' "
Harvard Advocate 97, no. 3: 72–75. Cambridge, Mass., Spring
1963 (cover states "summer" but the contents page states
"spring"). 75¢.

C60 "Martin's Folly"
Cleft 1, no. 1: 18–21. Edinburgh, June 1963. 1s.

C61 "Le Censura e il Romanzo"
Il Verri 8:82–92. Milan: Giangiacomo Feltrinelli, June 1963.
L800.
    Italian translation of "Censorship,"which first appeared in
Transatlantic Review, 1962 (**C51**). All sections are translated.

C62 "Grenzstadt"
Akzente 3:386–387. Munich: Carl Hanser, June 1963. DM60.
    A German translation by Katharina and Peter Behrens.

C63 "Unfinished Cigarette"
Birmingham Bulletin 2:27–30. Birmingham, Autumn 1963. 2s.

C64 "The Beginning Is Also the End"
Transatlantic Review 14:5–8. London, Autumn 1963. 4s.

C65 "Towers Open Fire"
Film 37: 4, 10. London, Autumn 1963. 1s 6d.

C66 "I Am Dying, Meester?"
City Lights Journal 1:46–48. Ed. Lawrence Ferlinghetti. San Francisco, [1963]. $1.50.
    Contained in *The Yage Letters*, (**A8**).

1964

C67 Letter to the editor
Times Literary Supplement, no. 3230: 73. London, Jan. 23, 1964.
9d.
    A letter to the editor defending his books against a review
entitled "Ugh" which appeared in TLS, no. 3220: 919 of Nov. 14,
1963, and which provoked a huge correspondence. The original
review contained quotes from WSB in its text.

C68 "Pry Yourself Loose and Listen"
Gnaoua 1:7–8. Ed. Ira Cohen. Tangier, Spring 1964. $1.00.

C69 "Notes on Page One"
Gnaoua 1:8–9. Ed. Ira Cohen. Tangier, Spring 1964. $1.00.

C70 "Ancient Face Gone Out"
Gnaoua 1:10–14. Ed. Ira Cohen. Tangier, Spring 1964. $1. 00.

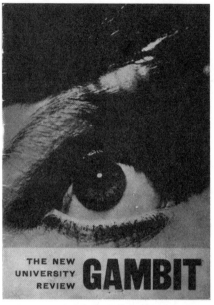

C58

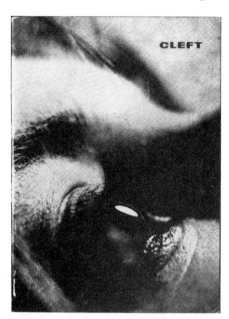

C60

C65

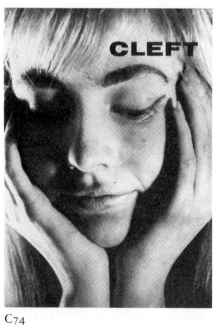

C74

C71 "Just So Long and Long Enough"
Gnaoua 1:14–16. Ed. Ira Cohen. Tangier, Spring 1964. $1.00

C72 "From a Distant Hand Lifted"
Transatlantic Review 15:54–60. London, Spring 1964. 4s.

C73 "They Just Fade Away"
Evergreen Review 8, no. 32: 62–63, 84–85. New York, April 1964.
$1.00.
   This item follows Brion Gysin's article "Cut-Ups: A Project for
Disastrous Success." This issue was banned from distribution in
the U.K.

C74 "A Distant Hand Lifted"
Cleft 1, no. 2: 4–7. Edinburgh, May 1964. 1s.

C75 "Giver of Winds Is My Name"
C 1, no. 9: 43–47. New York, Summer 1964. $1.00.
   First published text to use Egyptian glyphs.

C76 "Intersections Shifts and Scanning from *Literary Days* by Tom
Veitch"
C 1, no. 9: 27. New York, Summer 1964. $1.00.
   Literary Days was published by "C" Press.

C77 Quotes
   a. *Les Langues Modernes*, [July?] 1964:79–83. Paris.
   A partial transcript of a broadcast on the BBC of March 9, 1964,
by Eric Mottram called "William Burroughs and the Algebra of
Need" in which Mottram illustrated his text with long portions of
tape of WSB talking which he found in the BBC archives. Where
these tapes were originally recorded is unknown.
   The BBC talks dept. official transcript, a mimeographed Ts on
legal-size paper, 14 pp. clipped at top left, gives the date of the
original recording of the broadcast as Dec. 18, 1963. It is from this
transcript that Mottram edited the version which he sent to Pierre
Dommergues at *Les Langues Modernes*. The resulting article looks
at first glance like an interview as WSB's and Mottram's texts
follow each other through the pages, each introduced by their
name. In fact, WSB's contribution was only on tape and Mottram
was providing the linking material. However, this item is often
listed erroneously as an interview.
   The introduction to the piece in *Les Langues Modernes* is in

French and is by Pierre Dommergues; the text itself remains in English.

b. An offprint edition was issued: 6 pp. stapled and bound between glossy covers bearing the official title page for the magazine but no date. Number of copies unknown but thought to be very few.

C78 "Burning Heavens, Idiot"
Insect Trust Gazette 1:21–26. Philadelphia, Summer 1964. $1.00.

C79 "Grids"
Insect Trust Gazette 1:27–31. Philadelphia, Summer 1964. $1.00
Includes a facsimile manuscript of a grid layout.

C80 "Fluck You Fluck You Fluck You"
Fuck You / A Magazine of the Arts no. 5, vol. 7 [*sic*]: [xxii]. Ed. Ed Sanders. New York, September 1964. Free.
A three-column style layout dated March 31, 1964, in Tangier.

C81 "The Literary Techniques of Lady Sutton-Smith"
Times Literary Supplement no. 3258:682–683. London, Aug. 6, 1964. 9d.

C82 "Who Is the Third That Walks beside You?"
Art and Literature 2:9–11. Paris, Summer 1964. 8.50F.
A three-column style layout.

C83 "Tangier"
Esquire 62, no. 3 (370): 114–119. New York, September 1964.
Captions and notes to a photographic essay on Tangier by Robert Fréson.

C84 "The Border City"
Arcade 1: [3]. London 1964. 2s 6d. (second state was 3s.).
Subtitled "William Burroughs Special."

C85 "The Danish Operation"
Arcade 1: [19]. London, 1964. 2s 6d. (second state was 3s.).
Subtitled "William Burroughs Special."

C86 "The Cut"
Arcade 1: [21]. London, 1964. 2s 6d. (second state was 3s.).

C87 "Takis"
Signals 1, no. 3–4: 9. London, October 1964. 2s. 6d.

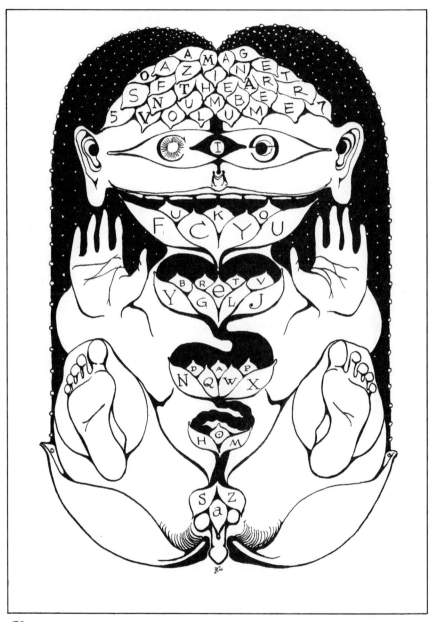

C80

C88 "We Called Her 'Mother' Wouldn't You?"
Mother 3:2–4. Northfield, Minn., November 1964. 50¢.
A three-column style manuscript reproduced in three-color facsimile and accompanied by its covering note.

C89 "Points of Distinction between Sedative and Consciousness-Expanding Drugs"
Evergreen Review 8, no. 34: 72–73. New York, December 1964. $1.00.

C90 "Text"
Rhinozeros 9:22–23. Ed. Rolf-Gunter Dienst. Berlin, 1964 DM1.50.
A fragment from the Edinburgh Conference material and a fold-in of WSB's texts with those from *Finnegan's Wake*. Translated into German by Anselm Hollo.

C91 "The Boys Magazine"
Chicago Review 17, no. 1 (whole no. 54): 130–131. Ed. Peter Michelson. Chicago, 1964. $1.00.

C92 "Martin's Mag"
Ambit 20:28–29. London, 1964. 2s 6d.
A three-column style layout.

Note: The year 1964 includes many of WSB's contributions to Jeff Nuttall's *My Own Mag.* This magazine is notorious for its lack of numbering and pagination (as well as having pages burned, slashed, and stained). It is in *My Own Mag* that WSB first introduced his own newspaper, *The Moving Times*, through which he began his collaborations with Claude Pélieu and Carl Weissner. I have used the sequence suggested by Bob Cobbing (who mimeographed the early issues) with the exception of transposing his no. 1 for his no. 2, which order still disagrees with the sequence given to me by the editor in 1968. The sequence here established agrees, however, with the editor's statements concerning the magazine in his biographical volume *Bomb Culture* (London, 1968) in which he says that he wrote to WSB only after the first issue was out. However, in the same book he says that issue 8 was the first to contain an issue of *Moving Times*. This does not agree with Cobbing's sequence, which shows the first issue of *Moving Times* as appearing in issue

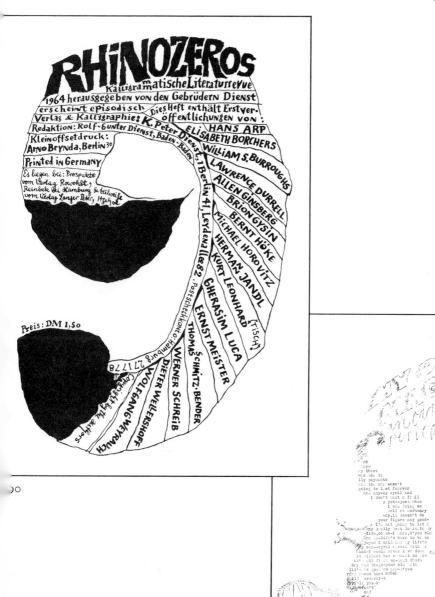

C93

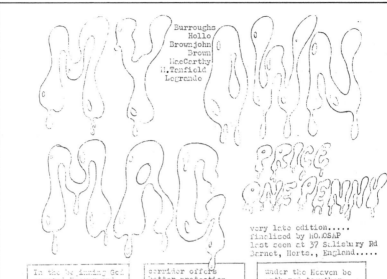

Burroughs
Hollo
Brownjohn
Brown
MacCarthy
H.Tanfield
Legrande

PRICE
ONE PENNY

very late edition.....
finalised by HOMOSAP
last seen at 37 Salisbury Rd
Barnet, Herts., England.....

In the beginning God created Heaven and a shelter proof against debris and radiation should exist in houses ready for the earth. And the earth was without form and void self protection.If there is no such shel -ter a cellar fitted out as a temporary shelter provides some protection.And darkness was upon the face of the deep. And the spirit of God moved upon the German Civil Defence Union will advise you on the face of the waters.And God said,"Let there be all questions concern -ing the building of a shelter light" and there was light. And God saw the light and that it was already trained will be able to take this opportunity to point out the survival possibilities which have been good : and God divided the light from the dark ness.And God called the light Day,and the darkness discussed during the training. For example a cellar

corridor offers better protection than a cellar adjac -ent to an outside he called night.And the evening and the morning were the first day.Wall.Simil -ar aspects should also be And God said,"Let there be a firmament in the midst of the waters Emergency seats and camp beds - emergen- cy seats and camp beds are necessary and let it divide the water from the waters.And God made the firmament for a long stay.It is prac -ticable if some of the campbeds could be used as and divided the waters which were under the firmament from the emergency stretchers.Waters which were above the firmament and it was and God With reg ard to emergency lighting,considerat- ion should called the firmament Heaven. And the evening and the morning were the second day be given to the fact that in temporary shelters, without an adequate ventilation And God said,"Let the waters

under the Heaven be gathered together system,lamps with batteries must be used unto one place and let the dry land appear" and it was so.In a God Emergency toilets should be provided according to the called the dry land Earth;and the gathering together of the waters called number of occupants. In the place of the standard models other suitable cont -ainers he Seas:and God saw that it was good.And God said, "Let the Earth may be provided.Self rescue outfit being forth grass,the herb yield -ing seed and the fruit tree yielding fruit in the evnt of people being buried under debris the after his kind,whose seed is in itself upon the earth":and it was .And following equipment is provided shovels,spades,axes, hatchets,chisels, heavy the earth brought forth grass, and herb yielding se after his kind,and -ers etc.Wirele -ievers - the -ing fruit

C94

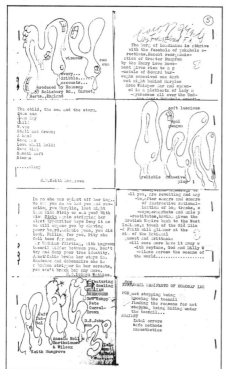

C95
C96

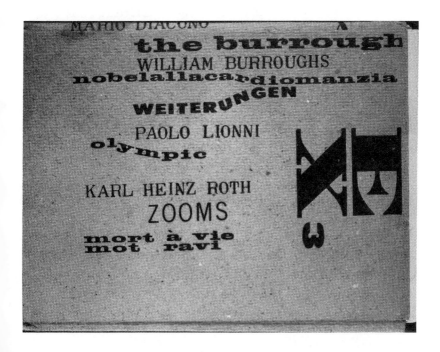

6. Cobbing's sequence also shows issue 8 preceded by two issues of *The Burrough*, which is essentially the same thing as *Moving Times* (they appear in issues 5 and 7). To try and avoid confusion I have given a brief description of each issue to further identify them.

C93 From H.B. William S. Burroughs"
My Own Mag [2:3]. Ed. Jeff Nuttall. Barnet, Herts., 4d. Issued January or February 1964.
The cover describes it as "An Odour-fill Periodical."

C94 "Warning Warning Warning Warning Warning Warning Warning Warning Warning"
My Own Mag [4:4]. Ed. Jeff Nuttall. Barnet, Herts., [1964]. 1d.
Contains a 32-square-grid manuscript. The cover describes the issue as "very late edition" and it is burned away in part at the bottom.

C95 "Afternoon Ticker Tape"
The Burrough, [1964: 1–2].
A magazine edited by WSB, mimeographed by Jeff Nuttall, and appearing as the last two pages of:
My Own Mag [5]. Ed. Jeff Nuttall. Barnet, Herts., [1964]. 3d.
Described on cover as "Cut-Up Issue," Most pages have been cut into eight squares which are stapled at edges to backing sheet.

C96 "Afternoon Ticker Tape"
The Burrough, [1964: 1–2].
A magazine edited by WSB, mimeographed by Jeff Nuttall.
Run-off pages from the *My Own Mag* insertion (**C95**) were sent by Nuttall to WSB in Tangier who issued them there in:
Ex 3 Tangier, 1964.
A folder containing a variety of loose and stapled sections in no fixed order, one of which was *The Burrough*.

C97 "Bring Your Problems to Lady Sutton Fix"
My Own Mag [6: 2, 4]. Ed. Jeff Nuttall. Barnet, Herts., [1964]. 3d.
The title of the magazine is on [p.3] and shows through a hole burned in the first page.

C97

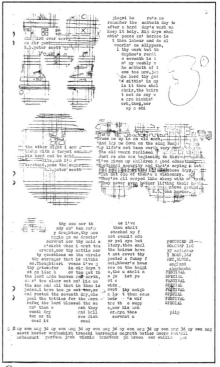

C99

C98 "Over the Last Skyscrapers a Silent Kite"
Moving Times, [1964: 1–2].
    A magazine edited by WSB and appearing as the last two pages
(pp. 7–9) of:
My Own Mag [6: 7–9]. Ed. Jeff Nuttall. Barnet, Herts, [1964]. 3d.
    The title of the magazine is on [p. 3] and shows through a hole
burned in the front page.

C99 "What in Horton Hotel Rue Vernet . . . "
The Burrough, [1964: 1–2].
    A magazine edited by WSB and appearing as the last two pages
of:
My Own Mag [7: 9–10]. Ed. Jeff Nuttall. Barnet, Herts., [1964].
3d.
    Described as "Special Festival" issue.

C100 "The Moving Times"
Moving Times (title of the piece as the title of the magazine), [1964:
1–2].
    A magazine edited by WSB and appearing in:
My Own Mag [8: 3–4]. Ed. Jeff Nuttall. Barnet, Herts., May 1964.
4½d.
    Described as a "Special Tangier Edition," the cover has a full-
page drawing of William Burroughs wearing a fez.

C101 "Extracts from Letter to Homosap"
My Own Mag [9: 11]. Ed. Jeff Nuttall. Barnet, Herts., November
1964. 6d.
    Has a "fall-out shelter," cover and a brown-green stain running
vertically down the front. A small square has been cut from bottom
of front page. Special "Post-election" issue.

C102 "Personals Special to *The Moving Times*"
Moving Times, [1964: 1].
    A magazine edited by WSB and appearing in:
My Own Mag [9: 12]. Ed. Jeff Nuttall. Barnet, Herts., November
1964. 6d.
    Has a "fall-out shelter," cover and a brown-green stain running
vertically down the front. A small square has been cut from bottom
of front page. "Special post-election issue."

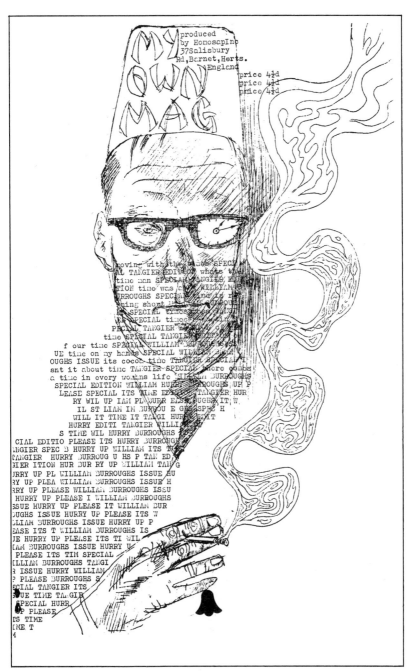

C100

C103

C102

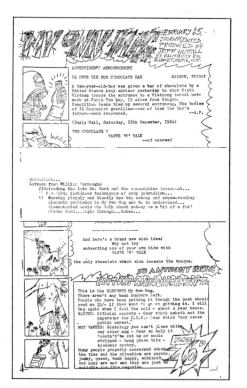

C110

C105

1965

C103 "William Burroughs Speaks!"
Marijuana Newsletter 1: 1, 3. LEMAR, New York: New York City.
Jan. 30, 1965. 25¢.
   Mimeographed at the Peace Eye Bookstore.

C104 "Fits of Nerves with a Fix"
C 1, no. 10: 70–71. New York, Feb. 14, 1965. $1.00.

C105 "Dec 29: Tuesday Was the Last Day for Singing Years"
Moving Times, [1965: 1–2].
   A magazine edited by WSB and appearing in:
My Own Mag 11:14. Ed. Jeff Nuttall. Barnet, Herts., February
1965. 6d.
   In the form of a letter to Jeff Nuttall.

C106 Letter to Jeff Nuttall
My Own Mag 11:12. Ed. Jeff Nuttall. Barnet, Herts., February
1965. 6d.

C107 Collage
Moving Times, [1965: 1].
   A magazine edited by WSB and appearing in:
My Own Mag 11:13. Ed. Jeff Nuttall. Barnet, Herts., February
1965. 6d.

C108 Letters and quotes from newsclippings:
   On Dr. Dent's apomorphine treatment, n.d.;
   To *Sunday Times*, Jan 17, 1965, written from the Hotel Chelsea in
      New York City
   To *Sunday Times*, n.d.
   Quotes from "Afternoon Ticker Tape," a news item in *St. Louis
      Globe Democrat*, and a news item from *St. Louis Post Dispatch*
   My Own Mag 11:11–12. Ed. Jeff Nuttall. Barnet, Herts., February
      1965. 6d.

C109 "Martin's Folly"
Moving Times, Presented as a single-sided poster sheet, London:
Project Sigma, 1965. 2s.
   Designed originally for display on the advertising walls of London Underground stations; however, this proved to be too expensive to do.

C110 "William Burroughs Answers Jim Bishop"
Marijuana Newsletter 2:3. New York, New York City. LEMAR:
March 15, 1965. 25¢.
A cut-up of a Jim Bishop article.

C111 "Last Awning Flaps on the Pier"
Intrepid 5:20. New York, March 1965.

C112 "The Last Words of Dutch Schultz"
My Own Mag 12:12–14. Ed. Jeff Nuttall. Barnet, Herts. May
1965. 9d.

C113 Letter to *Sunday Times*
Apomorphine Times [1965: 1–2].
A magazine edited by WSB and appearing in:
My Own Mag 12:15–16. Ed. Jeff Nuttall. Barnet, Herts., May
1965. 9d.

C114 "Chlorhydrate d'apomorphine chambre"
Lines 5:15. Ed. Aram Saroyan. New York, May 1965. 75¢.
A two-column style layout reproduced in facsimile.

C115 "Transcript of Dutch Schultz' Last Words"
Krea Kritiek 5: 15–21. S'Hertogenbosch, May 1965. f1.
Text, in English, reprinted from the *Valentine's Day Reading*
(**F**12).

C116 "November 20, 1962"
Brown Paper. Philadelphia, 1965. $2.50.
Unnumbered one-shot. One of 243 copies handprinted. A
folded sheet contained in the "manuscripts and notes" section,
being a flap on the back page containing loose sheets. The folded
sheet contains the following items:
[p. 1]: A parody of "Exterminator" by the editor Daniel Lauffer
[pp. 2–3]: A three-column style reply to the first item by WSB
dated March 13, 1964
[p. 4]: "November 20, 1962"

C117 "Composite Text"
Bulletin from Nothing 1:11–12. Ed. Claude Pélieu and Mary Beach. San Francisco, 1965. $1.50.

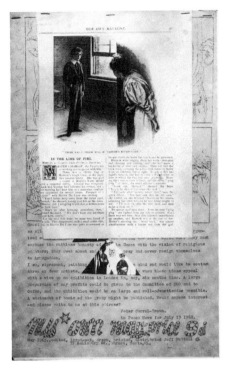

C112

C117

C122

C123

INCLUDING

Daisy Aldan
Carol Berge
William Burroughs
Ray and Bonnie Bremser
Pat Cosgrove
Frank Deffry
Diane DiPrima
Paul Goodman
Piero Heliczer
LeRoi Jones

Pat Knop
C. Kwiat
Carl Linder
Timoshenko Markovnik
Maurice Naughton
James Piscoti
John Sinclair
Philip Whalen
Jonathan Williams
and others

VOLUME I   ISSUE I

C124a

C118 Quotes
Evergreen Review 9, no. 36: 40–49, 87–88. New York, June 1965. $1.00
   Contained in "The Boston Trial of *Naked Lunch*," a transcript of the trial including statements by Allen Ginsberg and Norman Mailer. This issue banned from U.K. distribution.

C119 Untitled quote
Now Now [2]: back cover. San Francisco, 1965. $1.00.
   Quoted from the "Pay Colour" section of *The Soft Machine* (**A5**), it is reproduced in black, red, blue, and green. This issue also contains an article entitled "Where Cumith Bozo the Clown" on p. xiv by William Lee. This is not by WSB. William Lee is a taxi driver.

C120 "Pieces" (written in collaboration with Brion Gysin)
Mother 5: 63–67. Galesburg, Ill., Summer 1965. $1.00.
   Pages 64–66 are facsimile manuscripts.

C121 "File Ticker Tape"
Insect Trust Gazette 2: 17–22. Philadelphia, Summer 1965. $1.00.
   The piece is dated July 7, 1964.

C122 "The Dead Star"
My Own Mag, "Dutch Schultz Special," 13:7–13. Ed. Jeff Nuttall. Barnet, Herts., August 1965. 2s.
   One of 500 numbered copies in offset facsimile of the original manuscript.

C123 "Palm Sunday Tape"
Bulletin from Nothing 2:4–7. Ed. Claude Pélieu and Mary Beach. San Francisco, 1965. $1.00.

C124 "Coldspring News"

a. *The Spero* 1, no. 1: 15–16. Flint, Mich. Fenian Head Centre Press, 1965. $1.00.
   Designed as a poster in a three-column style newspaper layout, copyrighted 1964. Some copies have the item firmly bound in, others just tipped-in.

b. It was also issued separately in an unfolded state; those in the magazine were folded in three.

c. A later state exists which lacks the copyright information at the foot.

Note: "A Short Piece," which appears in *Icarus* 46, first appeared in the pilot issue of *Albatross* magazine [Dublin, December 1963]: 50–53. The pilot issue was not published as such though it was registered with the copyright libraries. When the editors M. L. Lowes and Iain Sinclair took control of the University of Dublin magazine *Icarus*, they used the material from the proposed *Albatross* in it. To conform with the University regulations, no mention of *Albatross* appeared in *Icarus*.

C125 "A Short Piece"
Icarus 46: 87–90. Dublin, [May 1965]. 2s 6d.

C126 "Beedige verklaring: Een getuigenis over een ziekte"
Randstad 9: 161–171. Amsterdam, 1965.

C127 "St. Louis Return"
Paris Review 35: 50–62. Paris, Fall 1965. 5F.
    Written originally for *Playboy*, but not published there. Page 50 is a facsimile manuscript.

C128 "The Last Post Danger Ahead"
Lines 6:31. Ed. Aram Saroyan. New York, November 1965. 75¢.
    A three-column style layout containing photographic collage material, reproduced in facsimile.

C129 "Method Text"
Now Now Now [3]:5. San Francisco, 1965.
    A facsimile reproduction of a three-column newspaper layout. Very large format magazine.

C130 "The Coldspring News (op de veranda achter zijn brerderij; heel watjaren wachten aan de grens; trieste knecht van de eilandkant)"
Krea 6: [22–28]. S'Hertogenbosch, 1965. f5.
A translation of "Coldspring News" **(C124)** into Dutch by Peter H. Van Lieshout.

C131 Quotes
Moving Times, [1965: 1].
    A magazine edited by WSB appearing in:
My Own Mag 14:11. Ed. Jeff Nuttall. Barnet, Herts, December 1965. 6d.
    In collaged material by Carl Weissner.

C129

C131

1966

C132 "Fun and Games, What?"
East Side Review 1: 74–77. New York, January 1966. $1.00.

C133 "Martins Torheit"
Mama 16: 4–7. Ed. Klaus Lea. Munich, March 1966. DM2.
A German translation of "Martin's Folly" (**C109**).

C134 "The Death of Opium Jones"
New Statesman 71, no. 1825: 304–305. London, March 4, 1966.
1s.

C135 "Literature and Drugs"
New Statesman 71, no. 1826: 338. London, March 11, 1966. 1s.
A letter to the editor.

C136 "Chappaqua, a Film by Conrad Rooks"
Royal's World Countdown 2, no. 6: 14. Hollywood, Calif., March,
1966. 25¢.
Taken from the press kit of the film (**F14**).

C137 "Nut Note on the Column Cutup Thing"
Moving Times, [1966: 1].
A magazine edited by WSB appearing in:
My Own Mag 15:15. Barnet, Herts., April 1966. 1s.

C138 "WB Talking"
Moving Times, [1966: 1].
A magazine edited by WSB appearing in:
My Own Mag 15:15. Barnet, Herts., April 1966. 1s.

C139 "Quantities of the Gas Girls"
Moving Times, [1966: 2].
A magazine edited by WSB appearing in:
My Own Mag 15:16. Barnet, Herts., April 1966. 1s.

C140 Untitled
Moving Times, [1966: 5].
A magazine edited by WSB appearing in:
My Own Mag 15:19. Ed. Jeff Nuttall. Barnet, Herts., April 1966.
1s.

EDITORIAL BIT.

It's about time I dropped all these pictures and metaphor s for a minute and made myself clear. About a year ago I put out a statement in which I used an irresolvable erection as a metaphor for life. Everybody thought I was bleating about impotence again. I don't think anybody got what I meant. Similarly my poems, constructions, events etc. etc. have all been variously interpreted as "protest", "schizophrenia", "pornography", "neo-dada", etc. etc., all of these being well wide of the mark. So I'm going to have to say it simply, very simply, to stick to the main points and ignore, for the moment, the paradoxes and complexities. This is what I have to say believe it or not: I LIKE IT HERE. I haven't got a particularly rosy view. "Naked Lunch" is an accurate picture of things, as far as I can see. But what cuts me off from my most regular contributor is that, if the worst comes to the worst, I'll settle for it . I think this is a fundamental difference between me and Alex Trocchi and the psychedelic thing. Certainly the situation needs changing. Certainly I hurl my unwieldy weight against the established order of things to change and improve it. Certainly I shall continue to do this all my life. But there's a catch. Not only do I want to change it. I also so want to preserve it in the first place. To keep it in existence to make it changeable. There's a sick idea floating about just below the surface of the underground scene. that the bomb would perhaps be quite a good thing, a necessary stage after which we could all float around being pure zen ghosts or something. Fuck that.
First of all I'll buy the established order of things rather than sail off into areas of consciousness where experience of the self is substituted entirely for experience of the world. I have evry wish to change the world but no wish to escape it. I think you have to accept it before you can change it, and if you don't change it, well it's been a good fight. The validity of being doesn't solely rest on the success of your projects. I've joined. I'm part of it. I come near madness with hate: of it but I BELONG.
I'm very much aware that living here, in flesh, on earth, in time, is living in circumstances that constantly obstruct human aspirations for freedom, total ecstacy,

Mich. Ayne, Mir
Bill Butler, po
Ted Berrigan, b
Joe Burke, psyc
            Fou
Better Books, 1
William Burrou

Jeff Berner, Wo
            Sa
Birth Press (E
Bob Cobbing, se
Ira Cohen, ed.
Dave Cunliffe,
Phil Cohen, ap
Peter Currel-B

Campaign for Nu
Centre 42, Fit
Pete Davey, po
George Dowden,
Phil Epstein,

Lawrence Ferli

Harry Fainligh
Freeman Synlic
Christopher Gr
Allen Ginsberg

Ray Gosling,
Charles Hatche

Mike Horowitz,
Jim Haynes,
Pete Hoida, po
Don Pierre Syl
Indica (hip
        and
Jacqueline de

John Keys, po
Mike Kustow,

Ted Kavanagh,

League of Lon
Klaus Lea, ed
Tim Leary, (C

John Latham,

ha, USA.

USA.
Philadelphia

don WCl, UK.
vd. Pasteur,

17th St.,

A.
on W9, UK.

Lancs, UK.
LondonN1, UK.
, Carn Green,
UK.

.

dsley Hosp-

Ave.,

K.
ncisco II,
USA.
UK.
- 9

New Departures")

ham, Glos, UK.
er, UK.
Long Hair

, Paris II,
.
don, N3, UK.

oscar for
WCI, UK.
London SW6, UK.

illbrook,
USA.
don WII, UK.

C141 "Martins Folly"
Residu 2: 17–18. London, Spring 1966. 12s. 6d.
Reprinted from the *Moving Times* wall-poster issue (**C109**).

C142 "Substitute Flesh"
Gorilla, early 1966: 43–49. Bonniers, Stockholm. S.K.16.50.
A long section from *The Ticket That Exploded* (**A6**) printed in
English. The rest of the magazine is in Swedish.

C143 "They Do Not Always Remember"
Esquire 65, no. 5 (390): 95. New York, May 1966. $1.00.

C144 "A Tape Recorder Experiment"
Klactoveedsedsteen 3: 20–21. Ed. Carl Weissner. Heidelberg, May
1966. DM3.
One of 120 copies of which nos. 1–40 contained an original
serigraph (not by WSB).

C145 Untitled Quote
Klactoveedsedsteen 3:22. Ed. Carl Weissner. Heidelberg, May 1966.
DM3.
Taken from *Nova Express* (**A10**). One of 120 copies of which
nos. 1–40 contained an original serigraph (not by WSB).

C146 "Salt Chunk Mary"
Intrepid 6:15–17. Buffalo, N.Y., 1966.

C147 "From William S. Burroughs, Writing of Norse's Exhibition in
Paris of Cosmographs"
Ole 5:48. Bensenville, Ill., [1966]. $1.00.
Reprinted from the exhibition leaflet entitled *Harold Norse Exhibi-
tion* (**F4**).

C148 "Exterminator!"
King, July 1966: 58–60. London. 7s. 6d.

C149 "Wish I Were There" (an assembled symposium title)
Venture 3, no. 4: 37. New York, August 1966. $2.95.

C150 "Afterbirth of Dream Now"
Grist 10:16. Lawrence, Kansas, 1966. $1.00.
Reprinted from *Now Now Now* magazine where it appears as
"Method Text" (**C129**).

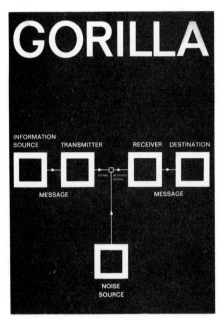

C142

C150

C151 "Tape Recorder Mutations" (with Claude Pélieu and Carl Weissner)
Klactoveedsedsteen 4: 32–36. Ed. by Carl Weissner. PANic Press, Heidelberg: November 1966. DM4.
Edition limited to 300 copies.

C152 Quote
Randstad 11–12:360. Amsterdam, 1966. f5.
Contained in an advertisement for the album *Call Me Burroughs* (**G1**) placed by Thomas Rap. The quote is four lines.

C153 Untitled quote from *The Soft Machine*
Evergreen Club News 1, no. 4: 4. New York, 1966. Distributed free to members.

C154 Untitled quotes
Moving Times [1966: 1–2].
A magazine edited by WSB appearing in:
My Own Mag 7: 18–19. Ed. Jeff Nuttall. Barnet, Herts., September 1966.
Appearing in a cut-up of WSB's work by Carl Weissner.

C155 "Towers Open Fire"
International Times 2:8. London, Oct. 31, 1966. 1s.
The film script, reprinted from *Film*, 1963. (**C65**).

C156 "Anti-Junk"
Books and Bookmen 12, no. 2: 19–21, 101. London, November 1966. 3s.

C157 "The Invisible Generation"
International Times 3:6. London, Nov. 14, 1966. 1s.

C158 "The Invisible Generation"
Los Angeles Free Press 3, no. 39: 1, 8. Los Angeles, Dec. 6, 1966. 15¢.
Reprinted from *International Times*, (**C157**).

C159 "The Invisible Generation"
London: *Project Sigma*, December 1966.
Single sheet, an offset reprint from *International Times*, 1966 (**C157**). Over 1,000 copies were made but the item was not given a *Sigma* index number and no evidence exists to show distribution except by *International Times* itself which provided the offprints.

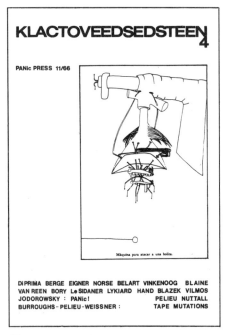

C151

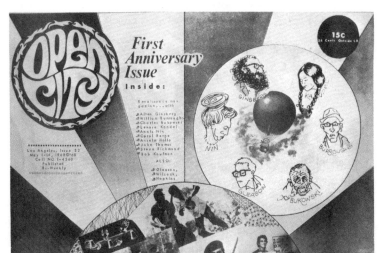

C163

C166

C160 "The Invisible Generation (Continued)"
International Times 5.5. London, Dec. 24, 1966. 5s.
   Poster 57 × 77 cm. on stiff card, designed by Michael English so
that part of the card could be cut out and assembled to make a
word-machine. First edition, silver ink silk-screened in edition of
approximately 200 copies printed Dec. 24, 1966. Second edition,
gold ink, silk-screened in edition of approximately 1,600 copies
printed Dec. 26, 1966. Card sizes vary slightly.

C161 "Fartings Jolly"
Moving Times, [1966: number of pages varies]. London.
   This magazine was assembled by Criton Tomazos to look like
My Own Mag. Many spare sheets from *My Own Mag* were bound
in, and it uses the *Moving Times* wall-poster issue as a cover but
with a hole cut in it and the bottom part trimmed off. The article
"Fartings Jolly" is by Tomazos and *not* by WSB. It is a parody of
"Martin's Folly." The full story appears in Bomb Culture by Jeff
Nuttall, (London, 1968).

1967

C162 "The Invisible Generation (Continued)"
International Times 6:6. London, Jan. 16, 1967. 1s.
   Reprint of the text issued as *International Times* 5.5, 1966
(**C160**).

C163 "They Do Not Always Remember"
Argosy 28, no. 3: 113–115. London, March 1967.
   Reprint from *Esquire*, 1966 (**C143**).

C164 "Exterminator"
Evergreen Review 11, no. 46: 54–56. New York, April 1967. $1.00.

C165 "The 'Priest' They Called Him"
Weekend Telegraph (Colour Magazine) 132:46. London, April 14,
1967. 4d.
   A section of the *Daily Telegraph*, no. 34825.

C166 "Old Fashioned Books"
Renaissance, [1967], n.p. Distributed as a supplement to *Open City*
52. Los Angeles, May 1–14, 1968.

Open City was weekly; the frequency of its "cultural supplement" is not known.

C167 "23 Skiddoo"
Transatlantic Review 25: 93–96. London, Summer 1967. 4s.

C168 "Adios of Saturn"
Great Society [1]:51. Ed. Ira Cohen. New York, June 1967. $1.00.
This piece is a cut-up by WSB of a poem by his son WSB III.

C169 "Academy 23: A Deconditioning"
Village Voice 12, no. 38: 5, 21. New York, July 6, 1967. 15¢.

C170 "Kicking Drugs: A Very Personal Story"
Harper's Magazine 235, no. 1406: 39–42. New York, July 1967.
75¢.

C171 "A Sample Section from *The Ticket That Exploded*
Evergreen Club News 2: 6–7. New York, July 1967. Distributed
free to members.
Prints an extract from the Grove Press edition of *The Ticket
That Exploded* (**A6b**).

C172 "23 Skidoo Eristic Elite"
International Times 18:4. London, Aug. 25, 1967. 1s. 6d.

C173 "The Third Mind"
Harper's Bazaar 3069: 132–135. New York, August 1967. 75¢.
Four pages of facsimile manuscript in the three-column style,
written in Tangier.

C174 "Parenthetically 7 Hertz"
Klacto/23 Special, September 1967: 43–45. Heidelberg. PANic
Press. Ed. Carl Weissner. DM1.50.
Piece dated April 1967.

C175 "Word Authority More Habit Forming than Heroin"
San Francisco Earthquake 1, no. 1: 25–31. Ed. Jan Herman. San
Francisco, Fall 1967. $1.00.

C176 "Academy 23: A Deconditioning"
City of San Francisco Oracle 1, no. 10: 3, 21,26. San Francisco,
October 1967. 25¢.
Reprinted from *Village Voice* (**C169**).

C174

C177 *"Nova Express* / Excerpts"
Aspen 5 & 6. New York, Fall/Winter 1967. $8.00.
   Contained in a box, among 28 sections of folded sheets and records. Item is present as a recording on 7-inch flexible disc taken from the *Call Me Burroughs* album originally published by the English Bookshop in Paris 1965 (**G1**). Two tracks comprising the whole of one side running at 33⅓ rpm.

C178 "The Future of Sex and Drugs"
(The Burroughs Academy Bulletin 1)
Mayfair 2, no. 10: 11–15. London, [October 1967]. 5s.

C179 "The Engram Theory"
(The Burroughs Academy Bulletin 2)
Mayfair 2, no. 11: 28–31. London, [November 1967]. 5s.

C180 "Where's Our Killer Whistle?"
(The Burroughs Academy Bulletin 3)
Mayfair 2, no. 12: 54–56. London, [December 1967]. 5s. 5s.

C181 "Cieux Brûlants, idiot" (fragment)
Opus International 4: 44–46. Paris, December 1967. 7.50F.
   Translated into French by Mary Beach and Claude Pélieu from "Burning Heavens, Idiot" in *Insect Trust Gazette*, 1964 (**C78**).

C182 "L'Avenir du roman"
La Quinzaine Litteraire 40:13. Paris, Dec. 1, 1967. 2.50F.
   Translated from "The Future of the Novel" in *Transatlantic Review*, 1962 (**C51**).

C183 "Censure"
La Quinzaine Litteraire 40:13. Paris, Dec. 1, 1967. 2.50F.
   Translated from "Censorship" in *Transatlantic Review*, 1962 (**C57**).

C184 "Accademia 23: Un Decondizionamento"
Pianeta Fresco 1: [109–112]. Milano, Dec. 12, 1967. L4000.
   A translation into Italian of "Academy 23: A Deconditioning" made by Giulio Saponaro. The item first appeared in *Village Voice*, 1967 (**C169**).

C185 "Day the Records Went Up"
Last Times, Winter 1967: 2–3, San Francisco. 25¢.

C186 "The Perfect Servant"
London Magazine 7, no. 9: 8–12. London, December 1967. 5s.

1968

C187 "Scientology Revisited"
(The Burroughs Academy Bulletin 4)
Mayfair 3, no. 1: 29–31, 80. London, January 1968. 5s.

C188 "Une Poème Moderne"
Asylum 3:31. Bootle, Lancs., January 1968. 2. 6d.
    Piece is dated Nov. 3, 1967. The magazine cover stock was issued in two states: amber and gray.

C189 "The Last Broadcast"
(The Burroughs Academy Bulletin 5)
Mayfair 3, no. 2: 28–29. London, February 1968. 5s.

C190 "By Far the Most Efficient and Precise Language We Possess Is the Common Cold"
(The Burroughs Academy Bulletin 6)
Mayfair 3, no. 3: 54–56. London, March 1968. 5s.

C191 "Johnny 23 / Story"
Evergreen Review 12, no. 52: 26–27. New York, March 1968. $1.00.

C192 "Academy 23: A Deconditioning"
Orpheus Magazine no. 3: 4–5. Phoenix, Arizona, [1968].
    Reprinted from *Village Voice*, 1967 (**C169**).

C193 "The Fire Breaks Out"
(The Burroughs Academy Bulletin 7)
Mayfair 3, no. 4: 32–34. London, April 1968. 5s.

C194 "Academy 23: A Deconditioning"
Warren-Forest-Sun 7:4, 10. Detroit, April 19, 1968. 10¢.
    Reprinted from *Village Voice*, 1967 (**C169**).

C195 "23 Skidoo Elite eristica"
Pianeta Fresco 2–3:2–5. Ed. Fernanda Pivano. Milan, 1968. L2800.
    Translated into Italian by Giulio Saponaro from *International Times* 1967 (**C172**).

C196 "In That Year of 1969, Astonished Motorists Were Hustled at Random into the Death Cells for Parking Offences"
(The Burroughs Academy Bulletin 8)
Mayfair 3, no. 5: 54–55. London, May 1968. 5s.

C197 "Flesket son eksploderte"
Vibra, Fri Norsk Presse 1:11. Oslo, 1968. N.K.2.00.
Norwegian translation of an extract from *The Ticket That Exploded* (**A6**).

C198 "Switch On and Be Your Own Hero"
(The Burroughs Academy Bulletin 9)
Mayfair 3, no. 6: 52–54. London, June 1968. 5s.

C199 "Johnny 23"
Ambit 37:11. London, 1968. 3s.

C200 "The Academy's Ultimate Offer—Immunity to Death"
(The Burroughs Academy Bulletin 10)
Mayfair 3, no. 7: 52–54. London, July 1968. 5s.

C201 "Do You Remember Tomorrow?"
(The Burroughs Academy Bulletin 11)
Mayfair 3, no. 8: 28–29. London, August 1968. 5s.

C202 Unidentified quote
a. *The Realist* 81. New York, August 1968. 35¢.
WSB is listed as a contributor, but the piece is not identified as there is no contents list and all items appear anonymously. WSB could not identify any of the contents as being by him.

b. Forty thousand copies of this issue of *The Realist* were offprinted and distributed free with a different front page, eliminating the *Realist* title and enlarging the headlines, "The Digger Papers," to become the title.

C203 "Parenthetically 7 Hertz"
Georgia Straight 2, no. 24: 7. Vancouver, Aug. 9, 1968. 15¢.
Reprinted from *Klacto / 23 Special*, 1967 (**C174**).

C204 "Oh God, Get Me Out of This!"
(The Burroughs Academy Bulletin 12)
Mayfair 3, no. 9: 32–34. London, September 1968. 5s.

C205 "Censura"
Revista de Bellas Artes 23:27. Mexico City, September 1968.
$1.00(U.S.).
A Spanish translation by Roberto Baresa of "Censorship" from
Transatlantic Review, 1962 (**C57**).

C206 "La novela del porvenir"
Revista de Bellas Artes 23: 24–26. Mexico City, September 1968.
$1.00 (U.S.).
A translation into Spanish by Roberto Baresa of "The Future of
the Novel" from *Transatlantic Review*, 1962 (**C51**).

C207 "Writers Report"
Rat 1, no. 16: 12. New York, Sept. 6, 1968. 20¢.
A report on the Democratic Convention in Chicago, printed
alongside reports by Allen Ginsberg, Jean Genet, and Terry
Southern. Dated Aug. 27, 1968,

C208 Untitled reprint of "Writers Report"
New York Free Press 1, no. 35: 13. New York, Sept. 5, 1968. 15¢.
A reprint of the above statement on Chicago which was issued in
the form of a report and may have been carried by many other
newspapers.

C209 "The Coldspring News"
San Francisco Earthquake 1, no. 4: 54–57. Ed. Jan Herman. San
Francisco, Summer/Fall 1968. $1.50.
Reprinted from *The Spero*, 1965 (**C124**).

C210 "Astronaut's Return"
Village Voice 13, no. 48: 12–13. New York, Sept. 12, 1968.

C211 "Wind Die You Die We Die"
(The Burroughs Academy Bulletin 13)
Mayfair 3, no. 10: 52–53, 62. London, October 1968. 5s.

C212 "O Say Can You See If Bently's Who He Appears to Be?"
Cavalier 18, no. 12: 43, 57. New York, October 1968. 60¢.

C213 "Smrt Opiového Jonese"
Světová Literature 13, no. 4: 176–178. Ed. Prague, František
Jungwirth. April 13, 1968. Kcs12.
Reprinted from *New Statesman*, 1966 (**C134**).

C214 "The Coming of the Purple Better One"
Esquire 70, no. 5(420): 89–91. New York, November 1968.
$1.00.

C215 "Day the Records Went Up"
Evergreen Review 12, no. 60: 47–50, 76–77. New York, November 1968. $1.00.

C216 "The Burroughs Academy: Bulletin 4—Scientology Revisited"
Georgia Straight 2, no. 38: 6–8. Vancouver, Nov. 22, 1968. 15¢.
The article, a reprint from *Mayfair* 1968 (**C187**) is preceded by a short facsimile TLs cover note from WSB.

C217 "Salt Chunk Mary"
San Francisco Earthquake 1, no. 2: 35–38. Ed. Jan Herman. San Francisco, Winter 1968. $1.00.
A reprint from *Intrepid*, 1966 (**C146**).

C218 "Last Awning Flaps on the Pier"
San Francisco Earthquake 1, no. 2: 38–40. Ed. Jan Herman. San Francisco, Winter 1968. $1.00.
A reprint from *Intrepid*, 1965 (**C111**).

C219 "Man, You Voted for a Goddam Ape"
(The Burroughs Academy Bulletin 14)
Mayfair 3, no. 12: 52–54. London, December 1968. 5s.

C220 "Suppressed Discoveries"
Rat 1, no. 23: 5, 14. New York, Dec. 13, 1968. 15¢.
A reprint from *Mayfair*, 1967 (**C180**).

1969

C221 "Rally Round the Secrets, Boys"
(The Burroughs Academy Bulletin 15)
Mayfair 4, no. 1: 52–54. London, January 1969. 5s.

C222 "Infiltration"
(The Burroughs Academy Bulletin 16)
Mayfair 4, no. 2: 52–53. London, February 1969. 5s.

C223 "The Brain Grinders"
(The Burroughs Academy Bulletin 17)
Mayfair 4, no. 4: 32–34. London, April 1969. 6s.

C224 "I'm Scared, I'm Scared, I'm Not"
(The Burroughs Academy Bulletin 18)
Mayfair 4, no. 5: 52–54. London, May 1969. 6s.

C225 Postcard dated Aug. 23, 1968
Package 3 University of Newscastle-upon-Tyne Students Union,
Spring 1969. Sheet 2 of a collection of 8 sheets enclosed in a
printed paper bag. Reproduced in a facsimile in a two-sided sheet
layout entitled "Bill Dropping in for Dinner" by Joseph Gilbert.

C226 "The Final Crusade of the Veteran Warriors"
(The Burroughs Academy Bulletin 19)
Mayfair 4, no. 6: 52–54, 56, 58. London, June 1969. 6s.

C227 "My Mother and I Would Like to Know"
Evergreen Review 13, no. 67: 35–37. New York, June 1969. $1.00.

C228 "The Last Words of Dutch Schultz"
Atlantic Monthly 223, no. 6: 72–83. Boston, June 1969. 75¢.

C229 "St Peters Building (1888)"
Architectural Design 39, no. 6: 314. London, June 1969. 7s. 6d.

C230 Untitled answer to a questionnaire
The Umi (The Sea) 1, no. 1: 17. Tokyo, Japan, June 1, 1969.
In English.

C231 "Mind Parasites!"
Rat 2, no. 13: 3, 19. New York, June 19, 1969. 15¢.
A book review of Colin Wilson's *The Mind Parasites*.

C232 "The Moving Times"
Moving Times, [1969].
Printed as part of:
VDRSVP. Nova Broadcast Press. San Francisco. Summer 1969.
Single large sheet of newsprint. Article begins on side 1 and
continues side 2. The sheet was distributed in two forms, inserted
in:

a. *Kaleidoscope*, 2d section, 2, no. 17: tipped in. Milwaukee, Wisc.,
July 4, 1969.

b. *San Francisco Earthquake* 5. Ed. Jan Herman. [1969]. A folder containing three sheets of folded newspaper of which VDRSVP is one.

Article is in the three-column newspaper layout style.

C233 "William Burroughs: *The Farm* by Clarence Cooper, New British Library. *Times Mirror.*"
Rat 2, no. 14: 23. New York, July 9, 1969. 15¢.
A book review.

C234 "The Voracious Aliens"
(The Burroughs Academy Bulletin 20)
Mayfair 4, no. 8: 32–34. London, August 1969. 6s.

C235 "*The Process*, a Novel by Brion Gysin"
Village Voice 14, no. 43: 7–8, 10. New York, Aug. 8, 1969. 25¢.
A book review.

C236 "Burroughs on *Bloodworld*"
Rat 2, no. 16: 32. New York, Aug. 12, 1969. 15¢.
A book review of *Bloodworld* by Lawrence Jennifer.

C237 "Days of Great Luxury Are Coming Back"
(The Burroughs Academy Bulletin 21)
Mayfair 4, no. 9: 54–56. London, September 1969. 6s.

C238 "Abstract"
Mikrokosmos 14:1. Witchita State University English Dept., 1969.

C239 "Disconnect Notice"
Rat 2, no. 18: 17. New York, Sept. 10, 1969. 15¢.
Article concerns Lomitol. This piece is answered by Richard Lingeman in the Oct. 8, 1969, issue of *Rat*. Lingeman is the author of *Drugs from A to Z* (New York: McGraw Hill, 1969), who felt that WSB had criticized him in this article.

C240 "Abstract"
Klacto/23 International 1:4. Ed. Carl Weissner. Frankfurt: Nova Press. Sept. 17, 1899 [*sic*].

C241 "The Invisible Generation"
Klacto/23 International 1:1. Frankfurt Nova Press, Sept. 17, 1899 [*sic*]. Ed. Carl Weissner.

This text is a postscript to "The Invisible Generation (Continued)" which appeared in *International Times*, 1966 (**C158**, **C160**).

C242 "Mind Parasites!"
Georgia Straight 3, no. 73: 16. Vancouver, Sept. 3, 1969. 25¢.
Reprinted from *Rat*, 1969 (**C231**). A book review.

C243 "Post Script to 'The Invisible Generation'"
Fruit Cup 0:9–10. Ed. Mary Beach. New York: 1969. $2.00.
Beach Books, Texts and Documents.
A reprint from *Klacto/23 International* (**C24**).

C244 "Abstract"
Fruit Cup 0:8–9. Ed. Mary Beach. New York: 1969. $2.00 Beach
Books, Texts and Documents.

C245 Quote
Rising Up Angry 1, no. 3: 12. Chicago, October 1969. 25¢.
Taken from *The Naked Lunch* (**A2**).

C246 "Abstract"
Best & Company [1]: 15–17. Ed. Bill Berkson. New York, 1969.
$1.50.

C247 "Academy 23"
Wormwood Review 9, no. 4(36): 19–26. Stockton, Calif. 1969.
$1.00.
Reprinted from *Village Voice*, 1967 (**C169**).

C248 "So Who Owns Death TV?"
ppH0069 Intercontinental [1969: 53–60]. Ed. Pradip Choudhuri.
Calcutta: Subhas Ghose. $1.00 U.S.
Contains a facsimile of the Beach Books edition of *So Who Owns
Death TV?* (**A13a**). Published in an edition of 3,000 copies.

C249 "Burroughs Back Again"
Rat 2, no. 19: 2. New York, Oct. 29, 1969. 25¢.
A letter replying to Richard Lingeman's letter in the Oct. 8,
1969, issue.

C250 "Burroughs: Woodstock"
Rat 2, no. 19: 13. New York, Oct. 29, 1969. 25¢.

C250

C251 "Two Abstracts"
Lip 1:1–4. Palo Alto, Calif., Fall 1969. $1.00.

C252 "Epitaphe pour un beatnik"
Le Nouvel Observateur 260:40. Paris, Nov. 3, 1969.
An obituary of Jack Kerouac.

C253 "Abstract"
Nola Express 42: 8–9. New Orleans, Nov. 7, 1969. 20¢.
Piece dated London, 1969.

C254 "Burroughs' Last Word on Lomitol"
Rat 2, no. 23: 2, 23. New York, Dec. 3, 1969. 25¢.
In the letters section. His letter concerns the correspondence
resulting from his articles "Disconnect Notice" and "Burroughs
Back Again" which appeared in *Rat*, 1969 (**C239, C249**).

C255 "Uncle Bill Burroughs (Alias Technical Tilly) on Scientology"
Rat 2, no. 24: 12–13. New York, Dec. 25, 1969. 25¢.
Reprinted from *Mayfair*, 1968 [see **C187**].

C256 "The Cold Spring News"
Intrepid 14/15:90. Buffalo, Winter 1969. $1.50.
Reprinted from *The Spero*, 1965 (**C124**). Only partially com-
plete.

C257 "Transcript of Dutch Schultz's Last Words"
Intrepid 14/15: 86–89. Buffalo, Winter 1969. $1.50.
Reprinted from the *Valentine's Day Reading* program (**F12**).

C258 "Roosevelt after Inauguration"
Intrepid 14/15: 81–85. Buffalo, Winter 1969. $1.50.
Reprinted from *Floating Bear*, (**C33**) 1961. Also includes the
annotations from *The Yage Letters* (**A8**) concerning this routine and
Ed Sanders's note which appear in the Fuck You Press edition of
the routine (**A9**).

C259 "Abstract"
Intrepid 14/15 6–7. Buffalo, Winter 1969. $1.50.
Piece dated May 1969.

C260 "Letter to Allen Ginsberg"
Intrepid 14/15:96. Buffalo, Winter 1969. $1.50.
Dated March 3, 1969.

C261 "Salt Chunk Mary"
Intrepid 14/15: 4–5. Buffalo, Winter 1969. $1.50.
Reprinted from *Intrepid*, 1966 (**C146**).

C262 "Last Awning Flaps on the Pier"
Intrepid 14/15: 2–3. Buffalo, Winter 1969. $1.50.
Reprinted from *Intrepid*, 1965 (**C111**). Piece dated Feb. 22, 1965.

C263 "On the E Meter"
Intrepid 14/15: 97–99. Buffalo, Winter 1969. $1.50.

C264 Note on Alfred Chester
Intrepid 14/15. Buffalo, Winter 1969. $1.50.

1970

C265 "Woodstock"
Georgia Straight 4, no. 91: 4. Vancouver, Jan. 7, 1970. 25¢.
Reprinted from *Rat*, 1969.

C266 "Discussion *Playboy* Panel: The Drug Revolution"
Playboy Magazine 17, no. 2: 53–74, 200–201. Chicago, February 1970. $1.00.
The panel consisted of H. J. Anslinger, WSB, J. Coburn, B. Ram Dass, L. Fieldler, J. Finlator, J. Fort, J. S. Oteri, and A. A. Watts. Though presented as a conversation between these people, in fact they never met; the questions were asked by mail.

C267 "The Transplant Apocalypse"
Mayfair 5, no. 2: 32–33. London, February 1970. 6s.

C268 "Mind Control"
Rat 2. New York, c. Feb. 1970. 25¢.

C269 "Mind Control"
It 74:9. Ed. Miles. London, Feb. 27, 1970. 2s.
Reprinted from *Rat* 2, 1970 (**C268**).

C270 "Without Your Name, Who Are You?
Mayfair 5, no. 3: 52–54. London, March 1970. 6s.
A reprint of the 1969 *Village Voice* review entitled "The Process" (**C235**).

C271 "Postscript—The Invisible Generation"
Corpus 5:20. Ed. Pierre Joris. New York, March 18, 1970. 25¢.
Reprinted from *Klacto/23 International*, 1969 (**C241**).

C272 "Burroughs on Scientology"
Los Angeles Free Press, second section, 7, no. 34: 34–35. Los Angeles, March 6, 1970. 35¢.
Reprinted from *Mayfair*, 1968 (**C187**).

C273 "Akademie 23—Eine Entwöhnung"
Highlife Hotcha. Ed. Urban Gwerder. Zurich, April 1970. 0.50SwF. Single sheet folded into four. The article occupies three of the eight panels.
A German translation taken from the R. D. Brinkmann and R. R. Rygulla anthology *Acid* (Darmstadt: Marz Verlag, 1969). The piece originally appeared in *Village Voice*, 1967 (**C169**).

C274 "W. S. Burroughs Alias Inspector J. Lee of the Nova Police"
Friends 5:15. London, April 14, 1970.

C275 "Sensible Job"
The Guardian, April 23, 1970:12. London. 8d.
In the "Letters to the Editor" section, being a letter in answer to Julian Mitchell's review of *The Job* which appeared in the April 16, 1970, issue.

C276 " . . . And a Final Word from William Burroughs"
Mayfair 5, no. 6: 36. London, June 1970. 6s.
WSB's last contribution to the controversial exchange concerning Scientology which appeared in *Mayfair*.

C277 "William Burroughs Answers Criticism of His Latest Book *The Job* Made by Julian Mitchell in a Recent *Guardian* Article"
IT 81:15. London, June 18, 1970. 2s.

C278 "Cut Ups as Underground Weapons"
Los Angeles Free Press, second section, 7, no. 36: 33. Los Angeles, June 26, 1970. 35¢.
Reprinted from *Friends*, July 10, 1970 (issued with late date, listed here as **C287** accordingly), where it is called "Storm the Reality Studios."

C279 "D.E. My Super-Efficiency System"
Mayfair 5, no. 7: 52–54, 56. London, July 1970. 6s.

C280 "M.O.B."
Contact 1: 10–11. London, July 1970. 30p.

C281 "The Unspeakable Mr. Hart (Part One)"
Cyclops 1:17. Ed. Graham Keen. London, July 1970. 3s.
A collaboration between WSB and illustrator Malcolm McNeill.

C282 Quote
Sundance 1:18. Ann Arbor, Mich., July 4, 1970. 25¢.
Taken from *The Naked Lunch* (**A2**).

C283 "Cut Ups as Underground Weapons"
Crawdaddy, section one, 4, no. 10: 8. New York, July 6, 1970. 35¢.
Reprinted from the *Los Angeles Free Press*, 1970 (**C278**), where the title comes from. The *Free Press* in turn reprinted it from *Friends*, July 10, 1970, where it is called "Storm the Reality Studios" (**C287**).

C284 "M.O.B."
Sigma Portfolio 37:2–3. London, 1970. Distributed to subscribers only.
Reprinted from *Contact*, 1970 (**C280**).

C285 "M.O.B."
East Village Other 5, no. 31: 3, 23. New York, July 7, 1970. 25¢.
Reprinted from *Contact*, 1970 (**C280**).

C286 "Open Letter to Mister Gordon Mustain"
East Village Other 5, no. 31: 3, 25. New York, July 7, 1970. 25¢.

C287 "Storm the Reality Studios"
Friends 9:7. London, July 10, 1970 (see **C278**).

C288 "Scrambles"
IT 83:9 London, July 17, 1970.

C289 "Outtakes"
Crawdaddy 4, no. 5: 26–27. Ed. Peter Stafford. New York, Summer 1970. 35¢.
Excerpts from *The Job* (**A16**).

C290 "The Unspeakable Mr. Hart (Part Two)"
Cyclops 2: 10–11. Ed. Graham Keen. London, August 1970. 3s.
A collaboration between WSB and illustrator Malcolm McNeill.

C291 "Storm the Reality Studios"
Nola Express 62:10. New Orleans, Aug. 21, 1970. 35¢.
Reprinted from *Friends* 1970 (**C287**).

C292 "This Man Has Been Scrambled"
Los Angeles Free Press, second section, 7, no. 34: 34–35. Los Angeles, Aug. 21, 1970.
Reprinted from *IT* 1970 (**C288**).

C293 "After the Inauguration"
Notes from Underground 3: 30–31. San Francisco, [1970]. 20¢.
Roosevelt after the Inauguration text with the names changed to those of contemporary politicians by John Bryan and Jan Herman, the editors.

C294 "The Unspeakable Mr. Hart (Part Three)"
Cyclops 3: 10–11. Ed. Graham Keen. London, September 1970. 3s.
A collaboration between WSB and illustrator Malcolm McNeill.

C295 "The Unspeakable Mr. Hart (Part Four)"
Cyclops 4: 10–11. London, October 1970. 3s.
A collaboration between WSB and illustrator Malcolm McNeill.

C296 "The Discipline of DE"
Rolling Stone 69: 34–35. San Francisco, Oct. 29, 1970. 50¢.

C297 "Ecoutez mes derniers mots"
Actuel 2:24. Paris, November 1970. 3F.
An extract from *Nova Express* (**A10**), translated by Mary Beach and Claude Pélieu. The magazine mistakenly credits Bob Kaufman instead of Claude Pélieu.

C298 "The Unspeakable Mr. Hart (Part One)"
Crawdaddy, section two, 5, no. 1: 33. New York, Nov. 22, 1970. 35¢.
Reprinted from *Cyclops*, 1970 (**C281**).

C299 "Twilights Last Gleamings"
Mayfair 5, no. 12: 61–62, 83. London, December 1970. 8s. 6d.

1971

C300 "Carrion Road"
Marijuana Review 1, no. 6: 12–13. Mill Valley, Calif., January
1971. 50¢.

C301 "Navigare Necesse Es. Vivare Nu Es Necesse"
Nola Express 73:5. New Orleans, Jan. 22, 1971. 35¢.
A quote from the opening of *The Job* (**A16**) accompanying a long
review of the book by Rich Mangelsdorff.

C302 Untitled poster
OU 38/39: poster. Ingatestone, Essex, Feb. 1971. The trade edition cost £3.50/48F.
Poster, blue and white on a gold ground, folded in four and
inserted with similar material in a folio. Issued in a variety of
editions: 1 example marked "A" contains the original manuscripts;
4 examples hors commerce; 10 examples marked "B"-"K"; 10
examples numbered 1–10 and a "trade" edition of 475 copies
numbered 26–500. All copies inspected show considerable crack-
ing of the ink on the poster. Contains a short quote from *Electronic
Revolution* (**A21**) in English and French. WSB was given some
unfolded copies to distribute.

C303 "Prisoners, Come Out"
The Last Supplement to The Whole Earth Catalogue, March 1971:74.
Menlo Park, Calif. $1.00.
Taken from *Nova Express* (**A10**).

C304 "Pages from Chaos"
Antaeus 2:83–85. Ed. Paul Bowles. Tangier, Spring 1971. $2.00.
WSB listed as a contributing editor.

C305 "Top Secret M.O.B."
Zoom 1:2. Frankfurt, May 1971.
German translation of "M.O.B." from *Contact*, 1970 (**C280**).

C306 "M.O.B."
La Veuve Joyeuse—Journal Souterrain pour Adulte Eclaire 1,2,3: Paris,
Spring 1971. 1.50F.
Translated into French from *Contact*, 1970 (**C280**).

C307 Untitled quote
UFO 1: Tipped-in poster. Ed. Carl Weissner. Göttingen: Expanded
Media Editions, June 1971. DM2.
Tipped in as an illustrated bonus poster. Thirty-two line quote is
in German.

C308 "UFO Space Bulletin—'Revolution durch Information'"
UFO 1:2. Ed. Carl Weissner. Göttingen: Expanded Media Editions, June 1971. DM2.
A German translation identified as being by "Bradley Martin /
Space Agent 23."

C309 "Deconditioning—Der Nicht-Chemische Trip"
UFO 1:7. Ed. Carl Weissner. Göttingen: Expanded Media Editions, June 1971. DM2.
A German translation.

C310 "A Nice Run Thing"
New Society 454:1011. London, June 10, 1971. 10p.
A book review of *Psychedelics* by Bernard Aaronson and
H. Humphrey Osmond.

C311 "Befreit euch, Gefangene"
Virginity 14/15. Ed. A. Schnurrer. Cologne, June–July 1971.
A 14-line extract from the Limes Verlag translation of *Nova
Express* (**D24**).

C312 "Windhand in die Tür verklemmt"
Gummibaum. Ed. the Frankfurter Autorenkollektiv. Frankfurt,
[1971]. Not seen.
German translation of "Wind Hand Caught in the Door," possibly a reprint from the German translation by Anselm Hollo which
appeared in *Rhinozeros*, 1961 (**C38**).

C313 "Who Is the Third That Walks beside You?"
East Village Other. New York, [1971]. / Not seen.

C314 "Who Is the Third That Walks beside You?"
Renaissance 8:17. Ed. Jan Herman. San Francisco, 1971.
This magazine also constitutes *Notes from Underground* 4. Reprinted from *East Village Other* (**C313**).

C315 "Who Is the Third That Walks beside You?"
Organ, July 1971: 35. Berkeley. 50¢.

The three-column style is incorrectly printed here. The sections labeled I, II, and III should each begin at the top of a column so that they can be read across as well as down. Reprinted from *East Village Other* (**C313**).

C316 "The Penny Arcade Peep Show / The Wild Boys Smile"
Suck 5: [10, 15]. Amsterdam, Summer 1971.
Extract from *The Wild Boys* (**A20**) in English.

C317 "Blütiger Nittwock"
UFO 2: 20–23. Ed. Carl Weissner. Göttingen: Expanded Media Editions. October 1971. DM2.
In German. The piece is signed with WSB's name.

C318 "The Writer"
Ink 19:20. London, Oct. 5, 1971. 10p.

C319 "Blue Movie / Who Are These Boys?"
Suck 6: 15–16. Amsterdam, 1971.
An extract from *The Wild Boys* (**A20**), in English.

C320 "William S. Burroughs Takes a Look at Sex Films"
Suck 6:15. Amsterdam, 1971.

C321 "The Dead Child"
Evergreen Review 15, no. 94: 33–34, 60–61. New York, December 1971. $1.00.
Extract from *The Wild Boys* (**A20**).

1972

C322 Statement on Claude Pélieu
Unmuzzled Ox 1, no. 2: 21. New York, February 1972. $1.00.
Piece dated Jan. 23, 1968. This piece was intended as an introduction to one of Claude Pélieu's books and was sent to him when he was living in San Francisco. The letter never arrived. How this statement reached *Unmuzzled Ox* is a mystery.

C323 "Abstract"
Out of Sight 44:7. Wichita, Kans. Feb. 14, 1972. May have been distributed free.

C324 "Abstract"
Ginger Snaps 1: 3–5. Exeter, Devon, March 1972. 30p.
One of 300 copies.

C325 "Valentine's Day Reading"
OU 40/41: Ingatestone, Essex, March 1972.
Contained in a box, along with eight posters and sheets. Item is present as approximately 9¾ minutes of Side A of a 10-inch 33⅓ rpm phono-disc. The recording is of WSB's reading at the East End Theater, New York, Feb. 14, 1965 (**G9**). Issued in a variety of editions: 1 example marked "A" contained originals plus 2 serigraphs; 4 examples hors commerce; 10 copies marked "B–K"; 10 examples numbered 1–10; and a "trade" edition of 475 copies.

C326 Quote
E.M.E. News 2. Ed. Carl Weissner. Göttingen, April 1972.
A quote in German.

C327 "Distant Heels"
Adventures in Poetry 9: [13–16]. New York, Spring 1972. $1.50.

C328 "Teil I Was ist Sucht?"
Honk 1:9. N.p., Germany, June 1972. DM1.
In German (See **B34**).

C329 "Do Not Disturb the Mongrels"
Bastard Angel 1:2. Ed. Harold Norse. San Francisco, June 1972. $1.50.

C330 "Page from Burroughs' St. Louis Journal"
Parvis à l'Echo des Cils, Paris: Jean-Jacques Pauvert. June 8, 1972: 30–33. 18.80F.
Three pages from the journal as printed in *Paris Review*, 1965 (**C127**). Plus an uncredited photograph on the fourth page.

C331 Untitled
Pot no. 7, no. 1: 4 [*sic*]. Heidelberg, July 1972. DM2.
In German. Origin unknown.

C332 "Tickertape"
Shantih International Writings, 2, no. 2: 77. New York, Summer 1972. $1.00.
Reprinted from the anthology *Cut Up or Shut Up* (See **B63**).

C333 "Lie, Lie, Lie"
Hard 1: 5–6. Cambridge, Mass., Summer 1972. $1.00

C334 "Electricals"
Antaeus 6: 55–57. Ed. Paul Bowles. Tangier, Summer 1972. $2.00.
WSB listed as contributing editor.

C335 "La Chute de l'art une poème moderne"
Contrasts, Summer 1972:6. Shiplake College, Henley-on-Thames.
30p.

C336 Quote
Rolling Stone 115:26. San Francisco, Aug. 17, 1972. 60¢.
Concerns cocaine and is dated 1959. Probably from *The Naked Lunch* (**A2**).

C337 "Ali's Smile"
Sixpack 2: 3–9. London, August 1972. 30p.
Reprinted complete from *Ali's Smile* (**A19**).

C338 "Soldier's Pay"
Fervent Valley 2: [2]. Placitas, N.Mex.: Duende Press, [1972].
$1.50.

C339 Quote
Big Table 8:3. Dortmund, October 1972. DM2.
In German.

C340 "Ich muss sterben, Miester?"
Big Table 8: 27–28. Dortmund, October 1972. DM2.
A German translation of "I Am Dying, Meester?" Taken from
City Lights Journal, 1963 (**C66**).

C341 "Inside Scientology"
Rolling Stone, Oct. 26, 1972: 66, 68. San Francisco. 60¢.
A book review of *Inside Scientology* by Robert Kaufman.

C342 "Inside Scientology"
Rolling Stone 121:46. London, Nov. 9, 1972. 20p.
Reprinted from the San Francisco edition of *Rolling Stone* of the
previous fortnight (**C341**).

1973

C343 "Your Name My Face"
Antaeus 8:33–37. New York, Winter 1973. $2.50.

C344 "Cut Up"
Electrolyz 2: 16–17. Merignac, March 1973. 2F.
A reprint of the cut-up piece by Brion Gysin from *Minutes to Go* (**A3**) originally extracted by *International Times* in 1967. The article states correctly that Brion Gysin is the author but the "sommaire" lists WSB as a coauthor. In French.

C345 '"My Legs Senor"'
Second Aeon 16/17:157. Cardiff, [1973].

C346 "Qui est le—marche à vos côtés—écrit 3e"
Poudrie de Dent. Paris, June 1973.
Translated by Calude Pélieu and Mary Beach from "Who Is the / Walks beside You / Written Third," which first appeared in Darazt, 1965 (**B16**).

C347 "Tant qu'on à la censure"
Oeuf 15/16/17:5. Geneva, Spring 1973. 1.50SwF.
Translated by Claude Péleiu and Mary Beach and first appearing in *Burroughs, Pélieu, Kaufman* (**D11**), this is an extract from "Censorship" first printed in *Transatlantic Review*, 1962 (**C51**).

C348 "Face to Face with the Goat God"
Oui 2, no. 8: 68, 92, 94. Chicago, August 1973 [issued July 1973]. $1.00.

C349 "Kerouac"
Soft Need 8: 17–21. Göttingen: Expanded Media Editions, September 1973. DM 6.80.
First English language version to be published of the Kerouac obituary which appeared in *Le Nouvel Observateur*, 1969 under the title of "Epitaphe pour un beatnik," (**C252**).

C350 "Die Stadt der Mutanten"
AQ 14: 16–21. Frankfurt, Autumn 1973. 8DM.
Translated by Carl Weissner into German.

C351 "William Burroughs Cut/up of Ezra Pound in 1959 Using Only the Very Own Words of Ezra Pound"
AQ 14:22. Frankfurt, Autumn 1973. 8DM.

C352 "Cut/up Made in 1973 Using the Words of William Burroughs and Arthur Rimbaud"
AQ 14:22. Frankfurt, Autumn 1973. 8DM.

C353 "Playback from Eden to Watergate"
Harpers 247, no. 1482: 84–86, 88. New York, November 1973. $1.00.

C354 "M.O.B."
GUM's Moving Review, December 1973:2. Glasgow University. 5p.
Reprinted from *Contact*, 1970 (**C280**).

C355 "Fits of Nerves with a Fix"
Adventures in Poetry [10]:10. New York, [1973].
This issue has no name, is not numbered, and all the contributions appear without names. The item is reprinted from *C*, 1965 (**C104**).

C356 "Abstract"
Via / Structure Implicit and Explicit 2: 76–79. The Student Magazine, Graduate School of Fine Arts, University of Pennsylvania, 1973.
The proofs of this magazine were made in 1972 if not earlier.

C357 "Story"
Sixpack 6:6. London, Winter 1973/74. 99p.
Not actually distributed until 1974.

D Foreign Editions

Danish

D1 *Junkie og uddrag af Yage brevene* (*Junkie* and *The Yage Letters*)
Copenhagen: Stig Vendelkærs Forlag, 1966. Farlige Bøger series.
Junkie translated by Harry Mortensen. *The Yage Letters* translated
by Mogens Toft. 18.5 × 11.3 cm. 208 pp. DK9.95.

Contains:

Bound in stiff laminated cards with red lettering on a white ground
with a black border. Pages trimmed.

D2 *Nøgen frokost* (*The Naked Lunch*)
Copenhagen: Gyldendal, March 14, 1967. Tr. Finn Holten Hansen. 21.1 × 13.4 cm. 260 pp. DK35.75.

Contains:

Bound in limp printed card with a limp card dust wrapper bearing title in pink and white lettering on gray ground. Pages uncut. 3,200 copies.

D3 *Nova ekspress* (*Nova Express*)
Copenhagen: Stig Vendelkærs Forlag, 1967. Farlige Bøger series. Tr. Erik Wiedemann. 18.5 × 11.3 cm. 168 pp. DK9.95.

Contains:
"Indholdsfortegnelse"	5
"Forord" by Erik Thygesen	7–10
"Forords-note" by WSB	11
Nova ekspress	13–168

Bound in stiff laminated cards with title in green lettering on white ground with a blue and black border. Pages trimmed.

Dutch

D4 *Junkie*
Amsterdam: Neulenhoff Edite, 1970. Meulenhoffreeks series, MR 14. Tr. Riekus Waskowsky. 20.0 × 11.4 cm. 158 pp.

Contains:
"Voorwoord" (Foreword)	7–12
Junkie	14–152
Advertisements	155–158

The front flap blurb continues on the inside of the flap, which opens to reveal two photographs of WSB. The blurb includes a chronology of WSB's publications and biography and includes quotes from *Burroughs, Pélieu, Kaufman* (**D11**), *The Job* (**A16**), and the *Paris Review* interview of 1965 (**E3**) as well as quotes from critical reviews. The critical reviews continue on the inside back flap, which also reproduces a facsimile page from the St. Louis Journal originally published in *Paris Review*, 1965 (**C127**).

Bound in stiff cards which open as above. Black lettering on an off-green ground with an illustration of a hospital bed.

D5 *Naakte Lunch* (*The Naked Lunch*)
Amsterdam: Meulenhoff Editie. January 1972. ISBN 90–290–91739.
Published as E 245 in the Meulenhoff catalogue. Tr. Joyce and Co. (Keith Snell and Erwin Garden). 20.0 × 12.6 cm. 288 pp.

Contains:
"Inhoud" (Contents)   5
"Introductie (Verklaring: Getuigenis Betreffende een ziekte)" ("Introduction [Deposition: Testimony concerning a Sickness] [**C12**])   7–17
Naakte lunch (*The Naked Lunch*)   19–232
"Appendix 1. Brief van een meester-verslaafde aan gevaarlijke drugs" ("Appendix 1. Letter from a Master Addict to Dangerous Drugs" [**C1**])   233–252
"Appendix 2. Het proces *Naakte Lunch* 1966" ("Appendix 2. The Case of *Naked Lunch* 1966")   253–280
"Nawoord van de vertalers" (Afterword by the translators, signed by Keith Snell and Erwin Garden)   282–286
Advertisement for *Junkie*   288

Bound in stiff wrappers with black letters on white ground with a reproduction of the Goya painting of Saturn eating a child.

D6 *Roosevelt na de ambtsinwijding* (*Roosevelt after Inauguration*)
Rotterdam: Cold Turkey Press, 1972. Tr. Jan Oudenaarde. 24.7 × 19.1 cm.(laminated cover). 24.5 × 19.4 cm.(mat cover). pp. [i–iv], 1–25, [i–iv].

Contains:
"William Burroughs praat over revolutionaire strijwijzen" (an interview with Dan Georgakas, London, August/September 1972).   1–8
Roosevelt na de ambtsinwijding (*Roosevelt after Inauguration* taken from *Floating Bear*, 1961 [**C33**])   11–13
"Burroughs' antwoord" (from *The Yage Letters* [**A8**] and from *Floating Bear*, 1961 [**C31**])   13–14
"De tijd in beweging" ("The Moving Times," from *The Moving Times* and *VDRSVP*, 1969 [**C232**])   16–20
"Martin's mag" (from *Ambit*, 1964 [**C92**])   20–23 [21–24]
Bibliography of WSB's works in Dutch   24[25]

Neatly mimeographed in an edition of 250 copies numbered on half title.

Bound in stiff blue card with title and press silkscreened in green. Spine stapled and covered by blue binding tape. Some copies have laminated covers and the size difference as above; however, this does not appear to constitute a special edition.

D7 *Wilde jongens: Een dodenboek (The Wild Boys: A Book of the Dead)*
Bussum: Uitgeverij Agathon, 1973. Tr. Micha Joseph. 19.9 × 12.4 cm. 174 pp.

Contains:
Wilde jongens (The Wild Boys)	5–172
"Inhoud" (Contents)	174

Bound in stiff cards with green lettering on a full-color illustration.

Finnish

D8 *Alaston lounas (Naked Lunch)*
Jyväskylä: K. J. Gummerus, 1971. Designated as no. 8453 in the Gummerus catalogue. Tr. Alun Perin. 21 × 13.7 cm. 232 pp.

Contains:
"Johdanto: Valaehtoinen todistajanlausunto sairaudesta" ("Deposition: Testimony concerning a Sickness" [C12])	5–14
Alaston lounas (Naked Lunch)	15–232

Bound in red cloth over boards with title silkscreened in white on spine. Issued in black, red, and white illustrated dust jacket. Pages trimmed.

A paperback edition was also issued on the same date in same design except 20.0 × 13.0 cm. and in wrappers with the dust jacket design.

French

D9 *Le Festin nu (The Naked Lunch)*
Paris: Editions Gallimard, 1964. Tr. Eric Kahane. 20.6 × 14.2 cm. pp. [i–vi], 1–260.

WILLIAM S. BURROUGHS

NØGEN FROKOST

PÅ DANSK VED
FINN HOLTEN HANSEN

GYLDENDAL

D2 (title page)

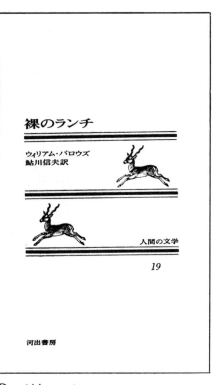

裸のランチ

ウィリアム・バロウズ
鮎川信夫訳

人間の文学

19

河出書房

D39 (title page)

William Burroughs

Nova Express

Bonniers

D50 (title page)

Contains:
"Introduction: Témoignage à propos d'une maladie" ("Introduc-
tion: Testimony concerning a sickness" [C12])   1–12
Le Festin nu (*The Naked Lunch*)   13–255
Contents   257

Bound in limp white cards folded to make inner flaps at top,
bottom and side. Title in red and black lettering on mat white
ground and with the characteristic NRF motif in red. Pages uncut.

The first printing was numbered 1–4,000; the second printing
was numbered 4,001–8,000; the third printing was numbered
8,001–12,000; the fourth printing was numbered 12,001–
16,000; and so on.

The book was subject to a resolution issued by the Minister of
the Interior on July 9, 1964, which imposed three conditions on its
sale. The triple interdiction prohibited sale to minors (under 18
years old), displaying or placing posters within public view, or any
other form of publicity. As books are not allowed to be displayed,
they have to be kept under the counter.

D10 *Les Lettres du Yage* (with Allen Ginsberg) (*The Yage Letters*)
Paris: Editions L'Herne, 1967. Les Livres Noirs series. Tr. Claude
Pélieu and Mary Beach. 21. 0 × 13.7 cm. 80 pp. Fr15.00.

Contains:
Preface   7–8
Les Lettres du Yage (*The Yage Letters*)   9–74
Bibliography   77

Bound in stiff black laminated wrappers. Cover bears two small
photographs of the authors and is folded to give flaps for blurb.

D11 *Burroughs, Pélieu, Kaufman*
Paris: Editions L'Herne, 1967. Cahiers de Herne 9. Tr. Mary
Beach and Claude Pélieu. Special editions: 28.2 × 21.0 cm. Trade
edition: 27.0 × 21.0 cm. pp. [x–xii], 1–308, [i–iv]. 36.00 F.

Contains:
"Sommaire"   vii–ix
"Les cowboys de l'apocalypse" by Pierre Bernard   x–xii

(The following items are by WSB)

(Sections on the work of Claude Pélieu and Bob Kaufman follow.
As more WSB work appears in the Pélieu section we give the
complete contents.)

(The following items are by Claude Pélieu.)

(The following two items are by WSB.)

(The following items are by Bob Kaufman.)

Plates: between pp. 52–53 are eight pages of glossy reproductions:
   i. Full-page photograph of WSB standing in front of the
      Académie Française by Brion Gysin c. 1960
   ii. Half-page photograph of WSB by H. Crowther taken 1964.
      Half-page reproduction of *APO–33*, Beach Books edition
      (**A12b**).
   iii. Full-page photograph of WSB, a still from the film *Chap-
      paqua* taken by David Larcher, 1966
   iv. As p. iii

v. Facsimile of ALs to Claude Pélieu, dated Nov. 21, 1966 (the first publication of this letter in any form)

vi–vii. Photographs of Allen Ginsberg

viii. Full-page photograph of WSB by Lüfti Oakük, 1966

There are eight pages of photographs and documents concerning Claude Pélieu between pp. 180–181 and a further eight pages concerning Bob Kaufman between pp. 276–277.

Bound in stiff white cards bearing red and purple lettering and a photograph of WSB. Very small photographs of the other two authors flank their names.

There is a special edition on better paper and numbered 1–40 and an hors commerce edition of 15 copies numbered A–O. These are all accompanied by a lithograph by Jean Helion. The page size is larger as they remain uncut, and the special edition lacks the black printing on the cover and consequently lacks the photographs of the authors and also lacks the reproduction of a collage by Claude Pélieu which appears on the back cover of the trade edition. The trade edition has its pages trimmed.

D12 *La machine molle (The Soft Machine)*

Paris: Christian Bourgois Editeur, March 8, 1968. Tr. Claude Pélieu and Mary Beach. Special editions: 21.1 × 12.6 cm. Trade edition: 20.0 × 12.0 cm. 224 pp. 20.70 F.

Contains:

La machine molle (The Soft Machine, from Grove Press edition [A5b])	7–219
Advertisements	223–224

The first edition consists of 17 numbered copies on Alfa Mousse paper numbered 1–17. There are also 7 hors commerce copies numbered H.C.1–H.C.7. The trade edition numbered 8,000.

Bound in stiff white cards, cellophane wrapped, and bearing a streamer reading 'BURROUGHS' in white letters on a purple ground. The cover has black lettering on a white ground. The special edition lacks the streamer and is slightly larger in size as its pages have not been cut. The trade edition has its pages trimmed.

A paperback edition was issued on April 24, 1971, as no. 545 in the 10/18 series by Christian Bourgois with a printing of 10,000 copies. 18.2 × 10.8 cm. 192 pp.

D13 *Le Ticket qui explosa (The Ticket That Exploded)*
Paris: Christian Bourgois Editeur, Oct. 3, 1969. Tr. Claude Pélieu
and Mary Beach. Special editions: 21.1 × 12.6 cm. Trade edition:
20.0 × 12.0 cm. 272 pp.

Contains:

"Advertissement remerciements"	7
Le Ticket qui explosa (The Ticket That Exploded, from the Grove Press edition [**A6b**])	9–266
Advertisements	268–270

The first edition consists of 20 numbered copies on Alfa Mousse
paper numbered 1–20. There are also 5 hors commerce copies on
the same paper and numbered H.C.1–H.C.5. The trade edition
numbered 3,000.

Bound in stiff white cards, cellophane wrapped, and bearing a
streamer reading 'BURROUGHS' in white letters on a purple
ground. The special editions lack the streamer and are slightly
larger in all-round size as their pages have not been cut. The trade
edition has its pages trimmed.

A paperback edition was issued in autumn 1972 as no. 700 in
10/18 series by Christian Bourgois, in a printing of 10,000. 18.2 ×
10.8 cm. 320 pp.

D14 *Apomorphine*
Paris: Editions L'Herne, Oct. 20, 1969. Les Livres Noirs series. Tr.
Claude Pélieu and Mary Beach. 21.0 × 13.5 cm. 104 pp.

Contains:

"Apomorphine" (the complete Beach Books text [**A12a**], printed
   sideways in the three-column style to give greater
   legibility)
	8–47

"Le jour où les dossiers ont explosé" ("Day the Records Went Up," from *Evergreen Review,* 1968 [**C215**])	49–64
"Nouvelles de Coldspring News" ("Coldspring News," from *The* *Spero,* 1965 [**C124**])	65–70
"Le Complot" ("The Conspiracy," from *Kulchur,* 1960 [**C19**])	71–76
"L'Exterminateur" ("Exterminator!" from *King,* 1966 [**C148**])	77–83

"Entre parenthèses Hertz" ("Parenthetically 7 Hertz," from
  Klacto /23 Special, 1967 [C174])   85–92
"*Chappaqua*, un film de Conrad Rooks" ("*Chappaqua*, a Film by
  Conrad Rooks," from a press release, Spring 1966
  [F14])   93–96
"Table des matières" (Table of Contents)   97

Bound in stiff black laminated wrappers. Cover bears a small
picture of the author taken from the film *Chappaqua*. Folded to
give flaps for the blurb.

D15 *Nova express*
Paris: Christian Bourgois Editeur, May 8, 1970. Tr. by Mary Beach
and Claude Pélieu. 20.0 × 12.0 cm. 224 pp.

Contains:
Note   7
Nova express   9–220

Bound in stiff white card wrappers with black lettering on mat
ground, cellophane wrapped, and bearing a streamer reading
'BURROUGHS' in white letters on a purple ground. There was
no special or hors commerce edition of this title as the complete
translation had previously appeared in *Burroughs, Pélieu, Kaufman*
(D11). For this same reason the edition was only 2,500.
  A paperback edition was issued on Jan. 3, 1972, as no. 662 in the
10/18 series by Christian Bourgois and Dominique de Roux. 18.2
× 10.8 cm. 192 pp. bearing a photograph of WSB on a red ground
with a black border. The edition was 10,000 copies.

D16 *Junkie*
Paris: Editions Pierre Belfond, Spring 1972. Tr. Catherine Cullaz
and Jean-René Major. 21.0 × 13.5 cm. 192 pp.

Contains:
Junkie   9–187

Bound in stiff cards. Black lettering on a light yellow ground.

D17 *Les Derniers Mots de Dutch Schultz* (*The Last Words of Dutch Schultz*)
Paris: Christian Bourgois Editeur, 1972. Tr. Mary Beach and Claude Pélieu. 20.0 × 12.0 cm. 160 pp.

Contains:
Les Derniers Mots de Dutch Schultz (*The Last Words of Dutch Schultz*)   9–139
"Table des matières" (Table of Contents)   141–143
Advertisements   149–155

Bound in limp green laminated cards bearing small photograph of WSB in black and white with green border. Lettering in black and white. Pages cut.

D18 *Les Garçons sauvages   Un Livre des morts* (*The Wild Boys: A Book of the Dead*)
Paris: Christian Bourgois Editeur, October 1973. Tr. Mary Beach and Claude Pélieu. 20.0 × 12.0 cm. 216 pp.

Contains:
Les Garçons sauvages (*The Wild Boys*)   7–213

Bound in stiff cards bearing a photograph of WSB by Mayotte Magnus on the front cover. The photograph credit is pasted on the back, having been omitted during printing. This constitutes the first state of issue. Lettering is in pink and orange on laminated black-and-white photographic ground. Pages are trimmed.

D19 *Révolution electronique* (*Electronic Revolution*)
Paris: Editions Champ Libre, 1974. Tr. Jean Chopin. 25.0 × 14.7 cm. pp. 1–124.

Contains:
Révolution electronique (*Electronic Revolution*. This translation first appeared in the Collection OU bilingual edition of this title, 1971 [**A21a**]).   7–62
Time (Translated from the "C" Press edition, 1965 [**A11a**].) The photographs collaged into the text are not by WSB and were not arranged by him. The four pages of calligrams drawn by Brion Gysin which appear in the first edition are replaced by a new set by Brion Gysin for this edition. They appear on pp. 80–83.)   65–110

Etoile morte (*The Dead Star* first published in *My Own Mag*, 1965 [**C122**].) This translation appears to have been taken from the Nova Broadcast Press edition, 1969 [**A14a**]. That edition rearranged the photographs by WSB which appear throughout the text and cut some into pieces. These cuts are retained in this translation, but the photographs are in yet another arrangement. The *My Own Mag* version was in facsimile of the original manuscript.) 111–123

Bound in stiff yellow cards folded to make flaps at front and back and bearing the title and a photographic design in red. Pages cut.

German

D20 *The Naked Lunch*
Wiesbaden: Limes Verlag, 1962. Tr. Katharina and Peter Behrens. 20.3 × 12.6 cm. 233 pp.

Contains:
The Naked Lunch (passages on pp. 72–73, 74, 76–77, 91–93 have been left in the original English) 5–228

Bound in purple cloth with an illustrated dust jacket with black letters on a white design over a purple ground.

There was an illegal reprint made of the first edition, details of which are not known at the present time except that it reproduced the first edition by offset.

Limes Verlag issued a second edition in 1966 in an edition of 1,500 copies, offset from the first edition and in the same format and binding but with the addition of "Anhang: Brief eines Mannes, der gefährlichen Drogen verfallen war" ("Appendix: Letter from a Master Addict to Dangerous Drugs," from *British Journal of Addiction*, 1957 [**C1a**]), pp. 229–256. A third and a fourth edition were issued, also offset from the first edition but also including the appendix from the second edition.

A paperback was issued in 1973 by Verlag Ullstein, Frankfort am Main, as Ullstein Buch no. 2843. 17.8 × 11.8 cm. 240 pp. DM 3.80. It has a photographic illustrated cover and retains the same passages in English as the first edition.

D21 *Junkie*
Wiesbaden: Limes Verlag, 1963. Tr. Katharina Behrens. 20.0 × 12.7 cm. 180 pp.

Contains:

"Vorwort" (Foreword: the Preface of the English language book,
    and not the Foreword by Carl Solomon [see **A1a,c**])   5–11
Junkie   13–178
Advertisements   180

Bound in red cloth (red ground with white threads interwoven
over it) and with a pictorial dust jacket with a design in red and
white with black lettering. The back panel is blank.
    A paperback edition was published as Ullstein Buch no. 2886 by
Verlag Ullstein, Frankfurt am Main, 1972. 17.7 × 11.6 cm. Text
reset; 160 pp. DM3.80.

D22 *Auf der Suche nach Yage* (with Allen Ginsberg) (*In Search of
Yage*, earlier title of *The Yage Letters*)
Wiesbaden: Limes Verlag, 1964. Tr. Katharina and Peter Behrens.
20.3 × 12.6 cm. 100 pp.

Contains:

"Inhalt" (Contents)   5
Auf der Suche nach Yage (*In Search of Yage*)   7–97
Advertisements   98–100

Hardbound in green/red cloth (green and red threads interwoven)
and issued in a white dust jacket with photographs of WSB and
Allen Ginsberg on the back.

D23 *Fernseh—Tuberkulose* (with Claude Pélieu and Carl Weissner)
(*Television Tuberculosis*, a translation of *So Who Owns Death T.V.?*)
Frankfurt am Main: Nova Press, 1969. Tr. Carl Weissner. 20.0 ×
13.0 cm. 24 pp.

Contains:

Photographs of happenings by Wolf Vostell (These do not appear
    in the Beach Books edition [**A13a**].)   covers i–ii, iii–iv
Claude Pélieu: "Onan City 19"; "Objektive Galactic Time";
    "Nueva Chicago"; "Demolition Plan 23"   3–8
    Untitled English language text printed white on black and with

four photographs of Claude Pélieu. Does not appear in Beach Books edition. 9

Carl Weissner: "So Who Owns Death TV?" (in English, printed white on black and with four photographs of Carl Weissner. Does not appear in the Beach Books edition) 10

So Who Owns Death TV? 11–15

Uncredited photograph of a collage 16

William Burroughs: Autograph statement on Dutch Schultz printed in white on black and with four photographs of WSB (in English; does not appear in Beach Books edition) 17

"Negativ Journale letzte Time" (untitled in Beach Books edition) 18–23

Newsclipping and ads printed white on black 24

Paperback with purple decorative wrappers. Stapled.

D24 *Nova Express*
Wiesbaden: Limes Verlag, 1970. Tr. Peter Behrens. 17.7 × 11.6 cm. 228 pp.

Contains:
"Vorbemerkung" (Foreword by WSB) 5
Nova Express 9–226
Advertisements 228

Hardbound in purple cloth and issued in a photographic dust jacket bearing a pink and purple design.

A paperback edition was published in 1973 by Verlag Ullstein, Frankfort am Main, as Ullstein Buch no. 2960. 17.7 × 11.6 cm. Text reset. 144 pp. DM2.80 later rising to DM3.70.

D25 *Die letzten Worte von Dutch Schultz (The Last Words of Dutch Schultz)*
Cologne: Verlag Kiepenheuer und Witsch, 1971. Pocket 24 in a paperback series. Tr. Hans Hermann. 18.0 × 12.0 cm. pp. i–vii, 1–112, i–viii.

Contains:
Blurb 1
Contents 5
Author's note 7
Die letzten Worte von Dutch Schultz 9–112

Front cover, first pasted-down endpaper, first free endpaper (as p. i), pp. ii–viii all have a black-and-white blowup newsphotograph of Dutch Schultz printed on them, bleeding at all edges. Pp. i–vii, last free endpaper, last pasted-down endpaper, and back cover again repeat the photograph of Dutch Schultz. P. vii at the front of the text and p. ii and the back cover after the text all have an additional collage element added to the photograph.

Paperbound in stiff card wrappers bearing the black-and-white photograph as described above.

D26 *The Soft Machine*
Cologne: Verlag Kiepenheuer und Witsch, 1971. Tr. Peter Behrens. 22.0 × 14.1 cm. 192 pp.

Contains:
"Inhalt" (Contents)	5
The Soft Machine (translated from the Grove Press edition [**A5b**])	7–192

Paperbound in stiff cards folded to give flaps on which is printed a blurb and printed in a blue and pink design composed of photographs of mouths.

A paperback edition was published in 1974 by Verlag Ullstein, Frankfurt am Main, as Ullstein Buch no. 3018. Text reset. 160 pp. DM3.80.

D27 *Die Elektronische Revolution (Electronic Revolution)*
Göttingen: Expanded Media Editions, August 1971. Tr. Carl Wiessner. Special edition: 16.2 × 10.5 cm. Trade edition: 16.0 × 10.3 cm. 124 pp. Trade edition, DM7.80.

Contains:
Die Elektronische Revolution (German translation)	7–64
The Electronic Revolution (original English)	67–111

Each section is preceded by a title page.

P. 2 bears a photograph of WSB by Brion Gysin. It is printed by offset in the trade edition but real prints of the photograph, printed on mat paper, have been stuck into the special edition which is also signed and numbered on the title page in an edition of 100 copies.

Bound in stiff back cards with a photographic dust jacket printed with a blue design and with orange letters superimposed over. The special edition has blue-stained edges in the manner of gilding.

Published in an edition of 1,000 copies, of which 100 were in the special edition.

D28 *Ali's Smile*
Göttingen: Expanded Media Editions no. 12, October 1973. Tr. Carl Wiessner. 19.0 × 14.0 cm. 40 pp. Paperback.

Contains:
Ali's Smile (in the original English)	iii–xvii
Advertisements	xix
Ali's Smile (in German translation)	xxi–xxxix
Advertisements	xl

Printed in green on orange/ochre paper with the text on one side of the page only (copyright page and ads, p. xl, are on verso of title page and p. xxxix respectively).

Paperbound in stiff cards with green photographic design on the front.

D29 *Der Job: Interview mit William S Burroughs von Daniel Odier* (*The Job*)
Cologne: Verlag Kiepenheuer und Witsch, 1973. Tr. Hans Hermann, except "The Invisible Generation," on pp. 152–162, which is translated by Peter Behrens. 22.0 × 14.1 cm. 188 pp. Paperback.

Contains:
Contents	5
Der Job (translated from the revised Grove Press edition [**A16a**])	7–187

Paperbound in stiff cards folded to give flaps on which is printed a blurb and printed flat black with white lettering.

Italian

D30 *La scimmia sulla schiena* (*Monkey on the Back*, a translation of *Junkie*)
Milan: Rizzoli Editore, March 14, 1962. Tr. Bruno Oddera. 22.4 × 14.5 cm. 252 pp.

Contains:

"Introduzione" by Fernanda Pivano (Introduction, dated Jan. 5, 1962)   5–24
Junkie   27–230
"Una cura che elimina la tossicomania" ("A Treatment That Cancels Addiction." This text was written by WSB in Cambridge, January 1961, and circulated in typescript and photocopy form. WSB gave Fernanda Pivano a copy shortly after it was written, and this Italian translation of it is the only published form of that text. A later version was published in the book *Health Bulletin: APO–33* [A12a] and the final text was published in *New Statesman*, March 4, 1966 [see C134]. The article also appears in the British edition of *The Soft Machine* [see A5d].)   231–250

Bound in stiff cloth boards printed with an orange, red, and black poppy design on a white ground. A glassine wrapper holds in place an orange streamer bearing the legend, in white letters, "Droga: Resoconto consapevole di uno scrittore."

A bookmark bearing a photograph of WSB and a blurb concerning the book was tipped in.

D31   *Il pasto nudo (Naked Lunch)*
Milan: Sugar Editore, February 1964. Tr. Claudio Gorlier and Donatella Manganotti. 21.0 × 14.2 cm. 296 pp.

Contains:

"Nota degli editori" (Publishers' note)   7
"Preface" by Oreste del Buono (Preface)   9–24
Il pasto nudo (Naked Lunch)   24–218
"Appendices: I. Glossario di donatella manganotti   221–230
II. William Burroughs, il profeta delle galassie ferite di Donatella Manganotti   231–270
III. Intervista con William Burroughs di Gregory Corso ed Allen Ginsberg   271–275
IV. Lettera di un super tossicomane"   277–292
(Appendixes: I. Glossary by Donatella Manganotti
II. "William Burroughs, Prophet of the Wounded Galaxies" by Donatella Manganotti
III. "Interview with William Burroughs by Gregory Corso and Allen Ginsberg," from *Journal for the Protection of All Beings*, 1961 [E1]

IV. "Letter from a Master Addict to Dangerous Drugs," from *British Journal of Addiction*, 1957 [**C1**])
"Indice" (Contents)   293

Bound in stiff boards printed with a photograph of WSB by Ian Sommerville on the front with greenish-blue letters superimposed. The same photograph is repeated on the first free endpaper and last pasted-down endpaper. No dust jacket. 3,000 copies were printed.

A second edition was issued in 1970 as I Giorni 30 and bound in the uniform fawn cloth of the series. The dust jacket has a photograph of WSB in black and white with yellow lettering superimposed. 306 pp. L3,000.

D32 *La morbida macchina (The Soft Machine)*
Milan: Sugar Editore, August 1965. I Giorni 13. Tr. Donatella Manganotti. 24.5 × 14.2 cm. 184, xii pp. L2,000.

Contains:
"Introduzione" by Giansiro Ferrata (Introduction)   iii–xi
"Nota del traduttore" by Donatella Manganotti (Note on the Translation)   7
La morbida macchina (The Soft Machine, translated from the Grove Press edition [**A5b**])   9–176
"Indice" (Contents)   177

Bound in fawn cloth. The dust jacket has a photograph of WSB by Robert Fréson reprinted from *Esquire*. Published in an edition of 3,000 copies.

D33 *Le lettere dello Yage: In amazzonia alla ricerca di una droga allucinatoria* (with Allen Ginsberg)(*The Yage Letters*)
Milan: Sugar Editore, March 1967. I Giorni 19. Tr. Donatella Manganotti. 21.0 × 13.4 cm. 112 pp. L1,500.

Contains:
"Nota" by Donatella Mangonotti (Note)   8
Le lettere dello Yage (The Yage Letters)   9–110
"Indice" (Contents)   111

Bound in fawn-colored cloth. The dust jacket has a montage of photographs of WSB and Allen Ginsberg. Published in an edition of 3,000 copies.

D34 *Sterminatore! (Exterminator!)*

Milan: Sugar Editore, 1969. I Giorni 28. Tr. Giulio Saponaro. 21.0 × 13.2 cm. 178 pp. L2,000.

Contains:

Bound in fawn cloth. The dust jacket is white with black silhouettes of two cockroaches on lower left. Title in black lettering is printed over red lettering to give a red shadow effect. Published in an edition of 3,000 copies. This volume contains a different set of stories from that in *Exterminator!* (**A23**).

D35 *Nova Express*
Milan: Sugar Editore, 1967. I Giorni 21. Tr. Donatella Manganotti. 21.0 × 13.2 cm. 208 pp. L2,200.

Contains:

"Nota del traduttore" by Donatalla Manganotti (Note on the Translation)	7–8
Nova Express	9–205
"Indice" (Contents)	207–208

Bound in fawn cloth. The dust jacket has a photograph of WSB. The book was issued with a streamer, black letters on an orange ground saying: "Il capolavera di Burroughs" ("A Masterpiece by Burroughs"). Published in an edition of 3,000 copies.

D36 *Il biglietto che è esploso (The Ticket That Exploded)*
Milan: Sugar Editore, 1970. I Giorni 31. Tr. Giulio Saponaro. 21.0 × 13.5 cm. 216 pp. L2,500.

Contains:

Il biglietto che è esploso (The Ticket That Exploded, from the Grove Press edition [**A6b**])	7–213

Bound in fawn-colored cloth. The dust jacket has a portrait of WSB in an oval on white ground cover as a miniature.

D37 *Le ultime parole di Dutch Schultz (The Last Words of Dutch Schultz)*
Milan: Sugar Editore, 1971. I Giorni 39. Tr. Giulio Saponaro. 21.3 × 13.4 cm. 104 pp. L1, L1,500.

Contains:

Le ultime parole di Dutch Schultz (The Last Words of Dutch Schultz)	7–100
"Indice" (Contents)	101

Bound in stiff white laminated boards with a colored design by Ugo Nespolo.

D38 *Ragazzi Selvaggi* (*The Wild Boys*)
Milan: Sugar Editore, 1973. I Giorni 44. Tr. Giulio Saponaro. 21.0
× 13.4 cm. 174 pp. L2,200.

Contains:
Ragazzi selvaggi (*The Wild Boys*)   5–171
"Indice" (Contents)   173

Bound in stiff pink laminated boards with a black drawing of
"Trashman" by Spain Rodrigues on front.

Japanese

D39 *Hakaka No Ranchi* (*The Naked Lunch*)
Tokyo: Kawade Shoboo, Autumn 1965. No. 19 in a series of
modern titles. Tr. Nobuo Ayukawa. 18.2 × 12.2 cm. pp. [i–ii],
1–350, [i–iv ads]. 420 yen.

Bound in crimson cloth with publisher's device stamped in gold on
cover and spine. Title in Japanese on spine and in English on front
cover (Japanese books read from right to left; therefore the front
cover would be the back cover to Western eyes). Glassine-
wrapped with title printed in gold on its front cover. A 6.0-cm.
wide blue streamer wrapped round repeating title and with critical
comments (probably the usual ones by Mailer and Terry Southern)
printed in white. The streamer is held in place by the glassine. Silk
bookmark bound in. 20,000 copies published on Sept. 25, 1965.

   A second edition was published on June 15, 1971, in an edition
of 3,000 copies at 750 yen. Bound in limp gray cloth-textured
boards. Glassine wrapped and with pastedown title strip in blue
and black with gold lettering. A streamer with blue lettering on a
black ground is held by the glassine wrapper. A bookmark is
bound in.

D40 *Mayaku Shokan* (*The Yage Letters*)
Tokyo: Shichosha Publishers, 1966. Tr. Ieda Takaaki and Suwa
Yu.

D41 *Junkie*
Tokyo: Shichosha Publishers, 1967. Tr. Nobuo Ayukawa.

Norse

D42 *Naken Lunsj (The Naked Lunch)*
Olso: Pax, 1967. Tr. Olav Angell.

Spanish

D43 *Almuerzo desnudo (The Naked Lunch)*
Buenos Aires, Argentina: Ediciónes Siglo Veinte, Jan. 20, 1971.
Tr. Anibal Leal. 20.6 × 15.0 cm. 272 pp.

Contains:
"Introducción—Deposición: Testimonio sobre una enfermedad"
   ("Introduction—Deposition: Testimony concerning a Sickness"
   [**C12**])   7–38
Almuerzo Desnudo (*The Naked Lunch*, taken from the Grove Press
   edition [**A2b**])   39–250
"Apendice: Carta de un empedernido adicto a las drogas pelig-
   rosas" ("Appendix: Letter from a Master Addict to Dangerous
   Drugs" [**C1**])   251–267

Bound in limp boards with blue and white design on cover. Pages
uncut.

D44 *Cartas del Yage* (with Allen Ginsberg) (*The Yage Letters*)
Buenos Aires: Ediciónes Signos, March 1971. Tr. M. Lassere. 17.9
× 13.8 cm. 88 pp.

Contains:
Cartas del Yage (*The Yage Letters*)   7–84
"Indice" (Contents)   85–87

Bound in limp boards with a gray design printed on a gray ground.
Pages cut.

D45 *Las últimas palabras de Dutch Schultz* (*The Last Words of Dutch
Schultz*)
La Bonanova, Palma de Mallorca: Las Ediciónes de los Papeles de
Son Armadans, published by El Departamento de Filosofía de
Universidad de Oviedo as Azanca 2, June 1, 1971. Tr. J. M.
Alvarez Flórez. 20.0 × 13.1 cm. 112 pp. Paperback.

Contains:

"Unas necesarias palabras editoriales"   5–14
"Algunas notas dispersas sobre la traducción" ("Some Scattered
    Notes on the Translations")   15–16
Las últimas palabras de Dutch Schultz (*The Last Words of Dutch
    Schultz*, taken from the Cape-Goliard edition [**A17**])   17–109

Paperbound in stiff red wrappers with the Azanca sun device on
the front and with white lettering. Pages are trimmed.

D46 *El trabajo* (Conversaciones con Daniel Odier) (*The Job: Conver-
sations with Daniel Odier*)
Barcelona: Editorial Mateau, January 1972. Collección Maldoror
no. 11. Tr. Antonio Desmonts. 11.9 × 10.7 cm. 198 pp. Paperback.

Contains:

"Presentación" by Salvador Clotas (Introduction)   7–20
El Trabajo (*The Job*), taken from the Grove Press edition
    [**A16a**])   21–194
"Indice" (Contents)   195

Paperbound in limp card with a green design on purple ground.

D47 *Espreso nova* (*Nova Express*)
Buenos Aires, Argentina: Ediciónes Minotauro, Nov. 30, 1972.
Colección Metamorfosis. Tr. Enrique Pezzoni. 19.6 × 11.3 cm.
160 pp.

Contains:

Espreso nova (*Nova Express*)   9–155
"Indice" (Contents)   157

Bound in limp green boards adapted from the Roy Kuhlman
design from the Grove edition [**A10a**). Pages cut.

D48 *Nova express*
La Bonanova, Palma de Mallorca: Las Ediciónes de los Papeles de
Son Armadans, published by El Departamento de Filosofía de
Universidad de Oviedo, as Azanca 5, Dec. 8, 1973. Tr. Martin
Lendinez. 20.0 × 13.1 cm. 184 pp.

Contains:

"Nota brevia" ("Brief Note" by WSB)   6

Paperbound in stiff laminated cards folded to make flaps upon which are printed the blurb. Cover bears a photographic black-and-white design in which the title information appears in white letters. A streamer 14.0-cm. wide is wrapped round, almost covering the cover. Printed on white glossy paper, it gives the title and author and the words: "Una obra capital de la literatura del siglo XX" printed in red.

Note that this is not a second edition of the Buenos Aires edition of 1972 but is a completely different translation.

Swedish

D49 *Tjacket (Junkie)*
Stockholm: Centerwall and Thuresson, 1967. Tr. Einar Heckscher.

D50 *Nova Express*
Stockholm: Alb. Bonniers Boktryckeri, 1968. Tr. Torsten Ekbom. 21.1 × 12.9 cm. 166 pp. SK29.50.

Contains:

Bound in stiff cards with lettering superimposed on an orange and black repeating design. Pages uncut.

E   Interviews

1961

E1 "Interview with William Burroughs" (WSB interviewed by Allen Ginsberg and Gregory Corso)
Journal for the Protection of All Beings 1:79–83. Ed. Lawrence Ferlinghetti. San Francisco: City Lights Books. 1961. $1.50.

1964

E2 "Tangier Cosmopolita William Burroughs un escritor que Refleja a la 'Beat Generation' pero que se ha mantenido al margen del movimiento 'Beatnik'" (WSB interviewed by a staff reporter)
España, no. 8752: 7. Tangier, Sept. 4, 1964.
    In Spanish. Has two uncredited photographs of WSB in Tangier.

1965

E3 "The Art of Fiction XXXVI: William Burroughs, an Interview" (WSB interviewed by Conrad Knickerbocker)
Paris Review 35:13–49. Paris, Fall 1965. 5F.
    P. 12 has a photograph of WSB by Charles Henri Ford.

E4 "The Hallucinary Operators Are Real" (WSB interviewed by staff reporters)
S. F. Horizons 2:3–12. Oxford, Winter 1965. 3s. 6d.

1966

E5 "Prophet or Pornographer?" (WSB interviewed by staff reporter).
Jaguar, January 1966. New York.

E6 "La Douce Machine à écrire"
Apparatus, December 1966:21–24. Brussels. 135F (Belgium).

A translation by Jean-Jacques Lebel of the interview with WSB by Allen Ginsberg and Gregory Corso in *Journal for the Protection of All Beings*, 1961, (**E1**).

E7 Untitled quote
Evergreen Club News 1, no. 4: 8. New York, [1966]. Distributed free to members.
   Taken from the interview with WSB by Conrad Knickerbocker in *Paris Review*, 1965 (**E3**).

1967

E8 "7: William Burroughs" (WSB interviewed by Conrad Knicker-bocker)
Pp. 141–174 in *Writers at Work: Third Series*. Prepared by George Plimpton. New York: Viking Press, 1967. 368 pp. $7.95.
   A selection of interviews from *Paris Review*. The WSB interview is from *Paris Review*, 1965 (**E3**).

E9 Untitled interview
Mayfair 2, no. 10: 5. London, October 1967. 5s.
   Appears in the "Mayfairers" column near the beginning. Un-characteristic words and phrases suggest that it was assembled from notes rather than a transcribed tape-recording. It is, however, presented with direct quotes. It serves as an introduction to the *Burroughs Academy* series of articles which begin in this issue.

1968

E10 "7: William Burroughs" (WSB interviewed by Conrad Knick-erbocker)
Pp. 141–174 in *Writers at Work: Third Series*. Prepared by George Plimpton. London: Secker and Warburg, 1968. 368 pp. 42s.
   A reprint using sheets or plates of the Viking Press edition (see **E8**). The interview is from *Paris Review*, 1965 (**E3**).

E11 "Västerlandets framtid" (WSB interviewed by Knut Lagrup)
Sydsvenska Dagbladet Snällposten, no. 1848: 4. Malmö, March 26, 1968.

Note: The Jeff Shiro interview with WSB first appeared in *Rat,* the New York City underground newspaper that Shiro edited. The Underground Press Syndicate (UPS) appears to have syndicated the first part of the interview only, for the second part, which followed a week later, does not appear in those newspapers which credit the interview to UPS. Most newspapers appear to have reprinted the interview from the *San Francisco Express Times* reprint as they mostly use this newspaper's titles for the two parts.

E12 "William Burroughs Interview" (WSB interviewed by Jeff Shiro)
Rat l, no. 18: 1, 10–11. New York, Oct. 4, 1968. 15¢.
Part One of an interview conducted at Terry Southern's apartment in New York City.

E13 "William Burroughs Interview" (WSB interviewed by Jeff Shiro)
Rat l, no. 19: 12–13. New York, Oct. 18, 1968. 15¢.
Part Two of an interview conducted at Terry Southern's apartment in New York City.

E14 "I'm Tired of Sitting on My Ass" (WSB interviewed by Jeff Shiro)
San Francisco Express Times 1, no. 38: 6, 12–13. San Francisco, Oct. 9, 1968. 15¢.
A reprint of Part One of the interview from *Rat,* 1968 (E12).

E15 "I Went Much Further than the So-called Radicals Part 2" (WSB interviewed by Jeff Shiro)
San Francisco Express Times 1, no. 41: 5. San Francisco, Oct. 30, 1968. 15¢.
A reprint of Part Two of the interview from *Rat,* 1968 (E13).

E16 "I'm Tired of Sitting on My Ass" (WSB interviewed by Jeff Shiro)
Georgia Straight 2, no. 36: 8–10. Vancouver, Nov. 8, 1968. 15¢.
A reprint of Part One of the interview from *Rat,* 1968 (E12).

E17 "I Went Much Further than the So-called Radicals Part II (WSB interviewed by Jeff Shiro)
Georgia Straight 2, no. 37: 7–8. Vancouver, Nov. 15, 1968. 15¢.
A reprint of Part Two of the interview from *Rat,* 1968 (E13).

E18 "William Burroughs Interview" (WSB interviewed by Jeff Shiro)
Love Underground Press 1, no. 11: 5, 8–9. Reno, Nev., Nov. 1, 1968. 20¢.
A reprint of Part One of the interview from *Rat*, 1968 (**E12**).

E19 "William Burroughs Interview" (WSB interviewed by Jeff Shiro)
Love Underground Press 1, no. 12: 4, 8–9. Reno, Nev., Nov. 15, 1968. 20¢.
A reprint of Part Two of the interview from *Rat*, 1968 (**E13**).

E20 "The Most Anti-political Revolt. . . . Ever. . . . in History" (WSB interviewed by Jeff Shiro)
Spokane Natural 2, no. 23: 12. Spokane, Nov. 8, 1968. 25¢.
A reprint of Part One of the interview from *Rat*, 1968 (**E12**). This journal did not reprint Part Two.

E21 "Interview: William Burroughs" (WSB interviewed by Jeff Shiro)
Los Angeles Free Press 5, no. 46(226): 27, 32. Los Angeles, Nov. 15, 1968. 15¢.
A reprint of Part One of the interview from *Rat* 1968 (**E12**). This journal did not reprint Part Two.

E22 "Burroughs: 'I'm Tired of Sitting on My Ass'" (WSB interviewed by Jeff Shiro)
The Scimitar 1, no. 7: 10–11. Ithaca, N.Y., Dec. 10, 1968. 20¢.
A reprint of Part One of the interview from *Rat* 1968 (**E12**). This journal did not reprint Part Two.

E23 "Interview" (WSB interviewed by Jeff Shiro)
Rat 1, no. 23: 5. New York, Dec. 13, 1968. 15¢.
This is a different interview from those of *Rat*, 1968 (**E12** and **E13**).

1969

E24 "Tactics of Deconditioning: William Burroughs Speaks" (WSB interviewed by Felix Scorpio)
IT 57:4–7. London, May 23, 1969.

Less than 1,000 copies of this issue were distributed because of problems with the printer.

E25 "In Search of the Connection" (WSB interviewed by Nina Sutton)
The Guardian, July 5, 1969:7. London. 6d.

E26 "Entretien avec William Burroughs" (WSB interviewed by Nina Sutton)
Plexus 28:32–43. Paris, October 1969.
A French translation of the interview from *The Guardian*, 1969 (E25). Article includes a photograph of WSB by Graham Keen.

E27 "Journey through Time-Space" (WSB interviewed by Daniel Odier)
Evergreen Review 13, no. 67: 39–41, 78–89. New York, June 1969. $1.00.

E28 "William Burroughs Interviewed by Driss Drissi"
Gaudie, series II, 6, no. 20: 6. Aberdeen University, April 30, 1969. 6d.

1970

E29 "Journey through Time-Space: An Interview with William S. Burroughs"
Pp. 504–534 in *The Radical Vision. Essays for the Seventies*. Ed. Leo Hamalian and Frederick R. Karl. New York: Thomas Y. Crowell Company, 1970. 625 pp.
Interview with Daniel Odier, which first appeared in *Evergreen Review* 13, 1969 (E27).

E30 *"Le Ticket qui . . . Junkie . . . Nova . . . Machine molle . . . Festin nu . . .* William Burroughs" (WSB interviewed by Jean-Francois Bizot)
Actuel 2:18–23. Paris, November 1970. 3F.

E31 "A Flower Pot from a High Window" (WSB interviewed by Michael March)
Crawdaddy 4, no. 5: 26–28 (and a brief quote on p. 1 of section two) New York, Summer 1970. 35¢.

E32 "Zwischen Marx und Haschish" (WSB interviewed by Nina Sutton)
Pardon 99, no. 2: 62–66. Frankfurt. February 1970. DM2.
A German translation of the interview from *The Guardian*, 1969 (**E25**).

1971

E33 "Burroughs Interview"
P. 42 in *The Open Conspiracy: What America's Angry Generation Is Saying*. Ed. Ethel Grodzins Romm. New York: Avon Books, January 1971. 256 pp. Paperback. $1.25.
A quote from the interview which appeared in *Rat*, 1968 (**E12**).

E34 "William Burroughs Mind Engineer" (WSB interviewed by Graham Masterson and Andrew Rossabi)
Penthouse 6, no. 6: 37–40, 60. London, June 1971. 30p.

E35 "William Burroughs Rapping on Revolutionary Techniques. London Interviewer Dan Georgakas Summer 1970 (August)"
Global Tapestry Journal, [1971: 45–50]. Blackburn, Lancs.

1972

E36 "Rolling Stone Interview: William Burroughs" (WSB interviewed by Bob Palmer)
Rolling Stone 108:34–39. San Francisco, May 11, 1972. 60¢.
The article is illustrated with a number of photographs of WSB.

E37 "William Burroughs 'I've Noticed a Regrettable Vagueness in Accounts of Hallucinogenic Drugs. In Time I Think These Just Lead to a Sort of Dreamland State.'" (WSB interviewed by Graham Masterson and Andrew Rossabi)
Penthouse 3, no. 7: 44, 46, 52. New York, March 1972. $1.00.
A reprint of the interview which first appeared in the English edition of *Penthouse*, 1971 (**E34**).

E38 "William Burroughs—Mind Engineer" (WSB interviewed by Graham Masterson and Andrew Rossabi)
Pp. 161–179 in *The Unexpurgated Penthouse*. Ed. Peter Haining.

London: New English Library, November 1972. 192 pp. Revised paperback edition.

The interview is taken from *Penthouse*, 1971 (**E34**), and is part of the new material added for the paperback edition. The original hardback edition was called *The Midnight Penthouse* and was published by Bernard Geis, London in 1968. The paperback edition was reprinted November 1972 and in July 1973.

E39 "Look at Uncle Bill" (WSB interviewed by Bill Butler) *Friendz* 31:18–19. London, July 14, 1972. 15p.

F Miscellaneous

1960

F1 Unititled piece on Takis
P.[7] in *Iris Clert présente l'impossible par Takis.* Paris: Iris Clert Gallery, 1960. 800 pp. Free exhibition catalogue.
    This piece opens with the line "Song cut along topographical magnetic lines . . ." from the *Minutes to Go* group of manuscripts.

1961

F2 "A Treatment That Cancels Addition"
A 13-page photocopied or Xerox-copied manuscript concerning itself with the apomorphine cure. Typewritten copies are also known to exist. This manuscript was written by WSB in January 1961 and circulated mainly to addicts and persons in the "drug-society" of that time. Copies were made of copies and the copy in the bibliographer's possession would seem to be at least a third-generation photocopy of a typescript.
    The text was later expanded and published as "The Death of Opium Jones," *New Statesman*, 1966 (**C134**).
    The original text was published in Italian translation as an appendix to the Italian edition of *Junkie, La scimmia sulla schiena* (**D30**).

F3 Untitled piece on Guy Harloff
Side [3] of *Guy Harloff at Galerie "La Cour d'Ingres."* Paris: Galerie "La Cour d'Ingress," Quai Voltaire, Dec. 8, 1961. Free exhibition catalogue.
    Printed on thick art card folded to make four sides.

F4 "Cosmographies Harold Norse"
P. [3] in *Harold Norse Exhibition.* March 17–April 5, 1961, Paris, at Cave de la Librairie Anglais.
    Rectangular yellow card, folded into three with WSB appearing on inside p. 3 and a French translation appearing on inside p. 1.

1962

F5 Statement on Takis

Pp. 3–4, 9, 10 in *Takis*. Milano: Galleria Schwarz, April 14, 1962. 12 pp. Distributed free during the exhibition.

Pages 3–4 contain the piece in Italian, p. 9 has the piece in French and p. 10 prints it in English. The text is the one opening with the lines: "Takis is working with and expressing . . . ".

F6 Transcription of a panel discussion

Pp. 5–8, 18–19, 29, 32–33 in *International Writers Conference*. Edinburgh, August 1962. 138 pp.

A mimeographed transcript of the proceedings of the conference. Foolscap bound with a filing ring through hole in top left corner. Number of copies unknown. WSB appears in the sections for Thursday, August 23, 1962: pp. 5–8 and for Friday, August 24, 1962: pp. 18–19, 29, 32–33.

F7 "From *Naked Lunch*"

Pp. 8–15 in *William Burroughs Naked Lunch*. October 1962 (for November 20, 1962). 16 pp. Free advance publicity announcement sheet for the Grove Press edition (**A26**).

Pp. 8–9 are taken from the "Meeting of International Conference of Technological Psychiatry" section of *The Naked Lunch* and pp. 10–15 from "The County Clerk" section.

1963

F8 Untitled rare book catalogue entry

Item 40 in *Roman Books Inc.* Fort Lauderdale, Fla., 1968. Rare book catalogue.

Contains a five-line quote from a letter. This catalogue is known as "The Outsiders" catalogue.

F9 Jacket blurb

A Clockwork Orange by Anthony Burgess. New York: Norton Paperback Library, 1963.

Noted on the back jacket of the sixth paperback edition. Other editions have not been inspected.

F10 Untitled piece on Takis

P. [3] in *Takis*. New York: Alexander Iolas Gallery, October 15, 1963. Exhibition catalogue.

34.5 x 26.5cm. Photograph inserted between folded printed cards. WSB appears on p. 3. This is the second printing of the text which opens with the words "Takis is working with and expressing with his sculpture . . . ," which first appeared in the Gallerie Schwarz catalogue (**E5**).

F11 Untitled
Pp. [4–9] in *Peinture poésie musique David Budd recontre William Burroughs et Earle Brown chez Rodolphe Stadler*. Paris: Galerie Stadler, March 14, 1964. 12 pp. Exhibition catalogue.

One sheet folded to make 12 panels (6 on each side). The two-column style piece by WSB occupies half of the catalogue and is present in both English and in a French translation made by Michel Thurlotte. Each photograph is printed alternately in red and orange ink. Page [2] has a brief biography of WSB and a portrait of him drawn by David Budd. A number of copies were signed by all three participants though whether or not this constituted a special edition is not known. The signatures are always in red ink.

F12 Theater program

THE AMERICAN THEATRE FOR POETS, INC. | presents February 14, 1965 | William Burroughs | *Valentine's Day Reading* | | THE EAST END THEATRE | 85 East 4th Street New York City.

28 × 21.5 cm. Distributed at the reading. 7 pp. plus cover page, all printed on one side only. Pp. [1]–6: "Transcript of Dutch Schultz's Last Words." p. [7]: a reprinting (not in three-column format) of "The Coldspring News" (**C124**).

1965

F13 Letter
In advertising poster for the second issue of *Now* magazine, which was designated as *Now Now* [San Francisco, 1965] (**C119**). Printed and published by the magazine's editor Charles Plymell. 56.00 × 43.00 cm.

A ten-line TLs concerning the magazine.

1966

F14 Untitled

Pp. 6, 8 in *Cast of Chappaqua*.28 pp.

This booklet is enclosed in a brown manilla envelope together with 15 25 × 20 cm. still photographs from the film, a list of available publicity material, and an 11-page essay by Conrad Rooks entitled "The New President" dated Aug. 26, 1966. This press kit to publicize the film was free. The cast of the film received copies of the booklet printed on a thicker laminated paper and enclosed within a red slipcase with their name printed in gold on the front. On WSB's copy his name was misspelled.

F15 "William Burroughs"

P. 4 in *Takis Magnetic Sculptures and the White Signals*. London: Indica Gallery, 1966. 12 pp. Free exhibition catalogue.

This is the piece on Takis which opens with the line: "Takis is working with and expressing in his sculpture thought forms of metal . . . "taken from *Signals*, 1964 (**C87**), and first published in the Galleria Schwarz catalogue, 1962 (**F5**). A variant cover lacks the illustration of Takis' sculpture.

F16 Quote

P. 5 in *ADAMI—Pictures with Connexions / Immagini con associa- zioni /Images avec associations*. Milano: Galleria Schwarz, Oct. 6, 1966. Exhibition catalogue. 24 pp.

The piece, which is taken from "Censorship," which first ap- peared in *Transatlantic Review*, 1962 (**C51**), is printed in the English, French, and Italian languages.

F17 Quote

P. 5 in *ADAMI—Pictures with Connexions / Immagini con associa- zioni / Images avec associations*. Milano: Galleria Schwarz, Oct. 6, 1966. Exhibition Catalogue. 24 pp.

The piece, which is from "Outskirts of the City," which first appeared in *Evergreen Review*, 1962 (**C44**), is printed in the English, French, and Italian languages.

F18 Untitled

P. [4] in *Brion Gysin at the Tangier Gallery*. Dated by Brion Gysin as Aug. 22, 1966. 8 pp. Exhibition catalogue.

A private-view invitation to an exhibition by Brion Gysin at the

Tangier Gallery, Passage Bestofol, 48 Blvd Pasteur, Tangier. Folded art paper to make four sides; loose tipped inside folded black paper on which is printed the exhibition announcement in gold title.

F19 Letter
In advertising poster for the book *Apocalypse Rose* by Charles Plymell published by Auerhahn Press, San Francisco. San Francisco, [Summer 1967]. Distributed free to bookstores.

A ten-line TLs is used as part of a collage by Plymell which the poster reproduces. Stiff art paper.

F20 Untitled piece on Takis
P. 4 in *Takis Magnetic Sculptures*. New York: The Howard Wise Gallery, April 7, 1967. Exhibition catalogue issued free to visitors and through the mail as a private-view invitation.

Usually found in its mailing envelope as issued. WSB's piece, reprinted from "L'Impossible par Takis" show at Iris Clert, 1960 (F1), is the text beginning with: "Song cut along typographical magnetic lines. . . ."

F21 Sleeve notes
Sheeper by Irving Rosenthal. New York: Grove Press, 1967. Published in a paperback edition as Evergreen Black Cat Book B–192, New York, 1968 at $1.25

The notes appear on the back cover of the paperback edition only.

1970

F22 Untitled piece on the work of Gette
P. 2 in *Gette's Crystals*. [Paris, 1970.] Exhibition catalogue.

Eight sheets printed on one side only, perfect bound. The first edition consisted of 5 copies on arches paper with a signed original by Gette at 600.00F.; 35 copies signed by Gette at 100.00F.; and a trade edition at 15.00F.

F23 "'A New Way of Looking at the Universe': Scientology Revisited by William S. Burroughs, Author of *Nova Express*, *The Soft Machine*, *Naked Lunch*, Is Now a Clear!"
In *Lemar Information Kit*. [1970.]

A large envelope containing over 20 separate stapled sheets and booklets. The item is present as a stapled eight-page booklet made from two sheets, folded and stapled, reprinted from *Mayfair*, 1968 (**C179**).

1971

F24 Quote concerning Henri Chopin
In *Audiopoems Henri Chopin*. [1971.] An announcement flyer for a recording.
One side only. Printed offset in blue ink on green paper. Contains five-line note by WSB on the middle right of page.

F25 Quote concerning Henri Chopin
Liner notes for *Audiopoems: Henri Chopin*. A 12-inch long-playing record. London: Tangent Records, [1971]. TG S 106.
The WSB piece is as a liner note on the back sleeve. It first appeared on the advance announcement flyer for this record (**F24**).

F26 Untitled
P. [3] in a flyer to announce the publication of *Last of the Moccasins* by Charles Plymell. [1971.]

F27 Electronic Revolution
Prepublication announcement flyer for *Electronic Revolution*. Ingatestone, Essex, [1971]. Free.
Single sheet, foolscap, red on white in facsimile typewriting and calligraphy. Gives publication of book (**A21**) as October 1971. Bilingual.

1972

F28 Quote
William S. Burroughs. Göttingen: Expanded Media Editions, 1972. Free.
An advertisement, single sheet folded into three with a quote from the German translation of *Electronic Revolution* on inside p. [1] and in original English on inside p. [2]. This is an advertising pamphlet for the German edition of *Electronic Revolution* (**D27**). It

has a photograph of WSB by Brion Gysin on the front cover. The same material was issued as a single sheet with the contents in a different arrangement as a second edition.

F29 Quote concerning Anthony Burgess
A Clockwork Orange by Anthony Burgess. New York: Ballentine Books, 1972. Seventh printing. Paperback. $1.25.
 The note appears on the back jacket as a blurb and reads: "One of the few books I have been able to read in recent years." Reprinted from the Norton edition of 1963 (**F9**).

1973

F30 "William Burroughs on the Painting of Brion Gysin"
Inside p. [3] and outside pp. [5–6] in *Permutations* by Brion Gysin. Paris: Galerie Weiller, March 20, 1973. Exhibition catalogue.
 Large sheet folded in half, then into three to make 12 sides. The inside is treated as three sides only. There also appears a French translation of the texts made by Claude Pélieu, pp. [1–2].

F31 "Statement of William Burroughs on Behalf of Michael X"
In untitled, large double-sided broadside, folded into four. New York: The International Committee to Save Michael X, 1973. Distributed free.
 Broadside contains statements and quotes from persons concerned with freeing Michael X from the death sentence. WSB quote dated September 1973.

F32 Quote
Souvenir Programme for the Official Lynching of Michael Abdul Malik, with Poems, Stories, Sayings by the Condemned. Ed. William Levy and John Michell. Cambridge: Cokaygne Press, 1973.
 Privately published by the Cokaygne Press as a fund raiser for Michael X. A poster which was issued to advertise the book also used the same quote: "A writer of considerable distinction."

G   Records and Tapes

G1 *Call Me Burroughs*

   a. *Call Me Burroughs.* 12-inch long-playing record published by Gaît Frogé at her English Bookshop, 42, rue de Seine, Paris 6ᵉ, Summer 1965.

      WSB reads excerpts from *The Naked Lunch* on side one and from *Nova Express* on side two. The tapes were recorded and edited by Ian Sommerville in Paris. The sleeve bears a large black-and-white photograph of WSB by Harriet Crowther with the title in gray lettering along the top designed by Tientje Louw. The black sleeve has two sets of liner notes: one in English by Emmett Williams and one in French by Jean-Jacques Lebel dated April 1965.

   b. *Call Me Burroughs.* An American edition of **G1a** was released by ESP-Disk record company of New York City in late 1966. It was identical to **G1a** in every way except that the front sleeve had the record company trademark of a white handprint on the top left corner and a reference number 1050. An extract from side two (*Nova Express*) lasting for 1.03 minutes is present on *The ESP Sampler* issued by the ESP record company in New York as ESP 1051 in 1967 at 99¢. Two extracts from side two are also present on an LP in *Aspen 5/6*, 1967 (**C117**).

   c. *Call Me Burroughs.* Issued as a C–60 cassette recording by Udo Breger, Göttingen, as Expanded Media Editions 6. DM9.80. The cassette has a wrapper designed by Hammond Guthrie.

G2 Excerpt from *Nova Express*

   A 23-minutes section read by WSB on *Klacto/23*, a tape issued by Carl Weissner and his *Klactoveedsedsteen* magazine in Frankfurt, September 1967.

      The recording was made by Weissner in Germany during a visit by WSB. The tape also has selections by others.

G3 Quote

   On Dashiell Hedayat, *Obsolete*, a 12-inch long-playing album released as Shandar SR 10009, Paris, 1971.

The short clip of tape of WSB appears at the end of the track "Love Song for Zelda" on face A and is WSB saying: "I have said the basic techniques of novia are very simple: consisting of creating and aggravating conflicts. No riots like injustice directed enemies" (12 seconds). The tape is thought to have been supplied by Daevid Allen and to have originated in the soundtrack of the film *Towers Open Fire*.

G4 Quote
  a. On Ravi Shankar, *Chappaqua*, Original Soundtrack Recording, 12-inch long-playing record released by Columbia Records/CBS, New York, c. May 1968, as Columbia Masterworks OS 3230. $5.98.

    The short appearance of WSB on the soundtrack occurs a little after the beginning of the last track on Side Two entitled "Theme" and is WSB saying, "An unworthy vessel, obviously—I withdraw from the case—" (5 seconds).

  b. The alternate soundtrack for the film was Ornette Coleman's *Chappaqua Suite*. It was not used, but was recorded and released in France and the U.S.A. WSB's voice is present on the U.S. edition only. Copies of the two editions could not be located for more complete descriptions.

G5 Conversation
On short tapes made as radio advertisements for the record *Brian Jones Presents the Pipes of Pan at Joujouka*. Produced by Kenny Everett for Rolling Stones Records in London, 1971.

    The tapes were made for use on American FM radio. Three ads were made, two of which include Burroughs. They consist of music from the record edited together with a sales message by Everett and conversational clips by WSB, Brion Gysin, Derek Taylor, and Everett.

G6 *Ali's Smile*
WSB reading the complete text of *Ali's Smile*. Brighton: Unicorn Press, October 1971. One side of 12-inch long-playing record accompanying the book (see **A19**).

G7 Excerpts from *The Wild Boys*
Issued on the 2-volume 12-inch long-playing record *The Dial-a-Poem Poets*, GPS001 (6.53 mins). $6.98.

    Recorded by John Giorno, Nov. 19, 1971, at WSB's flat in

London. Originally used as part of the Dial-a-Poem project whereby one could telephone a certain number and hear a poem.

G8 *Burroughs Reading*

A tape recorded in New York, Feb. 14, 1965, from *Valentine's Day Reading* (**F12**). Released on a 10-inch long-playing record as *OU* Revuedisque 40–41 (10.15 minutes), Ingatestone, March 1972 (see **C325**). One of 500 copies at £3.40.

OU magazine consists of a collection of artwork and documents, often with a record, in a folder. Some copies of the record were issued in a separate white cover at £2.00 (about 75 copies).

G9 *Burroughs Reading*

A tape recorded in New York Feb. 14, 1965, from *Valentine's Day Reading* (**F12**). Has the same opening segment identifying the time and date as **G8**. Released on a 10-inch long-playing record as *OU* Revuedisque 42–43–44 (8.40 minutes), Ingatestone, Oct. 10, 1973. One of 500 copies at £5.00

A few copies of the record were available separately but lacked any cover except a thin tissue inner sleeve.

Index

Index